C000173676

AMERICA'S
TEST KITCHEN

ALSO BY AMERICA'S TEST KITCHEN

The Complete Guide to Healthy Drinks
Everyday Bread
The Complete Small Plates Cookbook
Boards
The Complete Modern Pantry
The Outdoor Cook
Desserts Illustrated
Vegan Cooking for Two
Modern Bistro
Fresh Pasta at Home
More Mediterranean
The Complete Plant-Based Cookbook
Cooking with Plant-Based Meat
The Savory Baker
The New Cooking School Cookbook:
    Advanced Fundamentals
The New Cooking School Cookbook:
    Fundamentals
The Complete Autumn and
    Winter Cookbook
One-Hour Comfort
The Everyday Athlete Cookbook
Cook for Your Gut Health
Foolproof Fish
Five-Ingredient Dinners
The Ultimate Meal-Prep Cookbook
The Complete Salad Cookbook
The Chicken Bible
The Side Dish Bible
Meat Illustrated
Vegetables Illustrated
Bread Illustrated
Cooking for One
The Complete One Pot
How Can It Be Gluten-Free
    Cookbook Collection
The Complete Summer Cookbook
Bowls
100 Techniques
Easy Everyday Keto
Everything Chocolate
The Perfect Cookie

The Perfect Pie
The Perfect Cake
How to Cocktail
Spiced
The Ultimate Burger
The New Essentials Cookbook
Dinner Illustrated
America's Test Kitchen Menu Cookbook
Cook's Illustrated Revolutionary Recipes
Tasting Italy: A Culinary Journey
Cooking at Home with Bridget and Julia
The Complete Mediterranean Cookbook
The Complete Vegetarian Cookbook
The Complete Cooking for
    Two Cookbook
The Complete Diabetes Cookbook
The Complete Slow Cooker
The Complete Make-Ahead Cookbook
Just Add Sauce
How to Braise Everything
How to Roast Everything
Nutritious Delicious
What Good Cooks Know
Cook's Science
The Science of Good Cooking
Master of the Grill
Kitchen Smarts
Kitchen Hacks
100 Recipes
The New Family Cookbook
The Cook's Illustrated Baking Book
The Cook's Illustrated Cookbook
The America's Test Kitchen Family
    Baking Book
America's Test Kitchen Twentieth
    Anniversary TV Show Cookbook
The Best of America's Test Kitchen
    (2007–2023 Editions)
The Complete America's Test Kitchen
    TV Show Cookbook 2001–2023
Healthy Air Fryer
Healthy and Delicious Instant Pot

Mediterranean Instant Pot
Cook It in Your Dutch Oven
Vegan for Everybody
Sous Vide for Everybody
Air Fryer Perfection
Toaster Oven Perfection
Multicooker Perfection
Food Processor Perfection
Pressure Cooker Perfection
Instant Pot Ace Blender Cookbook
Naturally Sweet
Foolproof Preserving
Paleo Perfected
The Best Mexican Recipes
Slow Cooker Revolution Volume 2:
    The Easy-Prep Edition
Slow Cooker Revolution
The America's Test Kitchen
    D.I.Y. Cookbook

COOK'S COUNTRY TITLES

Big Flavors from Italian America
One-Pan Wonders
Cook It in Cast Iron
Cook's Country Eats Local
The Complete Cook's Country
    TV Show Cookbook

FOR A FULL LISTING OF
ALL OUR BOOKS:

CooksIllustrated.com
AmericasTestKitchen.com

PRAISE FOR AMERICA'S TEST KITCHEN TITLES

Selected as the Cookbook Award Winner of 2021 in the Health and Nutrition category

INTERNATIONAL ASSOCIATION OF CULINARY PROFESSIONALS (IACP) ON *THE COMPLETE PLANT-BASED COOKBOOK*

"An exhaustive but approachable primer for those looking for a 'flexible' diet. Chock-full of tips, you can dive into the science of plant-based cooking or just sit back and enjoy the 500 recipes."

MINNEAPOLIS STAR TRIBUNE ON *THE COMPLETE PLANT-BASED COOKBOOK*

"In this latest offering from the fertile minds at America's Test Kitchen the recipes focus on savory baked goods. Pizzas, flatbreads, crackers, and stuffed breads all shine here . . . Introductory essays for each recipe give background information and tips for making things come out perfectly."

BOOKLIST (STARRED REVIEW) ON *THE SAVORY BAKER*

"A mood board for one's food board is served up in this excellent guide . . . This has instant classic written all over it."

PUBLISHERS WEEKLY (STARRED REVIEW) ON *BOARDS: STYLISH SPREADS FOR CASUAL GATHERINGS*

"Reassuringly hefty and comprehensive, *The Complete Autumn and Winter Cookbook* by America's Test Kitchen has you covered with a seemingly endless array of seasonal fare . . . This overstuffed compendium is guaranteed to warm you from the inside out."

NPR ON *THE COMPLETE AUTUMN AND WINTER COOKBOOK*

"Here are the words just about any vegan would be happy to read: 'Why This Recipe Works.' Fans of America's Test Kitchen are used to seeing the phrase, and now it applies to the growing collection of plant-based creations in *Vegan for Everybody*."

THE WASHINGTON POST ON *VEGAN FOR EVERYBODY*

"If you're one of the 30 million Americans with diabetes, *The Complete Diabetes Cookbook* by America's Test Kitchen belongs on your kitchen shelf."

PARADE.COM ON *THE COMPLETE DIABETES COOKBOOK*

"Another flawless entry in the America's Test Kitchen canon, *Bowls* guides readers of all culinary skill levels in composing one-bowl meals from a variety of cuisines."

BUZZFEED BOOKS ON *BOWLS*

Selected as the Cookbook Award Winner of 2021 in the Single Subject category

INTERNATIONAL ASSOCIATION OF CULINARY PROFESSIONALS (IACP) ON *FOOLPROOF FISH*

"The book's depth, breadth, and practicality makes it a must-have for seafood lovers."

PUBLISHERS WEEKLY (STARRED REVIEW) ON *FOOLPROOF FISH*

"*The Perfect Cookie* . . . is, in a word, perfect. This is an important and substantial cookbook . . . If you love cookies, but have been a tad shy to bake on your own, all your fears will be dissipated. This is one book you can use for years with magnificently happy results."

HUFFPOST ON *THE PERFECT COOKIE*

"The book offers an impressive education for curious cake makers, new and experienced alike. A summation of 25 years of cake making at ATK, there are cakes for every taste."

THE WALL STREET JOURNAL ON *THE PERFECT CAKE*

"The go-to gift book for newlyweds, small families, or empty nesters."

ORLANDO SENTINEL ON *THE COMPLETE COOKING FOR TWO COOKBOOK*

Selected as the Cookbook Award Winner of 2021 in the General category

INTERNATIONAL ASSOCIATION OF CULINARY PROFESSIONALS (IACP) ON *MEAT ILLUSTRATED*

"True to its name, this smart and endlessly enlightening cookbook is about as definitive as it's possible to get in the modern vegetarian realm."

MEN'S JOURNAL ON *THE COMPLETE VEGETARIAN COOKBOOK*

GATHERINGS

CASUAL-FANCY MEALS TO SHARE

AMERICA'S TEST KITCHEN

Copyright © 2023 by America's Test Kitchen

All rights reserved. No part of this book may be reproduced or transmitted in any manner whatsoever without written permission from the publisher, except in the case of brief quotations embodied in critical articles or reviews.

Library of Congress Cataloging-in-Publication Data has been applied for.

ISBN 978-1-954210-14-1

"Champagne Cocktail," "Braised Celery," "Roast Leg of Lamb with Rosemary," "Lemon Tea Cake," and "Lemon Glaze (sub-recipe)" from JUBILEE: RECIPES FROM TWO CENTURIES OF AFRICAN AMERICAN COOKING: A COOKBOOK by Toni Tipton-Martin, copyright © 2019 by Toni Tipton-Martin. Used by permission of Clarkson Potter/Publishers, an imprint of Random House, a division of Penguin Random House LLC. All rights reserved.

AMERICA'S TEST KITCHEN
21 Drydock Avenue, Boston, MA 02210

Printed in Canada
10 9 8 7 6 5 4 3 2 1

Distributed by Penguin Random House
Publisher Services
Tel: 800.733.3000

FRONT COVER
PHOTOGRAPHY: Joseph Keller
FOOD STYLING: Chantal Lambeth

PICTURED ON FRONT COVER: Viet-Cajun Shrimp Boil (page 49)
PICTURED ON BACK COVER: Late-Summer Dinner with Close Friends (page 31), Spiced Panna Cotta with Candied Maple Pecans (page 196), Big-Batch Sazeracs (page 229)

EDITORIAL DIRECTOR, BOOKS: Adam Kowit

EXECUTIVE FOOD EDITOR: Dan Zuccarello

DEPUTY FOOD EDITORS: Leah Colins and Stephanie Pixley

EXECUTIVE MANAGING EDITOR: Debra Hudak

PROJECT EDITOR: Valerie Cimino

SENIOR EDITOR: Sara Mayer

TEST COOKS: Olivia Counter, Hanna Fenton, Hisham Hassan, Laila Ibrahim, José Maldonado, and David Yu

KITCHEN INTERN: Olivia Goldstein

DESIGN DIRECTOR: Lindsey Timko Chandler

DEPUTY ART DIRECTOR: Allison Boales

PHOTOGRAPHY DIRECTOR: Julie Bozzo Cote

SENIOR PHOTOGRAPHY PRODUCER: Meredith Mulcahy

SENIOR STAFF PHOTOGRAPHERS: Steve Klise and Daniel J. van Ackere

STAFF PHOTOGRAPHER: Kevin White

ADDITIONAL PHOTOGRAPHY: Joseph Keller and Carl Tremblay

FOOD STYLING: Joy Howard, Sheila Jarnes, Catrine Kelty, Chantal Lambeth, Gina McCreadie, Kendra McNight, Ashley Moore, Christie Morrison, Marie Piraino, Elle Simone Scott, Kendra Smith, and Sally Staub

PROJECT MANAGER, PUBLISHING OPERATIONS: Katie Kimmerer

SENIOR PRINT PRODUCTION SPECIALIST: Lauren Robbins

PRODUCTION AND IMAGING COORDINATOR: Amanda Yong

PRODUCTION AND IMAGING SPECIALISTS: Tricia Neumyer and Dennis Noble

COPY EDITOR: Deri Reed

PROOFREADER: Vicki Rowland

INDEXER: Elizabeth Parson

CHIEF CREATIVE OFFICER: Jack Bishop

EXECUTIVE EDITORIAL DIRECTORS: Julia Collin Davison and Bridget Lancaster

CONTENTS

WELCOME TO AMERICA'S TEST KITCHEN

This book has been tested, written, and edited by the folks at America's Test Kitchen, where curious cooks become confident cooks. Located in Boston's Seaport District in the historic Innovation and Design Building, it features 15,000 square feet of kitchen space including multiple photography and video studios. It is the home of *Cook's Illustrated* magazine and *Cook's Country* magazine and is the workday destination for more than 60 test cooks, editors, and cookware specialists. Our mission is to empower and inspire confidence, community, and creativity in the kitchen.

We start the process of testing a recipe with a complete lack of preconceptions, which means that we accept no claim, no technique, and no recipe at face value. We simply assemble as many variations as possible, test a half-dozen of the most promising, and taste the results blind. We then construct our own recipe and continue to test it, varying ingredients, techniques, and cooking times until we reach a consensus. As we like to say in the test kitchen, "We make the mistakes so you don't have to." The result, we hope, is the best version of a particular recipe, but we realize that only you can be the final judge of our success (or failure). We use the same rigorous approach when we test equipment and taste ingredients.

All of this would not be possible without a belief that good cooking, much like good music, is based on a foundation of objective technique. Some people like spicy foods and others don't, but there is a right way to sauté, there is a best way to cook a pot roast, and there are measurable scientific principles involved in producing perfectly beaten, stable egg whites. Our ultimate goal is to investigate the fundamental principles of cooking to give you the techniques, tools, and ingredients you need to become a better cook. It is as simple as that.

To see what goes on behind the scenes at America's Test Kitchen, check out our social media channels for kitchen snapshots, exclusive content, video tips, and much more. You can watch us work (in our actual test kitchen) by tuning in to *America's Test Kitchen* or *Cook's Country* on public television or on our websites. Listen to *Proof*, *Mystery Recipe*, and *The Walk-In* (AmericasTestKitchen.com/podcasts) to hear engaging, complex stories about people and food. Want to hone your cooking skills or finally learn how to bake—with an America's Test Kitchen test cook? Enroll in one of our online cooking classes.

However you choose to visit us, we welcome you into our kitchen, where you can stand by our side as we test our way to the best recipes in America.

- facebook.com/AmericasTestKitchen
- instagram.com/TestKitchen
- youtube.com/AmericasTestKitchen
- tiktok.com/@TestKitchen
- twitter.com/TestKitchen
- pinterest.com/TestKitchen

AmericasTestKitchen.com
CooksIllustrated.com
CooksCountry.com
OnlineCookingSchool.com

JOIN OUR COMMUNITY OF RECIPE TESTERS

Our recipe testers provide valuable feedback on recipes under development by ensuring that they are foolproof in home kitchens. Help the America's Test Kitchen book team investigate the how and why behind successful recipes from your home kitchen.

LET'S GET TOGETHER

INTRODUCTION

These aren't your parents' oldfangled dinner parties. The new ethos is that there's no "right" way to get together. Every host can write their own playbook and make their own rules. The idea of so-called perfect entertaining is much too subjective, and it implies a certain rigidity that we simply don't need anymore. Life has gotten less formal in lots of ways, and that definitely applies to how we gather together over food.

In that spirit, no will judge you if you invite people over and order everything in, something that has become much easier to do in recent years. But this book is for those of us who love to cook and want to share the food we make with friends. Cooks from across the departments of America's Test Kitchen have stepped out of the test kitchen in these pages, sharing personal recipes from their home kitchens and their favorite ways to entertain friends and family. And each cook shares their story of *why* their menu is meaningful to them.

These gatherings are of varying sizes, from intimate dinners for 4 (yes, just 4 people are enough to constitute a gathering) to bigger crowds of 10 to 12. They can take place anywhere, be it in your home, your backyard, a park, or even a vacation rental. The food can be served however works with your space and your preferences. And you can get as creative as you like with the menu. Keep things simple with a big bowl of pasta, a salad platter, and a fruit crisp that make the most of summer produce. Cook up a huge, messy shrimp boil for everyone to dive into with their hands, then serve piña coladas for dessert. If a trip to Spain isn't in the cards this year, bring everybody together over a small-plates feast inspired by one of the Basque Country's most renowned pintxos bars.

Although this new way to gather may be more informal (and definitely more fun), that still doesn't mean that having people over is effortless. It can be a bit intimidating for anyone, especially when your celebration centers around the food. (And as far as we're concerned, what celebration doesn't?) So each menu maker guides you through their game plan for success, including make-ahead choices and even when to skip a dish to streamline things. We think that there's a happy satisfaction in expending some effort to put together a meal so memorable that everyone will want to do it again (but not so much effort that *you* don't want to do it again). We believe that success comes not so much from trying to impress guests but more from having everyone feel well taken care of—and, naturally, very well fed.

So let's all get excited about entertaining again.

MEET THE MENU MAKERS

JACK BISHOP
CHIEF CREATIVE OFFICER

› **TOP TIP:** Do something unexpected. Serve a cheese you've never tasted. Do a taste-test of pickles from the farmers' market or of fancy chocolates. Create a tablescape using found elements from your yard. Eat the entire meal in cozy chairs by a fire pit. Mix it up and have fun!

› **A FAVORITE COOKBOOK:** *The Classic Italian Cook Book* by Marcella Hazan

› **SECRET WEAPON:** Salad is my superpower.

› **FAVORITE INGREDIENTS:** Extra-virgin olive oil, garden tomatoes, lobster, pasta, chocolate

SAM BLOCK
DIGITAL TEST COOK

› **TOP TIP:** Always, always, always, have a snack or two on the table before your guests arrive. Even if it's chips and dip or crackers and cheese, it gets your guests snacking and engaged so that you don't fall into "everyone must be starving" panic mode.

› **A FAVORITE COOKBOOK:** *The Flavor Bible* by Karen Page and Andrew Dornenburg

› **SECRET WEAPON:** Kitchen shears. I trim meat; cut bacon; and snip scallions, chives, and pepperoncini right into my salads, among other things.

› **FAVORITE INGREDIENTS:** Miso, gochujang, fish sauce (basically, anything that's fermented is all right by me)

MORGAN BOLLING
EXECUTIVE EDITOR, CREATIVE CONTENT, *COOK'S COUNTRY*

> **TOP TIP:** Don't forget to set the atmosphere beyond the food. String lights are an easy and inexpensive way to liven up any space. And come up with a fun playlist for your dinner party—bonus points for adding any songs that echo the food or the theme in some way!

> **A FAVORITE COOKBOOK:** *Deep Run Roots* by Vivian Howard

> **SECRET WEAPON:** I'm not sure if a charcoal grill can be called "secret," but using my trusty grill and rocking my matching charcoal earrings, I can cook anything.

> **FAVORITE INGREDIENTS:** Cured pork products (like salami, capicola, bacon), smoked paprika, any citrus

CAMILA CHAPARRO
SENIOR EDITOR, BOOKS

> **TOP TIP:** Make sure you have a clean kitchen and an empty dishwasher before guests arrive. It's easier said than done, but washing dishes as you go really pays off in terms of minimizing stress and avoiding ending the party with a gigantic mess.

> **A FAVORITE COOKBOOK:** *The New Basics Cookbook* by Sheila Lukins and Julee Rosso

> **SECRET WEAPON:** My husband, who loves to do dishes (at least, he claims to)

> **FAVORITE INGREDIENTS:** Any fresh herb, lime zest, Persian cucumbers, grape tomatoes, crispy shallots

LEAH COLINS
DEPUTY FOOD EDITOR, BOOKS

> **TOP TIP:** When entertaining, I always choose a dessert that I can make a few days ahead of time. Cookies are an easy, surefire go-to option. Alternatively, I might ask a guest to bring something of their choosing—and then be happy about whatever they bring.

> **A FAVORITE COOKBOOK:** *On Food and Cooking* by Harold McGee

> **SECRET WEAPON:** A kitchen timer! With two toddlers at home, a timer has saved many a recipe from being forgotten in the oven.

> **FAVORITE INGREDIENTS:** Eggs, potatoes, soy sauce

JULIA COLLIN DAVISON
EXECUTIVE EDITORIAL DIRECTOR

> **TOP TIP:** Coco Chanel has been quoted as saying, "Before you leave the house, look in the mirror and take one thing off." I use the same theory when planning food for a party. It's easy (and fun) to get carried away in the planning stages and come up with a menu that's too long or overly complicated, but this will bite you in the end. Better to streamline the food and give yourself some extra time to relax and enjoy your own party.

> **A FAVORITE COOKBOOK:** *Please to the Table* by Anya von Bremzen and John C. Welchman

> **SECRET WEAPON:** Chilled Champagne

> **FAVORITE INGREDIENTS:** Feta cheese, anchovies, smoked paprika

KEITH DRESSER
EXECUTIVE FOOD EDITOR, *COOK'S ILLUSTRATED*

> **TOP TIP:** Set up a DIY bar out of the kitchen flow, and when guests arrive, encourage them to fix themselves a drink. It doesn't have to be elaborate, but have it stocked with a few varieties of wine and a tub of beers on ice. I also like to have a variety of flavored seltzers on hand. Don't forget to include glassware and cocktail napkins as part of the setup.

> **A FAVORITE COOKBOOK:** I have a treasured binder of family recipes that is part cookbook, part nostalgia trip.

> **SECRET WEAPON:** My fully stocked bar

> **FAVORITE INGREDIENTS:** Lemons, sriracha (or any fermented hot sauce), cilantro, all cheeses

STEVE DUNN
SENIOR EDITOR, *COOK'S ILLUSTRATED*

> **TOP TIP:** Don't cook a recipe for the very first time when you have company. Give the whole menu a practice run so that you better understand the method and timing so you can prepare for the flow of the event.

> **A FAVORITE COOKBOOK:** *Taste & Technique* by Naomi Pomeroy

> **SECRET WEAPON:** My wife would say that it's my ability to organize myself in the kitchen so that I remain calm and composed regardless of how many things I have going on at once. I'd say it's all about advanced planning and placement.

> **FAVORITE INGREDIENTS:** Mustard, fish sauce, just about any pickled produce

MATTHEW FAIRMAN
SENIOR EDITOR, *COOK'S COUNTRY*

> **TOP TIP:** If the first guests arrive early while you're still setting up, enlist their help with the last few small tasks, from slicing bread to opening wine to lighting candles. It gives them something to do, breaks the ice, and establishes a relaxed, convivial feeling.

> **A FAVORITE COOKBOOK:** *The Flavor Bible* by Karen Page and Andrew Dornenburg

> **SECRET WEAPON:** Monosodium glutamate (aka MSG, sold under the brand name Ac'cent) has unfairly gotten a bad rap. I keep a pint container (labeled "SecretSalt") next to my salt crock, to add instant umami to any dish that needs it.

> **FAVORITE INGREDIENTS:** Soy sauce (I keep about a dozen varieties), fish sauce (I keep about a half dozen), chili crisp, shrimp and tomatoes fresh from the Low Country of South Carolina (my birthplace)

JOE GITTER
SENIOR EDITOR, BOOKS

> **TOP TIP:** Learn a new cocktail by heart and have any ingredients you need prepared, like simple syrup or citrus juice. As guests arrive, a confident shake in a cocktail shaker will impress everyone. And a stiff drink, quickly delivered, ensures a lively start to the night!

> **A FAVORITE COOKBOOK:** *An Everlasting Meal* by Tamar Adler

> **SECRET WEAPON:** Clear ice for my famous cocktails

> **FAVORITE INGREDIENTS:** Tarragon, hazelnuts, lemon zest, anchovies, Aria extra-virgin olive oil

BECKY HAYS
DEPUTY EDITOR, *COOK'S ILLUSTRATED*

> **TOP TIP:** Start an apron collection. If you have some fun, stylish offerings to help protect your guest's party clothes, they'll be even more excited to help out in the kitchen.

> **A FAVORITE COOKBOOK:** My grandmother's 1931 edition of *The Joy of Cooking* by Irma S. Rombauer

> **SECRET WEAPON:** Homemade stock

> **FAVORITE INGREDIENTS:** Artichokes, butter, corn, grapefruit, cherries

MARK HUXSOLL
TEST COOK, *COOK'S COUNTRY*

› **TOP TIP:** Whatever you're serving to drink, always have more glasses than guests. As people mingle, glasses may get mixed up or people might need fresh ones, and if things get really festive, there's always the possibility of breakage!

› **A FAVORITE COOKBOOK:** *Le Bec-Fin Recipes* by Georges Perrier

› **SECRET WEAPON:** My immersion circulator. It enables me to prep ahead so the hard work is done before guests even walk in the door.

› **FAVORITE INGREDIENTS:** Good-quality cultured butter, cheeses and charcuterie, any local and seasonal produce, natural wine. (A perfectly curated playlist is an ingredient, too!)

NICOLE KONSTANTINAKOS
DEPUTY FOOD EDITOR, *COOK'S COUNTRY*

› **TOP TIP:** Make sure to plan for a leisurely dinner. Everyone, including you, will enjoy it so much more. Consider taking a short break between the meal and dessert, and break out after-dinner drinks, nuts, or fresh fruit to encourage people to linger at the table.

› **A FAVORITE COOKBOOK:** *Chez Panisse Café Cookbook* by Alice Waters and the cooks of Chez Panisse

› **SECRET WEAPON:** Kitchen tongs (What *can't* they do?)

› **FAVORITE INGREDIENTS:** Olive oil, lemon, flake sea salt, furikake, Aleppo pepper flakes

BRIDGET LANCASTER
EXECUTIVE EDITORIAL DIRECTOR

› **TOP TIP:** Continue to be a gracious host even after the party is over. Keep tabs on any gifts or help that you receive from your guests, then be sure to send a thank-you note (via mail!) to tell them how much you appreciated their company.

› **A FAVORITE COOKBOOK:** *Nopi* by Yotam Ottolenghi and Ramael Scully

› **SECRET WEAPON:** My husband, a gifted, classically trained chef who can produce dinner masterpieces seemingly out of thin air. He's also a great storyteller and one of the funniest people I know, which makes him perfect for any get-together. A close second would be our multi-tap Kegerator, which keeps our various home brews on draft.

› **FAVORITE INGREDIENTS:** Fat (bacon fat, tallow, lard, schmaltz, olive oil), garlic, eggs, vanilla beans, wine

AMANDA LUCHTEL
TEST COOK, *COOK'S COUNTRY*

> **TOP TIP:** Have a progressive dinner party entirely in your own home. Serving each course or dish in a different room during dinner either a) allows you to quickly clean after your guests move to the next room for the next course, or b) enables you to leave a mess in that room and not worry about it until after your guests leave.

> **A FAVORITE COOKBOOK:** *Six Seasons* by Joshua McFadden

> **SECRET WEAPON:** The freezer. I store everything from chicken and vegetable scraps for stock to rolled cookie dough for freshly baked cookies, so I'm always ready for anything.

> **FAVORITE INGREDIENTS:** Soy sauce, lemon, mayo, jarred spicy marinara, honey

SARA MAYER
SENIOR EDITOR, BOOKS

> **TOP TIP:** If something stresses you, such as pre-dinner drinks or dessert, hand this assignment off to someone you trust and promise yourself that you will be happy with whatever they do. In the end, it's more about having fun than about whether someone does exactly what you would have done.

> **A FAVORITE COOKBOOK:** *Six Seasons* by Joshua McFadden

> **SECRET WEAPON:** Having a rotation of recipes that I know will always work and not making anything fancy when people come for dinner. Because of my job, guests usually expect something fancy but are always delighted when I make something like mac and cheese.

> **FAVORITE INGREDIENTS:** Chicken-apple sausage, hoisin sauce, Orrington Farms broth bases

LISA McMANUS
EXECUTIVE EDITOR, REVIEWS

> **TOP TIP:** Make sure your dining chairs are really comfortable; it doesn't matter how fancy they are or whether they match. The best conversations in the world happen after dinner is mostly over and people are still sitting around the table, talking and laughing over the strewn dishes and utensils. Once you all get up to move to the living room, the spell is broken.

> **A FAVORITE COOKBOOK:** *Pasta e Verdura* by Jack Bishop

> **SECRET WEAPON:** Not being 100 percent prepared. When the earliest guests arrive, I ask them to do something small—chop a garnish, open the wine, scooch the place settings over to add one more. It instantly gets them involved, and I find that everybody relaxes. Julia Child was famous for doing this, and I think it's brilliant.

> **FAVORITE INGREDIENTS:** Extra-virgin olive oil, Maldon salt, freshly ground pepper, La Dalia Pimentón de la Vera (a smoked paprika from Spain)

ERIN McMURRER
DIRECTOR OF CULINARY PRODUCTION, TV

› **TOP TIP:** I'm a list person. Making lists saves a ton of time and helps me to better organize myself. I make a shopping spreadsheet that lists all ingredients by category, as well as quantities, dates needed for prep work, and the source for purchasing. I also create a list of key tasks for the days leading up to my party and a separate day-of checklist.

› **A FAVORITE COOKBOOK:** *Plenty* by Yotam Ottolenghi

› **SECRET WEAPON:** A Kuhn Rikon Original Swiss Peeler

› **FAVORITE INGREDIENTS:** Flake sea salt, Aleppo pepper, lemon, extra-virgin olive oil, avocado

ASHLEY MOORE
FOOD STYLIST AND *COOK'S COUNTRY* CAST MEMBER

› **TOP TIP:** Embrace the cleanup. At any one of my family's get-togethers, the best part of the night is always doing the dishes. I realize how strange that sounds, especially since I am not a fan of doing them at home. But we crank up the stereo, pour fresh glasses of wine, and after we all pitch in to get the table cleared and dishes done, it's time to dance and sing into make-believe microphones (aka candlesticks).

› **A FAVORITE COOKBOOK:** A tiny ring-bound binder of my nana's recipes

› **SECRET WEAPON:** Being able to say, "Out of the kitchen, guys!" at a tone and audio level my boys actually listen to

› **FAVORITE INGREDIENTS:** Salt, extra-virgin olive oil, hot honey

CHRISTIE MORRISON
EXECUTIVE EDITOR, VIDEO AND COOKING SCHOOL

› **TOP TIP:** Ice, ice, baby. Buy some. Then buy some more. Buy more than you think you will possibly need. You will almost always definitely need it.

› **A FAVORITE COOKBOOK:** *Super Natural Every Day* by Heidi Swanson

› **SECRET WEAPON:** My mini whisk and my self-deprecating sense of humor

› **FAVORITE INGREDIENTS:** Maldon salt, lemons, pecorino cheese, in-season tomatoes, fresh dill

STEPHANIE PIXLEY
DEPUTY FOOD EDITOR, BOOKS

> **TOP TIP:** Don't forget to ask guests about dietary restrictions and allergies before you set your menu. It's the worst to go through the trouble of planning (and executing) a menu only to discover that a guest can't eat half of what you've made!

> **A FAVORITE COOKBOOK:** *The Art of Simple Food* by Alice Waters

> **SECRET WEAPON:** The Spotify playlists that my husband and I work out ahead of time—we make sure they're long enough to loop on shuffle for the whole night.

> **FAVORITE INGREDIENTS:** Lemon, Shaoxing wine, salt, any cheese

ELLE SIMONE SCOTT
EXECUTIVE EDITOR

> **TOP TIP:** Don't forget the little ones. My family always had a kids' table with easy-to-eat portions of the dinner just for them, cups with lids and straws (to prevent spills), and some games and crayons. It always leaves the kids feeling independent and still included.

> **A FAVORITE COOKBOOK:** Any edition of *The Joy of Cooking*

> **SECRET WEAPON:** Lots of quart- and pint-size containers with lids. I store anything and everything in them in the fridge and the pantry.

> **FAVORITE INGREDIENTS:** Finishing salts, dried mushrooms, mayonnaise, tinned fish

DAN SOUZA
EDITOR-IN-CHIEF, *COOK'S ILLUSTRATED*

> **TOP TIP:** When you're planning the timeline, make a point of carving out a few minutes for yourself just before serving. The goal is to reset and transition from cooking the meal to personally enjoying the meal.

> **A FAVORITE COOKBOOK:** *Filipinx* by Angela Dimayuga and Ligaya Michan

> **SECRET WEAPON:** Mayonnaise. It adds hidden richness to my sauce for sesame noodles, makes a sandwich come together, and adds body to any vinaigrette.

> **FAVORITE INGREDIENTS:** Tahini, clams, butter, fish sauce, my mom's preserved Meyer lemons

TONI TIPTON-MARTIN
EDITOR-IN-CHIEF, *COOK'S COUNTRY*

> **TOP TIP:** Don't wait for a special occasion to serve a special-occasion dish. Choose a treasured recipe and build the rest of your menu around it, then incorporate telling its story into your gathering.

> **A FAVORITE COOKBOOK:** *A Domestic Cook Book* by Malinda Russell

> **SECRET WEAPON:** My husband the dishwasher, who keeps things orderly as I cook

> **FAVORITE INGREDIENTS:** Garlic, lemon, salt, pepper

ERICA TURNER
ASSOCIATE EDITOR, *COOK'S ILLUSTRATED*

> **TOP TIP:** Give your guests a parting gift. It can be something as simple as spiced nuts or a cookie wrapped in a little bag or a small package of loose tea. It makes a delightful surprise and gives them a fond farewell that also helps them remember the evening.

> **A FAVORITE COOKBOOK:** Anything by Ina Garten

> **SECRET WEAPON:** A variety of sturdy rubber spatulas. Whether I'm cooking, baking, or just mixing a sauce or dip, they're so versatile and an absolute kitchen staple. Plus it feels so good to know you're not wasting a drop when you can get a clean scrape around a bowl or a jar.

> **FAVORITE INGREDIENTS:** Onions, garlic, tomatoes

DAN ZUCCARELLO
EXECUTIVE FOOD EDITOR, BOOKS

> **TOP TIP:** Choose dishes that allow you to step away from the kitchen so that you can enjoy being with your guests. I especially like to grill when I have people over so that everyone can be mingling. And serve family-style whenever possible—plattered items look really impressive and are easy to serve.

> **A FAVORITE COOKBOOK:** *The Good Housekeeping Illustrated Cookbook* (the 1980 edition, the book I learned to cook from)

> **SECRET WEAPON:** An instant-read thermometer. It's such a safety blanket, and I use it to temp everything to avoid overcooking, especially proteins.

> **FAVORITE INGREDIENTS:** Sherry vinegar, coarse sea salt, extra-virgin olive oil (all excellent for finishing dishes)

THE PRACTICALITIES

The first step in hosting any memorable gathering is to get the logistics in order. Since there are endless options for getting together these days, we've given you some guidance here to help you narrow down ideas and start to get the particulars of your gathering clear in your head.

PRE-PLANNING POINTERS

HOW MANY GUESTS DO YOU WANT TO INVITE?

You could keep it intimate with four people—go relaxed with Late-Summer Dinner for Close Friends (page 31), low-key with A Cozy Icelandic Evening (page 129), or craft a swooningly romantic Double-Date Night (page 209). Or plan a bash for 10 or 12 friends with Nacho Average Barbecue (page 63) or Oktoberfest at Home (page 173). Be honest with yourself about how much space (and ambition and time) you have to devote to entertaining.

WHAT TIME OF DAY DO YOU WANT TO HOST?

Evening is often the obvious choice. It's typically easiest to get folks together at the end of a day, and hosting on the weekend can give you the whole day to prepare. But we've also got some great menu options for other times of day: Mexican Brunch (page 217) and Midwestern Brunch (page 135), as well as a Vegetarian Luncheon (page 199) and The Great British Picnic (page 99), designed to while away a sunny afternoon, ideally on a patch of grass.

WHAT KIND OF FOOD DO YOU WANT TO SERVE?
WHAT STYLE OF PARTY DO YOU WANT TO HAVE?

If you want to go interactive and DIY, consider a Vegetarian Dumpling Party (page 79), a Bao Bar (page 71), or the Not Dog Party (page 145). For a grazing or small-plates style of meal, check out the Appetizers for Dinner Party (page 155) or A Night at La Cuchara de San Telmo (page 261). For a more traditional (but never boring) coursed-out, sit-down dinner, consider the Modern Tenderloin Dinner (page 37).

Or take it all outside with Summertime and the Grilling Is Easy (page 91). When choosing and planning food, don't forget to ask guests about any dietary restrictions.

WHAT KIND OF BEVERAGES DO YOU WANT TO SERVE? HOW MUCH DO YOU NEED?

Some of the menus include cocktail recipes or wine and beer pairing suggestions. But you should serve whatever you like and what you think will work best for your party. A good general guideline is to plan for three alcoholic drinks per guest for a dinner party lasting 3 hours. One 750-milliter wine bottle is 25⅓ ounces, so plan on getting approximately five 5-ounce pours from each bottle. (And don't forget to pay attention to how much people are drinking so that no one accidentally gets overserved.)

Make sure you have plenty of interesting nonalcoholic options as well, even if it's just a nice sparkling water. (Or see page 28 for some easy recipes.) It's smart to plan on three servings of nonalcoholic beverages per guest.

MAKE-AHEAD MOMENTUM

GAME PLANNING

Prepping and cooking ahead when possible ensures that you can maximize quality fun time with your guests. Every menu starts with a Game Plan that explains how the creator strategizes make-ahead options to get everything to the table smoothly and stress-free. In many cases, recipes have multiple make-ahead options, allowing you to customize them so that you can choose what works best with your own party-planning schedule.

PREP COMPONENTS AHEAD

Salads often aren't make-ahead candidates, but many of the salads in this book can have components prepped ahead and then assembled shortly before serving. For example, all of the elements for the Brunch Salad (page 140) can be prepped ahead. The farro for the Farro and Kale Salad with Fennel, Olives, and Pecorino (page 114) can be cooked a couple of days ahead. Sauces used in our recipes are also good candidates for prepping. In fact, all of the accompanying sauces for the pinxtos in A Night at La Cuchara de San Telmo (page 261) can be made ahead.

MAKE DISHES PARTIALLY AHEAD

Bringing main courses along to the point where all you need to do is cook them is a strong strategy for any gathering. For example, you can butterfly, skewer, and marinate the chicken for Grilled Lemon-Garlic Chicken with New Potatoes (page 94) a day in advance, so that all you have to do when it's time to cook is fire up the grill. You can assemble "The Italian" Stromboli (page 170) entirely ahead and freeze it. Then, just thaw and bake until golden and cheesy. The pastry, mousse, and sauce for the Raspberry Napoleons with Bittersweet Chocolate Sauce (page 214) can be made ahead, so all you'll need to do is assemble, serve, and wait for accolades.

MAKE DISHES ENTIRELY AHEAD

Experienced entertainers know that dessert is a make-ahead favorite. The Lemon Tea Cake (page 288) and Sticky Sweet Sow Bars (page 189) are among our desserts that can be made in their entirety well ahead of party time. And the No-Churn Lime-Pineapple Swirl Ice Cream (page 89), Guava Sorbet (page 77), and Vintage Triple-Layer "Christmas" Jell-O (page 241) *must* be made ahead.

SERVING STRATEGIES

HAVE A SURPLUS OF SERVEWARE

Have more glassware, plates, and silverware on hand than you think you'll need so that you don't get caught short having to wash anything during your get-together. If you don't have matching sets, don't sweat it! Embrace the appeal of mismatching. Alternatively, you can purchase inexpensive basic sets of 8 or 12 items for nearly everything you'll need for serving.

Assemble your serving platters and serving utensils well ahead of your gathering. That way you have time to make sure you have what you'll need for the menu you chose, or you can reach out to guests to ask them to lend something.

If you're serving buffet-style, even if just for starting snacks or appetizers, consider little tags or signs with the name of the dish. There's also a huge array of charms or markers for wine glasses and cocktail glasses, which is a fun thing to offer guests so they know which glass is theirs.

DECIDE HOW YOU'RE SERVING

These menus are designed to be very flexible: Bring everything to the table at once or serve dishes in stages; go buffet-style, or family-style, or plate and serve each guest—it's up to you.

If a buffet is in order, such as for Porkadise Found (page 183) or Appetizers for Dinner Party (page 155), make sure you have a large enough surface to present platters of food with plenty of room for guests to access it without a traffic jam.

Many of these menus are perfect for serving family-style, including Nonna's Sunday Supper (page 251), Autumn Vegetarian Salads + Dessert (page 191), and Midwestern Family Classics (page 237).

If you'd like to plate and serve each diner's meal for an elegant experience, especially appropriate for Double-Date Night (page 209) and Winter Comfort Dinner (page 273), enlist help from a willing guest (or two) to help that process go quickly and smoothly. People will be happy to help and feel involved.

USE YOUR APPLIANCE RESOURCES

Pull out your slow cooker to keep finished dishes warm without overcooking them, including the Icelandic-Style Creamy Fish Soup (page 131) in A Cozy Icelandic Evening, the Costillas al Vino Tinto (page 266) from A Night at La Cuchara de San Telmo, and the Smoky Chicken and Andouille Gumbo (page 232) from Gumbo Weather Get-Together.

If you have a warming oven, toaster oven, or "keep warm" stovetop burner, a gathering is the perfect time to put them to good use. Use a warming or toaster oven to warm up the Schiacciata (page 111) from Take Me Back to Tuscany or the Simple Crusty Bread (page 132) from A Cozy Icelandic Evening. Even just taking advantage of the residual heat from your regular oven can keep things warm.

Don't forget to check and see whether your chosen menu requires anything special. If you're planning to include the Fresh Juice Bar in the Midwestern Brunch (page 137), you'll need a juicer. If you want to make the from-scratch Fennel-Anise Pizzelle in Nonna's Sunday Supper (page 258), you'll need a pizzelle maker. Set up your blender for the Piña Coladas with Mint and Lime in the Viet-Cajun Shrimp Boil (page 51). A mini slow cooker will come in handy to keep the Vin Chaud warm during the Winter Comfort Dinner (page 275).

MENU MANAGEMENT

YOU DON'T HAVE TO MAKE THE WHOLE MENU

Think of these menus as aspirational ideals, and don't feel pressure to make every dish. The menu-makers often don't! Remember that this is *your* party, so tailor it to make it your own. The Not Dog Party (page 145) is a superfun and versatile spread. You can make only one (or neither) of the relishes, rather than both; and if you don't want to make smoked carrots for the dogs, go ahead and use your favorite store-bought regular or vegan hot dogs. You can still achieve Porkadise Found (page 183) if you choose to make either the Salami Get This Straight Salad or the Piggy Peppers, rather than both. There are three toppings for the polenta in Palomas and Polenta (page 119), but you can make two instead, or even just one.

Outsourcing dessert entirely is another great way to take some pressure off. When guests ask what they can bring, either suggest they bring their favorite store-bought dessert or assign them the menu's dessert recipe! (And just as important: Be at peace with your decision, come what may.)

TAKE ADVANTAGE OF STORE-BOUGHT SHORTCUTS

For example, in the Appetizers for Dinner Party (page 155), the Flatbreads, Two Ways start with store-bought pizza dough. And while the homemade Biscuit Crackers in that menu are a flaky, crunchy delight, you can certainly substitute your favorite store-bought crackers to pair with the Red Lentil Dip. Instead of making homemade Schiacciata for the Take Me Back to Tuscany menu (page 109), purchase focaccia from your local bakery.

OUTSOURCE COCKTAIL SNACKS

It's nice to have a little welcoming nibble already set out when guests arrive, something you don't have to think about while you attend to the last-minute details of your menu. The grocery store or local fancy market is your best friend here. Since you'll be focusing on the rest of the party menu, keep this part as simple as possible. It's impossible to go wrong with your favorite chips-and-dip combo or a vegetable tray with hummus. If you want a great make-ahead snack that would work for any get-together, check out the Sticky Spiced Nuts with Orange, Honey, and Rosemary on page 167.

WHAT TO TELL GUESTS TO BRING

It sounds obvious, but a bottle of wine or some flavored seltzer will *never* go to waste. Or if you're not well stocked with serving platters, ask a friend if they wouldn't mind lending one or two to the evening. A more creative response is to ask each guest to bring their own containers for leftovers. Or ask someone to bring a conversation game, like an Icebreaker card deck or Cards Against Humanity.

Alternatively, instead of asking guests to bring a thing, ask them to lend their skills. Can they mix or serve the cocktails? Would they be willing to help you serve the meal, or to stay afterward to help clean up? Could they make a music playlist to pair with the menu's theme?

One thing you shouldn't ask guests to bring: any item that you need for pre-dinner festivities. If they're late, you're stuck.

MIX AND MATCH A MENU

The menu makers designed gatherings around some of their favorite foods and party themes. We encourage you to do the same! Here's a list of all of the recipes in this book, organized by category and accompanied by the yield, so that you can mix and match dishes to create your own personalized get-together.

COCKTAILS AND NONALCOHOLIC DRINKS	SERVES
Cucumber Water (page 28)	6 to 8
› Cucumber Water with Lemon and Mint	
› Cucumber Water with Lime and Ginger	
› Cucumber Water with Orange and Tarragon	
Iced Black Tea (page 28)	8
› Iced Raspberry-Basil Black Tea	
› Iced Ginger-Pomegranate Black Tea	
› Iced Apple-Cinnamon Black Tea	
Piña Coladas with Mint and Lime (page 51)	10
Gin Camps (page 55)	4
English 75 (page 101)	8
Palomas for a Crowd (page 121)	8
Simple Green Juice (page 137)	1
Carrot-Pineapple-Ginger Juice (page 137)	1
Sparkling Spiked Lemonade (page 147)	8
Cider Bourbon Cocktails (page 157)	10
The Spiked Swine (page 185)	6
Pear-Mint Sparkling Iced Green Tea (page 201)	6
Bijou Cocktails (page 211)	4
Hibiscus Margaritas (page 219)	6

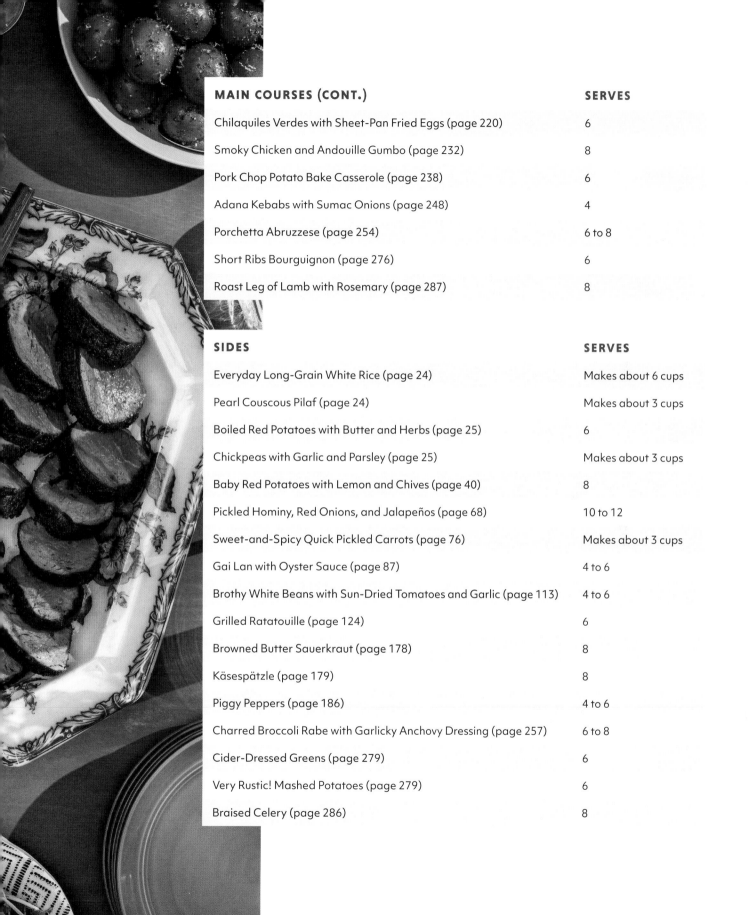

DESSERTS

RESCUE RECIPES

These ultrasimple recipes are adaptable to many different menus and are an easy way to stretch your food to accommodate any last-minute extra (or just extra-hungry) guests.

EVERYDAY LONG-GRAIN WHITE RICE

Makes about 6 cups
Total Time: 40 minutes
Perfectly light and tender, this rice has just the right texture to make it a great side dish or bed for any number of saucy dishes. Letting the cooked rice sit, still covered, off the heat for 10 minutes ensures that any extra moisture is absorbed. Omit the salt if you're serving the rice with a salty dish.

   2   cups long-grain white rice
   3   cups water
  ½   teaspoon table salt (optional)

1 Place rice in fine-mesh strainer and rinse under running water until water running through rice is almost clear, about 1½ minutes, agitating rice with your hand every so often.

2 Combine rice; water; and salt, if using, in large saucepan and bring to simmer over high heat. Stir rice with rubber spatula, dislodging any rice that sticks to bottom of saucepan. Cover, reduce heat to low, and cook for 20 minutes. (Steam should steadily emit from sides of saucepan. If water bubbles out from under lid, reduce heat slightly.)

3 Remove from heat; do not uncover. Let stand, covered, for 10 minutes. Gently fluff rice with fork. Serve.

PEARL COUSCOUS PILAF

Makes about 3 cups
Total Time: 30 minutes
Canola oil keeps this simple pilaf neutral enough to work with anything. You can substitute extra-virgin olive oil or butter, if you prefer. You can also double the recipe, if desired. The couscous can be refrigerated for up to 3 days.

    1   teaspoon canola oil
    1   cup pearl couscous
 1¼   cups water
   ⅛   teaspoon table salt

1 Cook oil and couscous in large saucepan over medium heat, stirring frequently, until about half the grains are golden brown, about 3 minutes. Stir in water and salt and bring to boil. Reduce heat to low, cover, and simmer until couscous is tender and water is absorbed, 9 to 12 minutes.

2 Off heat, let sit for 10 minutes. Fluff couscous with fork and season with salt and pepper to taste. Serve.

BOILED RED POTATOES WITH BUTTER AND HERBS

Serves 6

Total Time: 35 minutes

Look for small red potatoes, measuring 1 to 2 inches in diameter. If using larger potatoes, halve or quarter them and adjust the cooking time as needed. Feel free to use whatever fresh herb matches the culinary theme of your menu.

- 2 pounds small red potatoes, unpeeled
- 2 tablespoons unsalted butter
- 1 tablespoon minced fresh chives, tarragon, or parsley

Cover potatoes by 1 inch water in large saucepan and bring to boil over high heat. Reduce to simmer and cook until potatoes are tender, 20 to 25 minutes. Drain potatoes well, then toss gently with butter in large bowl until butter melts. Season with salt and pepper to taste, sprinkle with chives, and serve.

CHICKPEAS WITH GARLIC AND PARSLEY

Makes about 3 cups

Total Time: 30 minutes

Ultraversatile canned chickpeas cooked with garlic, onion, and vegetable broth work as part of a plate-sharing arrangement with any number of party menus. The chickpeas can be refrigerated for up to 3 days.

- ¼ cup extra-virgin olive oil, divided
- 4 garlic cloves, sliced thin
- ⅛ teaspoon red pepper flakes
- 1 onion, chopped fine
- ¼ teaspoon table salt
- 2 (15-ounce) cans chickpeas, rinsed
- 1 cup vegetable broth
- 2 tablespoons minced fresh parsley
- 2 teaspoons lemon juice

1 Cook 3 tablespoons oil, garlic, and pepper flakes in 12-inch skillet over medium heat, stirring frequently, until garlic turns golden but not brown, about 3 minutes. Stir in onion and salt and cook until softened and lightly browned,

5 to 7 minutes. Stir in chickpeas and broth and bring to simmer. Reduce heat to medium-low, cover, and cook until chickpeas are heated through and flavors meld, about 7 minutes.

2 Uncover, increase heat to high, and continue to cook until nearly all liquid has evaporated, about 3 minutes. Off heat, stir in parsley and lemon juice. Season with salt and pepper to taste and drizzle with remaining 1 tablespoon oil. Serve.

EASIEST-EVER BISCUITS

Makes 10 biscuits

Total Time: 30 minutes

The dough for these biscuits is moist and scoopable, and it rises up in the oven to produce golden biscuits that are rich and tender. The biscuits come together very quickly, so start heating your oven before gathering your ingredients. They are wonderful brushed with a bit of melted butter, but you can skip that step if you're serving the biscuits with a rich accompaniment. The biscuits can be stored in a zipper-lock bag at room temperature for up to 24 hours. Reheat them in a 300-degree oven for 10 minutes.

3 cups (15 ounces) all-purpose flour
4 teaspoons sugar
1 tablespoon baking powder
¼ teaspoon baking soda
1¼ teaspoons table salt
2 cups heavy cream
2 tablespoons unsalted butter, melted (optional)

1 Adjust oven rack to upper-middle position and heat oven to 450 degrees. Line rimmed baking sheet with parchment paper. In medium bowl, whisk together flour, sugar, baking powder, baking soda, and salt. Microwave cream until just warmed to body temperature (95 to 100 degrees), 60 to 90 seconds, stirring halfway through microwaving. Stir cream into flour mixture until soft, uniform dough forms.

2 Spray ⅓-cup dry measuring cup with vegetable oil spray. Drop level scoops of batter 2 inches apart on prepared sheet (biscuits should measure about 2½ inches wide and 1¼ inches tall). Respray measuring cup after every 3 or 4 scoops. If portions are misshapen, use your fingertips to gently reshape dough into level cylinders. Bake until tops are light golden brown, 10 to 12 minutes, rotating sheet halfway through baking. Brush hot biscuits with melted butter, if using. Serve warm.

COMPOUND BUTTER

Makes about ½ cup
Total Time: 10 minutes

Enliven any bread with some sophisticated butter. Simply whip 8 tablespoons softened unsalted butter in a bowl with a fork until light and fluffy, then mix in any of the following ingredient combinations and season with salt and pepper to taste. Cover with plastic wrap or roll into a log and refrigerate for up to 4 days. (You can also freeze compound butter, wrapped tightly in plastic wrap, for up to 2 months.)

HERB BUTTER

Use ¼ cup chopped fresh herbs of your choice. If you like, add 1 minced garlic clove, 2 tablespoons minced shallot, or 4 teaspoons rinsed and minced capers.

HERB-MUSTARD BUTTER

Use 3 tablespoons minced fresh herbs and 5 tablespoons whole-grain mustard.

HERB-LEMON BUTTER

Use 3 tablespoons minced fresh herbs and 4 teaspoons grated lemon zest.

THAI CURRY BUTTER
Use ½ cup Thai red curry paste.

NORI BUTTER
Use 2 teaspoons nori powder.

SCALLION BUTTER
Use 1 tablespoon finely chopped scallion.

CHEESY BUTTER
Use ¾ to 1 cup crumbled cheese such as feta, blue, or goat cheese.

SIMPLEST SALAD

Serves 4 to 8

Total Time: 5 minutes

This essential green salad requires the bare minimum of ingredients, no measuring, no whisking, and (virtually) no thought. Rubbing the bowl with a halved garlic clove adds just a hint of flavor. Use whatever vinegar you have on hand or you prefer. Try to use interesting and flavorful leafy greens such as mesclun, arugula, Bibb, or romaine.

- ½ garlic clove, peeled
- 8 ounces (8 cups) lettuce, torn into bite-size pieces if necessary
  Extra-virgin olive oil
  Vinegar

Rub inside of salad bowl with garlic. Add lettuce. Slowly drizzle oil over lettuce, tossing greens very gently, until greens are lightly coated and just glistening. Season with vinegar, salt, and pepper to taste, and toss gently to coat. Serve.

MAKE-AHEAD VINAIGRETTE

Makes about 1 cup

Total Time: 5 minutes

If you'd like to jazz up the Simplest Salad with something beyond oil and vinegar, have a make-ahead vinaigrette on hand in the refrigerator (it keeps for up to 1 week). Mayonnaise and mustard are natural emulsifiers, and the molasses also acts as a stabilizer, meaning the vinaigrette will stay emulsified during storage. Don't use blackstrap molasses.

- 1 tablespoon regular or light mayonnaise
- 1 tablespoon molasses
- 1 tablespoon Dijon mustard
- ½ teaspoon table salt
- ¼ cup white wine vinegar
- ½ cup extra-virgin olive oil, divided
- ¼ cup vegetable oil

1 Combine mayonnaise, molasses, mustard, and salt in 2-cup jar with tight-fitting lid. Stir with fork until mixture is milky in appearance and no lumps of mayonnaise or molasses remain. Add vinegar, seal jar, and shake until smooth, about 10 seconds.

2 Add ¼ cup olive oil, seal jar, and shake vigorously until combined, about 10 seconds. Repeat with remaining ¼ cup olive oil and vegetable oil in separate additions, shaking vigorously after each addition until combined. Vinaigrette should be glossy and lightly thickened after all oil has been added, with no pools of oil on surface. Season with salt and pepper to taste. (Vinaigrette can be refrigerated for up to 1 week; shake to recombine before using.)

VARIATIONS

MAKE-AHEAD SHERRY-SHALLOT VINAIGRETTE
Add 2 teaspoons minced shallot and 2 teaspoons minced fresh thyme to jar with mayonnaise. Substitute sherry vinegar for white wine vinegar.

MAKE-AHEAD BALSAMIC-FENNEL VINAIGRETTE
Toast 2 tablespoons fennel seeds in small skillet over medium heat until fragrant, 1 to 3 minutes. Crack them with mortar and pestle or on counter using bottom of heavy skillet. Add fennel seeds to jar with mayonnaise. Substitute balsamic vinegar for white wine vinegar.

MAKE-AHEAD CIDER-CARAWAY VINAIGRETTE
Toast 2 teaspoons caraway seeds in small skillet over medium heat until fragrant, 1 to 3 minutes. Crack them with mortar and pestle or on counter using bottom of heavy skillet. Add caraway seeds to jar with mayonnaise. Substitute cider vinegar for white wine vinegar.

CUCUMBER WATER

Makes 8 drinks

Total Time: 10 minutes, plus 30 minutes chilling

If you want something a little more exciting than tap water or store-bought seltzer, try this elegant flavored water or one of its jazzed-up variations. Any type of cucumber will work well.

8   cups water, divided
12 ounces cucumber, sliced thin, plus extra for garnish

1   Combine 1 cup water and three-quarters of the cucumber in 8-cup liquid measuring cup or large bowl. With potato masher or muddler, muddle cucumber until broken down and all juice is expressed, about 30 seconds. Stir in 3 cups water. Cover and refrigerate until flavors meld and mixture is chilled, 30 minutes to 1 hour.

2   Strain infused water into pitcher, pressing on solids to extract as much liquid as possible. Discard solids. Stir in remaining 4 cups water and garnish with extra cucumber. (Water can be stored in refrigerator for up to 1 day; garnish with cucumber just before serving.) Serve in ice-filled glasses.

VARIATIONS

CUCUMBER WATER WITH LEMON AND MINT

Muddle ½ thinly sliced lemon and ¾ cup fresh mint leaves with cucumber. Garnish with extra thinly sliced lemon and mint leaves.

CUCUMBER WATER WITH LIME AND GINGER

Muddle 1 thinly sliced lime and 1 tablespoon grated fresh ginger with cucumber. Garnish with extra thinly sliced lime.

CUCUMBER WATER WITH ORANGE AND TARRAGON

Muddle ½ thinly sliced orange and ¾ cup fresh tarragon leaves with cucumber. Garnish with extra thinly sliced orange and tarragon leaves.

ICED BLACK TEA

Makes 8 drinks

Total Time: 15 minutes, plus 1 hour steeping and 1 hour chilling

For this full-flavored iced tea, steep the tea leaves first in boiling water, then add ice water and steep some more. The longer cold steep continues to extract flavor but doesn't make the tea bitter. You can sweeten this to taste. Both caffeinated and decaffeinated tea work well. For an iced green tea recipe, see page 201.

3   tablespoons black tea leaves
6   cups boiling water
2   cups ice water
    Lemon wedges

Place tea in medium bowl. Add boiling water and steep for 4 minutes. Add ice water and steep for 1 hour. Strain through fine-mesh strainer into pitcher or large container (or strain into second bowl and transfer to pitcher). Refrigerate until chilled, at least 1 hour or up to 3 days. Serve in ice-filled glasses, garnished with lemon wedges.

VARIATIONS

ICED RASPBERRY-BASIL BLACK TEA

Omit lemon. Mash 1½ cups thawed frozen raspberries, 3 tablespoons chopped fresh basil, 2 tablespoons sugar, and 2 teaspoons lemon juice in bowl until no whole berries remain. Add mixture to tea with ice water. Garnish each serving with basil sprig.

ICED GINGER-POMEGRANATE BLACK TEA

Add ⅔ cup pomegranate juice, 2 tablespoons sugar, and 1½ to 2 tablespoons grated fresh ginger to tea with ice water. Substitute lime wedges for lemon.

ICED APPLE-CINNAMON BLACK TEA

Omit lemon. Add ½ cinnamon stick to medium bowl with tea. Add 1 cored and shredded red apple and 1 tablespoon sugar to tea with ice water.

Jack Bishop's

LATE-SUMMER DINNER WITH CLOSE FRIENDS

SERVES 4

» "CAPRESE" SALAD WITH FRIED GREEN TOMATOES AND BASIL VINAIGRETTE

» PENNE WITH CARAMELIZED ZUCCHINI, PARSLEY, AND SUMAC

» SALTY APPLE-RASPBERRY CRISP WITH WALNUTS

Jack Bishop

As we get older, my wife and I are less interested in big dinner parties. Yes, there's something exciting about cooking dinner for 10 or 12 and throwing people together who haven't met before. Lauren and I hosted plenty of these evenings, especially in our 30s and 40s. But in recent years, we've really come to enjoy the special dinner for four. There's something so comfortable about this kind of evening with close, long-time friends. And it's so much easier! No planning, shopping, and cooking for days. During the summer, I let my garden serve as inspiration. That means tomatoes, zucchini, and herbs. We'd probably put out some good olives, prosciutto, and halved dried figs with drinks, but keep the dinner light. The salad and pasta are meant to be served as two separate courses, but both are pretty substantial. At this time of year, dessert must feature fruit. Raspberries honor summer, while apples are a nod to the cold weather ahead. And store-bought vanilla ice cream is definitely the way to go.

MY GAME PLAN

UP TO 6 HOURS AHEAD
› Make the dressing for the "Caprese" Salad with Fried Green Tomatoes and Basil Vinaigrette. (I don't recommend making it a day ahead, because the vinegar might start to discolor the vibrant green color.)

UP TO 4 HOURS AHEAD
› Slice the mozzarella for the caprese salad.
› Shave the Parmesan for the Penne with Caramelized Zucchini, Parsley, and Sumac.
› Bake the Salty Apple-Raspberry Crisp with Walnuts. (Leave it on the counter and reheat it for 10 minutes in a 350-degree oven before serving.)

UP TO 2 HOURS AHEAD
› Cook the zucchini for the penne (leave it in the covered skillet).

"CAPRESE" SALAD WITH FRIED GREEN TOMATOES AND BASIL VINAIGRETTE

Serves 4

Total Time: 45 minutes

WHY I LOVE THIS RECIPE By September it becomes pretty clear that some of the tomatoes in my garden will never ripen. Rock-hard tomatoes (the kind that will literally bounce) don't make very good eating. However, any green tomatoes with a little give (don't expect them to be soft like ripe tomatoes) are good candidates for slicing, coating with panko, and frying in olive oil. This caprese-inspired salad does just that, jazzed up with a basil dressing.

BASIL VINAIGRETTE

- 1 cup packed fresh basil leaves
- ¼ cup fresh parsley leaves
- 2 tablespoons white wine vinegar
- 1 teaspoon Dijon mustard
- ½ teaspoon table salt
- ¼ teaspoon pepper
- 6 tablespoons extra-virgin olive oil

FRIED GREEN TOMATOES

- 1 pound green tomatoes
- ½ teaspoon table salt
- 2 cups panko bread crumbs
- ¼ teaspoon pepper
- 2 large eggs
- 1 tablespoon water
- ½ cup extra-virgin olive oil, divided

- 1 pound fresh mozzarella, sliced thin

1 FOR THE VINAIGRETTE Process basil, parsley, vinegar, mustard, salt, and pepper in blender until herbs are roughly chopped, scraping down sides of blender jar as needed. With blender running, add oil in slow, steady stream until dressing is emulsified, about 1 minute. Scrape dressing into measuring cup (for easy pouring) and set aside. (Dressing can be refrigerated for up to 6 hours; bring to room temperature before serving.)

2 FOR THE TOMATOES Remove ¼-inch slice from stem end of each tomato. Cut tomatoes crosswise into ¼-inch-thick slices. Arrange tomatoes in single layer on rimmed baking sheet and sprinkle with salt; let sit for 15 minutes.

3 Combine panko and pepper in shallow dish. Beat eggs and water in second shallow dish. Transfer tomatoes to paper towels and thoroughly pat dry. Wipe baking sheet clean. Working with 1 tomato slice at a time, dip in egg, then coat with panko mixture, pressing gently to adhere. Return tomato slices to now-empty sheet.

4 Line large plate with paper towels. Heat ¼ cup oil in 12-inch nonstick skillet over medium-high heat until shimmering. Fry half of tomatoes until golden brown and crisp on both sides, about 2 minutes per side. Transfer tomatoes to prepared plate. Wipe skillet clean with paper towels. Repeat with remaining ¼ cup oil and tomatoes.

5 Whisk vinaigrette to recombine. Shingle mozzarella and fried tomatoes on individual plates and drizzle with vinaigrette. Serve immediately.

> **JACK'S TIPS**
> › Don't bother with this recipe unless you have high-quality fresh mozzarella. A serrated knife makes slicing the cheese a bit easier.
>
> › The parsley maintains the bright green color of the vinaigrette. A dash of mustard adds welcome zing and helps keep the dressing from separating. If you make it hours in advance, it might require 5 seconds of whisking, but otherwise it will stay emulsified for quite a while.

PENNE WITH CARAMELIZED ZUCCHINI, PARSLEY, AND SUMAC

Serves 4

Total Time: 1 hour

WHY I LOVE THIS RECIPE This easy pasta incorporates three simple lessons I've learned from years in the kitchen. First off, cooking zucchini until it is jammy is transformative. The skillet will be ridiculously full at the outset and the cooking time will seem very long. But trust me: This works. Second, a tablespoon of minced parsley is lovely but whole leaves, used in abundance, act almost like a salad green. The grassy bitterness of all the parsley in this recipe offsets the intense sweetness of the zucchini. Finally, don't underestimate the power of a single well-chosen spice. I love the lemony, floral notes of sumac.

¼	cup extra-virgin olive oil, plus extra for drizzling
3	pounds zucchini or yellow summer squash, halved lengthwise and sliced ½ inch thick
½	teaspoon table salt, plus salt for cooking pasta
3	garlic cloves, minced
1	teaspoon ground sumac, plus extra for sprinkling
12	ounces penne or other short tubular pasta
2	cups fresh parsley leaves
2	ounces shaved Parmesan cheese (1 cup)

1 Heat oil in 12-inch nonstick skillet over medium-high heat until shimmering. Add zucchini and salt and cook, stirring occasionally, until zucchini softens and is just beginning to brown, 15 to 20 minutes. Reduce heat to medium and continue cooking, stirring often, until zucchini is jammy and lightly browned, 25 to 30 minutes. Stir in garlic and cook until fragrant, about 1 minute. Off heat, stir in sumac and season with salt and pepper to taste.

2 Meanwhile, bring 4 quarts water to boil in large pot. Add 1 tablespoon salt and pasta and cook until just shy of al dente. Reserve 2 cups cooking water and drain pasta. Return pasta to pot and add zucchini mixture, parsley, and 1¼ cups reserved cooking water. Cook over medium heat until pasta is al dente, 1 to 2 minutes, adjusting consistency of sauce with additional cooking water as needed. Top individual portions with a handful of Parmesan, sprinkle with extra sumac, and drizzle with extra oil. Serve.

JACK'S TIPS

> Using a nonstick skillet ensures that the browning stays on the zucchini rather than the pan.

> Pasta recipes often suggest reserving a little cooking water to adjust the consistency of the finished sauce, but I always reserve more than suggested. I like to undercook my pasta and then let it finish cooking in the sauce. The cooking water lubricates everything and helps the pasta absorb the sauce's flavors.

> I'm obsessed with shaved Parmesan. While grated Parm adds a savory flavor backbone, it also tends to melt and disappear. I like the visual, textural, and flavor impact of big shavings of cheese. Use a sharp vegetable peeler to turn a wedge of Parmigiano-Reggiano into a mound of fluffy curls.

SALTY APPLE-RASPBERRY CRISP WITH WALNUTS

Serves 4 to 6

Total Time: 1¼ hours

WHY I LOVE THIS RECIPE   I often use the bitterness of walnuts to help keep dessert sweetness in check. Sprinkling the finished crisp with flake sea salt adds another layer of complexity. Depending on the type of apple you use, you may notice some extra juice collecting in the bottom of the dish while portioning. Make sure to drizzle this over the crisp—it's delicious! Leftover crisp makes a fantastic next-day breakfast.

¾	cup walnuts
1	cup (5 ounces) all-purpose flour
⅓	cup (2⅓ ounces) packed light brown sugar
¼	teaspoon table salt
6	tablespoons unsalted butter, cut into ½-inch pieces and softened slightly
1½	pounds Macoun or Empire apples, cored and cut into ¼-inch slices
10	ounces (2 cups) raspberries
½	teaspoon flake or coarse sea salt
1	pint vanilla ice cream

1   Adjust oven rack to middle position and heat oven to 375 degrees. Place nuts in skillet over medium heat and toast, shaking skillet often, until fragrant, 3 to 5 minutes. Immediately transfer nuts to cutting board, let cool slightly, and chop.

2   Combine nuts, flour, sugar, and table salt in medium bowl. Add butter and use your fingers to work butter into dry ingredients until mixture resembles nubby streusel, about 1 minute.

3   Arrange apples in 8-inch square baking dish and top evenly with raspberries. Sprinkle streusel mixture over top and pat down slightly to compress. (Baking dish will be very full.) Bake until fruit is beginning to bubble around edges and topping is lightly browned, 45 to 50 minutes.

4   Transfer dish to wire rack, sprinkle crisp with sea salt, and let cool for 30 minutes. Serve with ice cream.

JACK'S TIPS

›   I think local apples with a balance of sweetness and acidity, such as Macouns or Empires, work best here. But I don't mind an apple that will soften in the oven or even become saucy, like McIntosh. I do suggest avoiding Granny Smiths— they are too firm and dry.

›   I prefer fresh raspberries, but this dessert will be *just fine* if you use 10 ounces frozen berries. Thaw them on the counter for an hour, leaving behind any of the liquid they shed.

›   Can we talk about salt? I'm obsessed with flake Maldon sea salt. The crystals of this English salt are gossamer thin and extra crunchy. This salt has a permanent place on my dining table, where it's the only way to finish food. Its crispy-crunchy texture also makes it the perfect choice for sweet-salty desserts like this one.

Julia Collin Davison's

MODERN TENDERLOIN DINNER

SERVES 8

» **EASY BEEF TENDERLOIN WITH HARISSA SPICE RUB**
Cilantro-Mint Relish

» **BABY RED POTATOES WITH LEMON AND CHIVES**

» **ARUGULA AND BABY KALE SALAD WITH DATES, ORANGES, AND ALMONDS**

» **CHOCOLATE POTS DE CRÈME WITH DULCE DE LECHE AND BOURBON WHIPPED CREAM**

Julia Collin Davison

I enjoy serving simple, rustic-looking food with big, interesting flavors, especially when company is coming for dinner. I like to keep things casual but don't skimp on the meal itself. I've also learned over the years that I hate being stuck in the kitchen after my guests have arrived, so I choose recipes that can be prepped well ahead of time (with plenty of time left to clean up the kitchen). Beef tenderloin is my go-to for a fancier meal because it doesn't require much attention and is incredibly easy to cook well. To give this mildly flavored beef some punch, and help me skip the messy step of browning, I add a simple harissa-flavored spice rub, and I serve the roast with an herb-packed relish. Boiled red potatoes flavored with lemon zest and a kale-arugula salad studded with dates and almonds round out the meal in a nice way. Pots de crème is my go-to dessert for nearly all occasions because it just never disappoints.

MY GAME PLAN

UP TO 3 DAYS AHEAD
〉 Make the Chocolate Pots de Crème with Dulce de Leche (through the end of step 4).

UP TO 1 DAY AHEAD
〉 Tie and salt the beef and make the spice rub for the Easy Beef Tenderloin with Harissa Spice Rub. (Note that you must tie and salt the beef at least 6 hours ahead of time.)
〉 Make the Cilantro-Mint Relish.

UP TO SEVERAL HOURS AHEAD
〉 Make the dressing, toast the almonds, and prep the oranges for the Arugula and Baby Kale Salad with Dates, Orange, and Almonds. You can also assemble the greens and cover with damp paper towels.
〉 Scrub the potatoes for the Baby Red Potatoes with Lemon and Chives and place in a pot of water with salt.

EASY BEEF TENDERLOIN WITH HARISSA SPICE RUB

Serves 8

Total Time: 2¼ hours, plus 6 hours chilling

WHY I LOVE THIS RECIPE This impressive beef tenderloin is simply rubbed with spices and then roasted in a low oven to a perfect medium-rare. The spices not only add flavor but also give the tenderloin a beautiful, deep red crust, so there is no need to sear the roast. Rubbing a little honey over the tenderloin helps the spices stick nicely and adds a welcome counterpoint to the savory spices. A final burst of broiler heat at the end of cooking helps toast the spice crust before serving.

1	(4- to 5-pound) trimmed beef tenderloin roast, tied at 1-inch intervals
1	tablespoon kosher salt
	Vegetable oil spray
2	tablespoons paprika
1	tablespoon ground coriander
1	tablespoon ground dried Aleppo pepper
1	teaspoon ground cumin
1	teaspoon garlic powder
¾	teaspoon caraway seeds
3	tablespoons honey, warmed

1 Pat roast dry with paper towels, then rub with salt. Wrap roast with plastic wrap and refrigerate for at least 6 hours or up to 24 hours.

2 Adjust oven rack to middle position and heat oven to 250 degrees. Spray wire rack with oil spray and set inside aluminum foil–lined rimmed baking sheet. Combine paprika, coriander, Aleppo pepper, cumin, garlic, and caraway seeds in small bowl. Unwrap roast, pat dry with paper towels, and set on prepared rack. Brush top and sides of roast with honey, then sprinkle evenly with spice mixture, pressing gently to adhere. Spray roast lightly with oil spray. Roast until meat registers 115 degrees (for medium-rare) or 125 degrees (for medium), 1½ to 2 hours.

3 Remove roast from oven and heat broiler. Broil roast until spice crust has toasted slightly and meat registers 120 to 125 degrees (for medium-rare) or 130 to 135 degrees (for medium), 5 to 10 minutes. Transfer roast to carving board and let rest for 20 minutes before slicing and serving.

JULIA'S TIPS

› Look for a fatter, shorter roast over a longer, skinnier one. If your roast is particularly narrow, begin checking for doneness at least 30 minutes early in step 2. If you're buying an untrimmed tenderloin to trim yourself, be sure it weighs 6 to 7 pounds.

› You may need to tuck the tapered end of the roast underneath by 3 to 5 inches to create a more even shape before tying.

CILANTRO-MINT RELISH

Makes about 1¼ cups

Total Time: 10 minutes

WHY I LOVE THIS RECIPE   I make versions of this rustic, fresh sauce all the time by switching up the herbs. Cilantro and mint are wonderful alongside the harissa-spiced beef. Mincing the garlic to a paste mellows out its sharp bite.

1	cup chopped fresh cilantro
½	cup chopped fresh mint
4	scallions, sliced thin
½	cup extra-virgin olive oil
3	garlic cloves, minced to a paste
2	tablespoons lemon juice
¼	teaspoon table salt

Combine all ingredients in serving bowl and set aside until ready to serve. (Sauce can be refrigerated for up to 24 hours; bring to room temperature before serving.)

BABY RED POTATOES WITH LEMON AND CHIVES

Serves 8

Total Time: 30 minutes

WHY I LOVE THIS RECIPE   I'm not a fan of fancy potato dishes. I much prefer the flavor and ease of boiled or roasted potatoes, especially if we're having company.

3	pounds baby red potatoes, unpeeled
½	teaspoon table salt, plus salt for cooking the potatoes
6	tablespoons unsalted butter
¼	cup minced fresh chives
1	teaspoon grated lemon zest
½	teaspoon pepper

1   Place potatoes in large Dutch oven and add water to cover by 1 inch. Add 1 teaspoon salt and bring to boil over medium-high heat. Reduce heat to medium and simmer until potatoes are tender, 10 to 15 minutes.

2   Drain potatoes and return to pot. Add butter, chives, lemon zest, ½ teaspoon salt, and pepper and toss gently until butter is melted and potatoes are well coated. Cover and keep warm until ready to serve.

ARUGULA AND BABY KALE SALAD WITH DATES, ORANGES, AND ALMONDS

Serves 8

Total Time: 15 minutes

WHY I LOVE THIS RECIPE   The flavors of this salad—the almonds and oranges in particular—work well alongside the beef and potatoes, while the dates add a lovely sweetness. I'm a fan of arugula and baby kale because they have actual flavor and don't wilt over the course of the dinner.

2	oranges
¾	cup pitted dates, chopped
⅓	cup cider vinegar
⅓	cup extra-virgin olive oil
¾	teaspoon table salt
¼	teaspoon pepper
5	ounces (5 cups) baby kale
5	ounces (5 cups) baby arugula
2	heads Belgian endive (10 ounces), trimmed and sliced thin
⅓	cup sliced almonds, toasted

1   Cut away peel and pith from oranges. Quarter oranges, then slice crosswise into ¼-inch-thick pieces.

2   Stir dates, vinegar, oil, salt, and pepper together in small bowl, breaking up date pieces as needed.

3   Combine kale, arugula, and endive in large bowl. Just before serving, drizzle dressing over salad and toss to coat. Transfer to serving platter or individual plates and top with oranges and almonds. Serve.

JULIA'S TIPS

> I like using smaller red potatoes that measure between 1 and 1½ inches in diameter. If your potatoes are larger, cut them into 1½-inch pieces before cooking.

> To time them perfectly, place the potatoes in a pot of water with salt ahead of time; start cooking them when the tenderloin is between 105 and 110 degrees.

> A mini food processor makes quick work of chopping the fresh herbs.

CHOCOLATE POTS DE CRÈME WITH DULCE DE LECHE AND BOURBON WHIPPED CREAM

Serves 8

Total Time: 1 hour, plus 4 hours chilling

WHY I LOVE THIS RECIPE Chocolate pots de crème became an instant favorite of mine when a recipe first appeared in *Cook's Illustrated* back in 2006. I've learned over the years that you shouldn't mess with the proportions of the base recipe, but you can add all sorts of toppings to change up the flavors. This version with dulce de leche and bourbon whipped cream is one of my all-time winning combos, and it brings down the house every time.

10	ounces bittersweet chocolate, chopped fine
5	large egg yolks
5	tablespoons plus 2 teaspoons sugar, divided
¼	teaspoon table salt
2¼	cups heavy cream, divided
¾	cup half-and-half
1	tablespoon vanilla extract
½	teaspoon instant espresso powder mixed with 1 tablespoon water
1	cup dulce de leche, warmed
1	teaspoon bourbon

1   Place chocolate in large heatproof bowl; set fine-mesh strainer over bowl and set aside.

2   Whisk egg yolks, 5 tablespoons sugar, and salt in medium bowl until combined, then whisk in 1½ cups heavy cream and half-and-half. Transfer mixture to medium saucepan and cook over medium-low heat, stirring constantly and scraping bottom of pot with wooden spoon, until thickened and silky and custard registers 175 to 180 degrees, 8 to 12 minutes. (Do not let custard overcook or simmer.)

3   Immediately pour custard through strainer over chocolate. Let mixture stand to melt chocolate, about 5 minutes. Whisk gently until smooth, then whisk in vanilla and espresso mixture. Divide custard mixture evenly among eight 5-ounce ramekins. Gently tap ramekins against counter to remove air bubbles.

4   Let pots de crème cool completely, then cover with plastic wrap and refrigerate until slightly firm, about 2 hours. Spoon 2 tablespoons dulce de leche over top of each pot de crème, cover, and refrigerate until fully chilled, at least 2 hours or up to 3 days. (Before serving, let pots de crème stand at room temperature for 20 to 30 minutes.)

5   Using hand mixer or standing mixer fitted with whisk attachment, beat remaining ¾ cup heavy cream, remaining 2 teaspoons sugar, and bourbon on low speed until foamy, about 30 seconds. Increase speed to medium and continue beating until beaters leave trail, about 30 seconds. Increase speed to high and whip until nearly doubled in volume and soft peaks form, 30 to 45 seconds. Dollop pots de crème with whipped cream and serve.

JULIA'S TIPS

> You can substitute ½ teaspoon vanilla extract for the bourbon, if desired.

> To warm the dulce de leche, microwave in bowl at 50 percent power, stirring occasionally, until thin and pourable, 2 to 4 minutes.

Matthew Fairman's

VIET-CAJUN SHRIMP BOIL

SERVES 10

» **FRESH SPRING ROLLS WITH MANGO AND MARINATED TOFU**
Hoisin-Peanut Dipping Sauce

» **VIET-CAJUN SHRIMP BOIL**

» **PIÑA COLADAS WITH MINT AND LIME**

Matthew
Fairman

Southeast Louisiana has a thriving Vietnamese food scene, which serves as the inspiration for my New Orleans–centric dinner party. People down here in the gumbo belt (the Gulf Coast stretching from Houston to the Florida panhandle) have long understood the irresistible, lip-smacking pleasures of diving into a mountain of Cajun boiled crawfish, but there's a new style bubbling up. The Viet-Cajun seafood boil—where the spicy boil gets doused with a citrusy, garlicky, gingery lemongrass butter—has elevated this classic to unbelievably delicious new heights. Before moving to New Orleans, I had never tasted anything like it, and now I'm unable to resist it. This is party food where you drop your inhibitions, roll up your sleeves, dig in with your hands, and don't stop peeling and eating (except to ice your palate with a cold beverage) until your elbows drip with butter. I like to cook and serve outdoors, but it's equally achievable in a large pot indoors. Since the boil is unabashedly spicy, salty, and rich, I pair it with two cooling foils: spring rolls bright with mango, cucumber, and herbs; and frozen piña coladas tinged with mint and lime that I offer for dessert. (With the shrimp boil itself, I go for beer.)

MY GAME PLAN

UP TO 1 MONTH AHEAD
❯ Make the simple syrup for the Piña Coladas with Mint and Lime.

UP TO 3 DAYS AHEAD
❯ Make the garlic butter for the Viet-Cajun Shrimp Boil (reheat the butter and stir in the fish sauce mixture before serving).
❯ Make the Hoisin-Peanut Dipping Sauce.

UP TO 4 HOURS AHEAD
❯ Make the Fresh Spring Rolls with Mango and Marinated Tofu.
❯ Combine all the ingredients for the shrimp boil (except for the shrimp and corn) in the pot. Then just turn the heat on about an hour before you want the boil to be ready.

UP TO 1 HOUR AHEAD
❯ Blend and freeze the piña coladas.

FRESH SPRING ROLLS WITH MANGO AND MARINATED TOFU

Serves 10

Total Time: 1 hour, plus 30 minutes chilling

WHY I LOVE THIS RECIPE With fresh herbs, sweet mango, crisp cucumber, crunchy peanuts, chewy noodles, and marinated tofu, these rolls feature an irresistible mix of flavors and textures. The stir-together marinade of fish sauce, brown sugar, and lime juice seasons both the tofu and the noodles, layering in complex umami. Served chilled with a creamy hoisin-peanut dipping sauce, they're also refreshing and get your palate ready for the spicy shrimp to follow.

5	tablespoons lime juice (3 limes)
3	tablespoons fish sauce
2	teaspoons packed brown sugar
14	ounces super-firm or extra-firm tofu, patted dry
1	English cucumber (1 pound), peeled, seeded, and cut into 3-inch-long matchsticks (2 cups)
1	large mango (1 pound), peeled, pitted, and cut into 3-inch-long matchsticks (2 cups)
4	ounces rice vermicelli
	Table salt for cooking noodles
2	teaspoons vegetable oil
5	leaves red leaf lettuce or Boston lettuce, halved crosswise
10	round rice paper wrappers (8 inches in diameter)
1½	cups fresh cilantro leaves
1½	cups fresh Thai basil leaves or mint leaves, small leaves left whole, medium and large leaves torn into 1-inch pieces
⅔	cup roasted, salted peanuts, chopped
1	recipe Hoisin-Peanut Dipping Sauce (page 48)

MATTHEW'S TIPS

› Building the rolls on a damp dish towel keeps the rice paper wrappers from sticking to the work surface. Wrapping the finished rolls with lettuce makes them easy to hold and eat.

› If you can't find Thai basil, don't substitute regular basil; its flavor is too gentle for this filling. Mint makes a better substitute.

1 Whisk lime juice, fish sauce, and sugar in small bowl until sugar has dissolved. Cut tofu crosswise into 10 planks, then cut each plank in half lengthwise. Place tofu in 13 by 9-inch baking dish and drizzle ¼ cup lime juice mixture over top; refrigerate tofu for at least 30 minutes or up 24 hours. (Remaining lime juice mixture can be refrigerated for up to 24 hours.)

2 Toss cucumber and mango with 2 tablespoons lime juice mixture. Let cucumber mixture sit for 30 minutes, then drain and set aside.

3 Bring 2 quarts water to boil in medium saucepan. Add vermicelli and 1 teaspoon salt and cook until noodles are tender but not mushy, 2 to 4 minutes. Drain noodles and rinse under cold running water until cool. Drain again thoroughly and transfer to medium bowl. Add oil and remaining 2 tablespoons lime juice mixture and toss to coat noodles. Using kitchen shears, cut noodles into approximate 3-inch lengths; set aside.

4 Place lettuce on platter; set aside for serving. Remove tofu from marinade and pat dry with paper towels. Spread clean, damp dish towel on work surface. Fill 9-inch pie plate with 1 inch room-temperature water.

5 Working with one wrapper at a time, immerse wrapper in water until just pliable, about 10 seconds; lay softened wrapper on towel. Scatter about 2 tablespoons cilantro leaves and 2 tablespoons basil leaves over center of wrapper, leaving 1½-inch border around wrapper. Arrange 2 tofu pieces horizontally on wrapper, leaving 2-inch border at bottom. Arrange ¼ cup cucumber-mango mixture on top of tofu. Sprinkle with 1 tablespoon peanuts. Top with scant ¼ cup noodles.

6 Fold bottom of wrapper up and over filling. Fold both sides of wrapper in over filling and press gently to seal. Applying gentle pressure to wrap filling tightly, roll filling up over itself until wrapper is fully sealed. Place spring roll seam side down on 1 lettuce piece on platter. Cover with second damp dish towel. Repeat with remaining wrappers and filling. Serve with dipping sauce, wrapping lettuce around exterior of each roll. (These are best served immediately, but they can be covered with a clean, damp dish towel and refrigerated for up to 4 hours.)

ACCOMPANIMENT

HOISIN-PEANUT DIPPING SAUCE

Makes about 1 cup
Total Time: 5 minutes

¼   cup smooth peanut butter
¼   cup hoisin sauce
¼   cup water
2   tablespoons tomato paste
2   teaspoons sriracha
1   garlic clove, minced

Whisk all ingredients together in small bowl.
(Sauce can be refrigerated for up to 3 days;
bring to room temperature before serving.)

VIET-CAJUN SHRIMP BOIL

Serves 10

Total Time: 1 hour

WHY I LOVE THIS RECIPE This seafood boil is the pinnacle of warm-weather party food, and it's delightfully casual to make. Though there are quite a few ingredients, the garlic butter can be made ahead of time and the boil comes together simply in one giant pot. It's the kind of low-stress, high-reward recipe that you'll want to make again and again for fun, casual gatherings and backyard parties for all occasions. Plus, it easily can be halved to feed fewer people for dinner any night of the week. I often make this using an outdoor cooking setup with a propane burner and large stockpot, but it works well indoors too. Serve with plenty of crusty French bread for sopping up the garlic butter.

SHRIMP BOIL

3	pounds small red potatoes, unpeeled
2	pounds andouille or kielbasa sausage, cut into 3-inch lengths
6	celery ribs, cut into 1-inch pieces
2	onions, halved
1	cup Zatarain's Crawfish, Shrimp, and Crab Boil seasoning
½	cup paprika
¼	cup cayenne pepper
¼	cup celery salt
¼	cup table salt
3	lemons, halved
8	pounds extra-large head-on shrimp (10 to 15 per pound)
4	ears corn, husks and silk removed, cut into thirds

VIET-CAJUN GARLIC BUTTER

¼	cup fish sauce
¼	cup lime juice (2 limes)
¼	cup orange juice (1 orange)
8	garlic cloves, smashed and peeled
2	(2-inch) pieces ginger, peeled and chopped coarse
1	lemongrass stalk, trimmed to bottom 6 inches and chopped coarse
24	tablespoons (3 sticks) unsalted butter
2	tablespoons Zatarain's Crawfish, Shrimp, and Crab Boil seasoning
2	tablespoons sugar
2	tablespoons lemon-pepper seasoning
1	tablespoon celery salt
2	(18 by 14-inch) disposable aluminum roasting pans

1 **FOR THE SHRIMP BOIL** Add 2½ gallons water, potatoes, sausage, celery, onions, Zatarain's seasoning, paprika, cayenne, celery salt, and salt to 24-quart stockpot. Squeeze lemon juice into pot, add spent lemon halves, and stir to combine. Bring mixture to boil, then reduce heat to medium-high and cook until potatoes are fully tender, about 15 minutes. Off heat, add shrimp and corn and let steep until shrimp are opaque throughout, about 7 minutes.

2 **FOR THE GARLIC BUTTER** Meanwhile, combine fish sauce, lime juice, and orange juice in bowl. Process garlic, ginger, and lemongrass in food processor until very finely chopped, about 20 seconds, scraping down sides of bowl as needed. Melt butter in large saucepan over medium heat. Add garlic mixture, Zatarain's seasoning, sugar, lemon-pepper seasoning, and celery salt and cook until sizzling rapidly and fragrant, about 2 minutes; set aside.

3 Using slotted spoon or wire spider skimmer, transfer shrimp boil to roasting pans, draining thoroughly before adding to pans; discard onions and lemons. Whisk fish sauce mixture into garlic-butter mixture, then drizzle over shrimp boil and toss to coat. Serve.

MATTHEW'S TIPS

› To make this in one pot, you'll need a big one— 24 quarts, which is admittedly not a common kitchen item. Reasonably priced versions are available, but alternatively, you can split the shrimp boil ingredients evenly among two (or even three) smaller pots.

› Use potatoes measuring 1 to 2 inches in diameter.

› I prefer head-on shrimp here; however, 6 pounds of headless shrimp can be substituted.

› Any smoked sausage will work well.

› I developed this recipe using Zatarain's Crawfish, Shrimp, and Crab Boil seasoning. Other powdered crab boil seasonings will work, but avoid seasonings containing whole spices.

› For serving, you can use large, deep pans or platters instead of the disposable roasting pans, if you prefer.

PIÑA COLADAS WITH MIND AND LIME

Makes 10 cocktails

Total Time: 30 minutes

WHY I LOVE THIS RECIPE Whether they're sipping on a Hurricane in the French Quarter or picking up frozen daiquiris from drive-throughs all over town, New Orleanians love their cocktails. My homage to the Crescent City's penchant pairs with my Vietnamese-influenced menu. Frozen pineapple has the flavor of fresh while reducing the amount of ice needed. Coconut cream brings richness, and the rum duo packs just the right punch.

½ cup sugar

⅓ cup warm tap water

2 (13.5-ounce) cans coconut cream, chilled, divided

8 ounces white rum, chilled, divided

6 ounces coconut rum, chilled, divided

¼ cup fresh mint leaves, divided, plus mint sprigs for garnish

1 ounce lime juice, divided

¼ teaspoon table salt, divided

24 ounces (6 cups) frozen pineapple chunks, divided

16 ounces (4 cups) ice cubes, divided

Fresh pineapple slices

1 Whisk sugar and warm water together in bowl until sugar has dissolved. Let cool completely, about 10 minutes. (Syrup can be refrigerated for up to 1 month.)

2 Working in two batches, add coconut cream, white rum, coconut rum, simple syrup, mint leaves, lime juice, salt, pineapple, and ice to blender (in that order) and process until smooth, about 1 minute, scraping down sides of blender jar as needed; transfer mixture to pitcher. (Mixture can be frozen for up to 1 hour. Stir until consistency is uniform before serving.) Serve in chilled old-fashioned or small hurricane glasses, garnished with pineapple slices and mint sprigs.

MATTHEW'S TIPS

> I like to serve this as a dessert cocktail, but you could certainly serve it to start the menu, if you like.

> To add drama, float some aged rum on top.

Dan Souza's

MY MAINE EVENT

SERVES 4

» **GIN CAMPS**

» **ROASTED OYSTERS ON THE HALF SHELL WITH DIJON CRÈME FRAÎCHE**

» **MAINE-STYLE LOBSTER ROLLS**

» **HOUSE SALAD**

» **LIME POSSETS WITH RASPBERRIES**

Dan Souza

If my mom were to invite you over for a summer-time lunch, you would surely be served a gin and tonic, fresh local seafood, whatever is begging to be picked from her sprawling garden, Cape Cod potato chips, and something sweet-tart and homemade for dessert. This menu is my take on her special brand of warm, friendly hospitality. I've added my own touches and tweaks through-out for a meal that would feel just as at home on a well-dressed dinner table as it would on a sun-drenched porch. The stars here are the lobster rolls: sweet lobster meat dressed simply with mayonnaise and salt and piled into buttery griddled buns. Don't let their short ingredient list (or that hot dog bun) fool you—these are special. The rest of my meal reflects that casual-yet-special vibe: my twist on a refreshing gin and tonic, gently roasted oysters gilded with Dijon crème fraîche, a slightly gussied-up green salad, and fruity, creamy lime possets. As with any good menu, many components can be made in advance so that day-of entertaining is fun and stress-free. So, round up your three favorite people and show them your love. Oh, and don't forget the potato chips.

MY GAME PLAN

UP TO 2 DAYS AHEAD
〉 Make the Lime Possets with Fresh Raspberries.

UP TO 1 DAY AHEAD
〉 Make the Dijon Crème Fraîche for the Roasted Oysters.
〉 Cook, crack, and pick the lobsters and cut up the lobster meat for the Maine-Style Lobster Rolls.
〉 Make the vinaigrette for the House Salad.

UP TO A FEW HOURS AHEAD
〉 Scrub the oysters.
〉 Wash and prep the salad components.

GIN CAMPS

Makes 4 cocktails

Total Time: 10 minutes

WHY I LOVE THIS RECIPE A gin and tonic is a refreshing aperitif before any meal and a family favorite whenever we get together for dinner. The Gin Camp (short for Campari) is my simple twist on the classic, featuring a measured amount of lime juice (rather than a wedge) for pitch-perfect acidity along with the addition of bittersweet Campari: The complex amaro adds citrus and spice notes and turns the cocktail a beautiful blush hue.

6	ounces London dry gin
2	ounces Campari
2	ounces lime juice, plus 4 strips lime peel for garnish
16	ounces tonic water

1 Combine gin, Campari, and lime juice in 2-cup liquid measuring cup. (Gin mixture can be refrigerated for up to 1 hour.)

2 Fill 4 chilled collins glasses halfway with ice. Divide gin mixture among glasses and top each with 4 ounces tonic water. Using spoon, gently lift gin mixture from bottom of glasses to top to combine. Top with additional ice. Pinch lime peel over each cocktail and rub outer edge of glass with peel, then garnish with lime peel and serve.

DAN'S TIPS

› To make lime peels, use a Y-shaped vegetable peeler to remove a 2- to 3-inch strip, working lengthwise and avoiding white pith as much as possible.

› Tanqueray is my go-to gin for this cocktail, but go ahead and use your favorite brand of London dry gin.

ROASTED OYSTERS ON THE HALF SHELL WITH DIJON CRÈME FRAÎCHE

Serves 4

Total Time: 45 minutes

WHY I LOVE THIS RECIPE Eating raw oysters on the half-shell is one of my life's true pleasures. So when my dear colleague Lan Lam was developing a technique for roasting oysters, I was deeply skeptical. Not of her ability, of course, but of the very concept of cooking these precious bivalves. Raw oysters display an incredible range of flavors, from cucumber and melon to seaweed and rich minerality. Roasting flattens these delicate characteristics, but as Lan proved, it also transforms oysters into true comfort food. My luxurious version is topped with a spoonful of Dijon crème fraîche and showered with fresh chives.

5	tablespoons crème fraîche
4	teaspoons Dijon mustard
16	oysters, 2½ to 3 inches long, well scrubbed
2	tablespoons minced chives

1 Stir crème fraîche and mustard in bowl until well combined. Cover and refrigerate until needed. (Sauce can be refrigerated for up to 24 hours.)

2 Adjust oven rack to middle position and heat oven to 450 degrees. Gently crumple and uncrumple one 24-inch length of aluminum foil. Place in 18 by 13-inch rimmed baking sheet. Nestle oysters, cupped side down, into foil on sheet and bake until oysters open slightly, about 5 minutes. (It's OK to continue with oysters that don't open.) Let oysters rest until cool enough to handle, about 5 minutes.

3 To shuck oysters, fold dish towel several times. Grip towel in hand that will be holding oyster, with towel sandwiched between your palm and your thumb. Using your thumb, hold oyster in place on towel with hinge facing toward your palm. Insert tip of oyster knife into gap where oyster has opened. Work tip of knife into hinge using twisting motion. When shells begin to separate, twist knife to pop hinge. Run knife along top shell, scraping adductor muscle from shell to release oyster. Slide knife under oyster to scrape adductor muscle from bottom shell. Discard top shell and return oyster to foil, being careful not to spill much liquid. Repeat with remaining oysters.

4 Distribute sauce evenly among oysters, about 1 teaspoon per oyster. Bake until thickest part of largest oyster registers 160 to 165 degrees, 5 to 8 minutes. Let rest for 5 minutes. Sprinkle with chives and serve.

DAN'S TIPS

› New England oysters are my favorites here, naturally, but you should use whatever is fresh and locally available to you.

› Using oysters that are 2½ to 3 inches long ensures that they will cook evenly.

› You'll need an oyster knife and a large serving platter.

SHUCKING OYSTERS

1. Fold dish towel several times. Grip towel in hand that will be holding oyster, steadying oyster and protecting your palm.

2. Using your thumb, hold oyster in place on towel with hinge facing toward your palm. Insert tip of oyster knife into gap where oyster has opened slightly.

3. Work tip of knife into hinge using twisting motion. When shells begin to separate, twist knife to pop hinge.

4. Run knife along top shell, scraping adductor muscle from shell to release oyster. Slide knife under oyster to scrape adductor muscle from bottom shell.

MAINE-STYLE LOBSTER ROLLS

Serves 4

Total Time: 1¼ hours

WHY I LOVE THIS RECIPE   On the scale of ways to express love, I believe that serving a lobster roll is just a notch below proposing marriage. You buy expensive crustaceans and do all the work in the kitchen so that your guests can experience nothing but a warm, butter-griddled roll giving way to sweet, barely dressed lobster. I grew up eating these gifts all over my mom's home state of Maine, where the best lobster rolls feature an ingredient list you can count on one hand.

3	(1¼-pound) live lobsters
¼	teaspoon table salt, plus salt for cooking lobsters
2	tablespoons mayonnaise
4	New England–style hot dog buns
3	tablespoons unsalted butter, melted

1   Place lobsters in large bowl and freeze for 30 minutes. Bring 2 gallons water to boil in large pot over high heat.

2   Add ⅓ cup salt and lobsters to pot, arranging with tongs so that all lobsters are submerged. Cover pot, leaving lid slightly ajar, and adjust heat to maintain gentle boil. Cook for 8 minutes. Holding lobster with tongs, insert thermometer through underside of tail into thickest part; meat should register 140 degrees. If necessary, return lobster to pot for 2 minutes longer, until tail registers 140 degrees.

3   Transfer lobsters to rimmed baking sheet and set aside until cool enough to remove meat, about 10 minutes. Remove small legs from all three lobsters, then remove meat from lobsters. (Save small legs and any lobster roe for snacking on later.) Cut tail meat into ½-inch pieces and claw and knuckle meat into 1-inch pieces. (Lobster meat can be refrigerated in airtight container for up to 24 hours.)

4   Whisk mayonnaise and ⅛ teaspoon salt together in large bowl. Add lobster and toss gently to combine. Season with salt to taste.

5   Place 12-inch nonstick skillet over low heat. Brush both sides of buns with melted butter and sprinkle with remaining ⅛ teaspoon salt. Place buns buttered side down in skillet. Increase heat to medium-low and cook until crisp and brown, 2 to 3 minutes. Flip and continue to cook until crisp and brown on second side, 2 to 3 minutes. Transfer buns to large platter. Spoon lobster salad into buns and serve.

DAN'S TIPS

› Depending on the size of your hot dog buns, you may have extra dressed lobster left over after filling the buns. Too much of a good thing doesn't exist here; bring the extra to the table and let everyone pile more onto their rolls.

› If you don't have access to top-loading New England–style buns, go ahead and butter, salt, and toast the interiors of 4 side-loading buns instead of the exteriors.

› Kettle-style potato chips are a must for serving, IMO, preferably Cape Cod brand if you can find them.

HOUSE SALAD

Serves 4

Total Time: 15 minutes

WHY I LOVE THIS RECIPE A tossed salad of fresh-from-the-garden butter lettuce, tomatoes, and cucumber is a fixture at my parents' table. You could call it their house salad. Many vinaigrettes would work well here, but lemon shines brightest, and they often use that. In a daring break from tradition, I take a cue from supersavory Caesar salad and spike my vinaigrette with a few dashes of fish sauce for umami and depth. And since that move already puts me in the proverbial doghouse, I continue to break the rules by tossing in frilly frisée for crisp texture and loft.

DRESSING

- 1 tablespoon lemon juice
- ½ teaspoon mayonnaise
- ½ teaspoon Dijon mustard
- ¼ teaspoon fish sauce
- Pinch table salt
- Pinch sugar
- 3 tablespoons extra-virgin olive oil

SALAD

- 1 head Bibb lettuce (8 ounces), torn into bite-size pieces
- 1 small head frisée (4 ounces), torn into bite-size pieces
- 8 ounces cherry tomatoes, halved
- ½ seedless English cucumber, peeled, halved lengthwise, and sliced thin

1 FOR THE DRESSING Whisk lemon juice, mayonnaise, mustard, fish sauce, salt, and sugar in medium bowl until mixture is milky in appearance and no lumps of mayonnaise remain. Whisking constantly, very slowly drizzle oil into vinegar mixture until glossy and lightly thickened, with no pools of oil visible. (If pools of oil are visible on surface as you whisk, stop addition of oil and whisk until mixture is well combined, then resume whisking in oil in slow stream.) Season with pepper to taste. (Vinaigrette can be refrigerated for up 24 hours; whisk to recombine before serving.)

2 FOR THE SALAD Combine lettuce, frisée, tomatoes, and cucumber in large bowl. Drizzle with dressing and toss gently until greens are evenly coated. Season with salt to taste. Serve immediately.

LIME POSSETS WITH RASPBERRIES

Serves 4

Total Time: 50 minutes, plus 3 hours chilling

WHY I LOVE THIS RECIPE My favorite summer dessert is fresh fruit topped with cold heavy cream and a sprinkle of sugar. I serve it all summer long. But on occasions when I want something a little more refined, I make posset. This rich, tart-sweet custard with British roots comes together quickly with just four ingredients (and no eggs) and can be made a couple days in advance. I love how the lime's bracing acidity adds verve and balance to the just-set cream, and I hope you and your guests will too.

2 cups heavy cream

⅔ cup (4⅔ ounces) sugar

1 tablespoon grated lime zest plus 6 tablespoons juice (3 limes)

5 ounces (1 cup) raspberries

1 Combine cream, sugar, and lime zest in medium saucepan. Bring to boil over medium heat and cook, stirring frequently to dissolve sugar, until mixture is reduced to 2 cups, 6 to 12 minutes. If mixture begins to boil over, briefly remove from heat.

2 Off heat, stir in lime juice. Let mixture sit until cooled slightly and skin forms on top, about 20 minutes. Strain mixture through fine-mesh strainer into 4-cup liquid measuring cup. Divide mixture evenly among four 6-ounce ramekins.

3 Refrigerate, uncovered, until set, at least 3 hours. (Chilled possets can be wrapped in plastic wrap and refrigerated for up to 2 days. Unwrap and let sit at room temperature for 10 minutes before serving.) Garnish with raspberries and serve.

DAN'S TIPS

› You will need four 6- or 8-ounce ramekins, shallow water glasses, or mason jars.

› Don't leave the cream mixture unattended in step 1, as it can boil over easily.

› Reducing the cream mixture to exactly 2 cups creates the best consistency. Transfer the liquid to a 2-cup heatproof liquid measuring cup once or twice during boiling to monitor the amount.

Morgan Bolling's

NACHO AVERAGE BARBECUE

SERVES 10 TO 12

» NACHOS!

» GRILL-SMOKED PORK BUTT

» ANCHO CHILE BARBECUE SAUCE

» PICKLED HOMINY, ONIONS, AND JALAPEÑOS

» BIG-BATCH GREEN CHILE QUESO

» CANDIED BACON S'MORES

Morgan Bolling

My best friend, Lauren, introduced me to the glorious concept of a nacho table. To make one, you cover an entire table in butcher's paper, blanket the paper with tortilla chips, and then add a ton of toppings. You can deck out the chips all the same way or divide the nachos up into different sections so that everyone can choose their own nacho experience from the same table. If you go with the latter, you can label the butcher's paper with what each section contains. I've now done some variation on this party with Lauren and other friends multiple times. For this version, I grill-smoke a pork butt; this brings the party outside, where you can revel in the messiness, and it gives the nachos a smoky element. On that theme, I like to put out a DIY s'mores bar for dessert (with candied bacon as an extra party trick). You can relight the grill for the marshmallows, or get your fire pit going if you have one. This is definitely nacho average barbecue!

MY GAME PLAN

UP TO 1 WEEK AHEAD
〉 Make the Ancho Chile Barbecue Sauce.

UP TO 3 DAYS AHEAD
〉 Cook and shred the Grill-Smoked Pork Butt.

UP TO 2 DAYS AHEAD
〉 Make the Pickled Hominy, Onions, and Jalapeños.
〉 Cook the bacon for the Candied Bacon S'mores.

UP TO 1 DAY AHEAD
〉 If you're not cooking the pork butt ahead, season and refrigerate the pork. (Note that you must do this at least 18 hours ahead.)

UP TO SEVERAL HOURS AHEAD
〉 Prep your chosen nacho toppings as needed.

NACHOS!

WHY I LOVE THIS RECIPE These nachos are so customizable and a great opportunity to get creative with both the toppings and how you assemble them. I often make half the nachos vegetarian and put all the pork on the other half. You can even lay out just the chips and put all the toppings in bowls to allow people to dress their own portions of nachos. Either way, it's such a fun party food.

START WITH

1	roll butcher's paper
5	(12-ounce) bags tortilla chips
1	recipe Grill-Smoked Pork Butt (page 66)
1	recipe Ancho Chile Barbecue Sauce (page 67)
1	recipe Pickled Hominy, Onions, and Jalapeños (page 68)
1	recipe Big-Batch Green Chile Queso (page 68)

IF YOU WANT, ADD

Canned beans (black, pinto, or refried)

Shredded cheese (Monterey Jack, pepper Jack, or cheddar)

Salsa (store-bought or homemade)

Guacamole (store-bought or homemade)

Mexican crema or sour cream

Fresh garnishes (sliced scallions, sliced radishes, lime wedges, cilantro, radishes)

Hot sauce

TO SET UP NACHO TABLE Cover large table with butcher's paper, then spread chips evenly over top, leaving plenty of space around edges for plates, utensils, and elbows. Sprinkle pulled pork evenly over half or all of chips, as desired, and drizzle with barbecue sauce. Sprinkle pickled hominy mixture over chips, then drizzle with queso. Top with additional garnishes as desired and serve immediately with tongs, spatulas, and plenty of napkins.

MORGAN'S TIP

› Be sure to buy butcher's paper or another food-safe paper. Some craft papers are not meant for direct contact with food.

GRILL-SMOKED PORK BUTT

Serves 10 to 12

Total Time: 5¾ hours, plus 18 hours chilling

WHY I LOVE THIS RECIPE I grew up in North Carolina, so barbecued pork has a special place in my heart. This recipe is designed to start on the grill and finish in the oven (rather than requiring a smoker) but still produces deeply smoky pork thanks to the wood chunks. Adding some of the juices to the pork when shredding makes it extra-rich. This does take some time to prepare, but it will make for the most spectacular nachos you've ever had. Plus, it can be done up to 3 days ahead.

1	(5- to 6-pound) bone-in pork butt roast, trimmed
2	tablespoons kosher salt
1½	tablespoons pepper
4	(3-inch) wood chunks
1	(13 by 9-inch) disposable aluminum roasting pan

1 Pat pork butt dry with paper towels. Place on large sheet of plastic wrap and rub all over with salt and pepper. Wrap tightly in plastic and refrigerate for 18 to 24 hours.

2A **FOR A CHARCOAL GRILL** Open bottom vent completely. Light large chimney starter three-quarters filled with charcoal briquettes (4½ quarts). When top coals are partially covered with ash, pour evenly over half of grill. Place wood chunks evenly on coals. Set cooking grate in place, cover, and open lid vent completely. Heat grill until hot and wood chunks are smoking, about 5 minutes.

2B **FOR A GAS GRILL** Distribute wood chunks evenly on grill grates above primary burner. Turn all burners to high, cover, and heat grill until hot and wood chunks are smoking, about 15 minutes. Turn primary burner to medium-high and turn off other burner(s). (Adjust primary burner as needed to maintain grill temperature of 300 degrees.)

3 Clean and oil cooking grate. Unwrap pork and place fat side down in disposable pan. Place disposable pan on cooler side of grill. Cover grill (with lid vent directly over pork if using charcoal) and cook until pork registers 120 degrees, about 2 hours. Thirty minutes before removing pork from grill, adjust oven rack to middle position and heat oven to 300 degrees.

4 Transfer disposable pan from grill to rimmed baking sheet. Cover pan tightly with aluminum foil and transfer pan (still on sheet) to oven. Cook until fork inserted in pork meets little resistance and meat registers 200 degrees, 2½ to 3 hours.

5 Remove foil from pan (be careful of steam) and let pork rest for 30 minutes. Transfer pork to carving board. Strain accumulated juices from pan through fine-mesh strainer set over bowl; discard solids. Using tongs, remove blade bone from roast. Chop pork into bite-size pieces.

6 Whisk strained pork juices to recombine. Toss pork with 1 cup juices in now-empty pan and season with salt and extra juices to taste. Cover and keep warm in 200-degree oven for up to 1 hour. (Pork can be refrigerated for up to 3 days; reheat in 200 degree oven, stirring occasionally.)

MORGAN'S TIPS

› Plan accordingly: The pork butt needs to be seasoned at least 18 hours before it is cooked, and between the grill and the oven, the total cooking (and resting) time is 5¾ hours.

› I like hickory wood chunks, but you can use any variety you prefer. You also can swap in 2 cups wood chips, wrapped in heavy-duty aluminum foil with holes poked in the top.

ANCHO CHILE BARBECUE SAUCE

Makes about 1⅓ cups

Total Time: 30 minutes

WHY I LOVE THIS RECIPE Ancho chile powder gives this sauce a deep smokiness, making it way better than your average store-bought barbecue sauce. This sauce is also a real bridge builder, uniting the thematic flavors of barbecued pork and nachos.

1	tablespoon vegetable oil
½	onion, chopped fine
2	tablespoons ancho chile powder
2	teaspoons smoked paprika
1	garlic clove, minced
1	cup ketchup
½	cup Worcestershire sauce
5	tablespoons packed light brown sugar
3	tablespoons cider vinegar
1	tablespoon soy sauce
1½	teaspoons hot sauce
½	teaspoon pepper

1 Heat oil in medium saucepan over medium heat until shimmering. Add onion and cook until softened, about 5 minutes. Stir in chile powder, paprika, and garlic and cook until fragrant, about 30 seconds.

2 Stir in ketchup, Worcestershire, sugar, vinegar, soy sauce, hot sauce, and pepper. Bring to simmer and cook, stirring occasionally, until sauce is thickened and flavors meld, 5 to 7 minutes. Let cool completely before serving. (Sauce can be refrigerated for up to 1 week; bring to room temperature before serving.)

MORGAN'S TIP

> You can substitute a different type of pure ground chile powder (such as chipotle chile powder), if you like.

PICKLED HOMINY, ONIONS, AND JALAPEÑOS

Serves 10 to 12

Total Time: 45 minutes

WHY I LOVE THIS RECIPE I love both pickled onions and pickled jalapeños, so naturally I was excited to combine them. Hominy is a corn product made from dry kernels; it has a really nice nutty taste and chewy texture and adds another dimension to the pickling mixture. These pickles are quick, but they also can be made a couple days in advance.

1	(15-ounce) can white hominy, rinsed
1	red onion, halved and sliced thin
2	jalapeño chiles, stemmed and sliced into thin rings
2	cups cider vinegar
⅓	cup sugar
1	tablespoon kosher salt

Combine hominy, onion, and jalapeños in large bowl. Bring vinegar, sugar, and salt to boil in medium saucepan. Pour vinegar mixture over hominy mixture. Push onions and hominy to submerge and let flavors meld for at least 30 minutes. (Pickled hominy mixture can be refrigerated for up to 2 days.)

MORGAN'S TIP
› You can use just 1 jalapeño or omit chiles entirely if you're spice averse.

BIG-BATCH GREEN CHILE QUESO

Makes about 8 cups

Total Time: 15 minutes

WHY I LOVE THIS RECIPE You don't want to make this topping in advance, but that's fine because this molten, lightly spicy queso comes together superfast. Microwaving the cheeses is the easiest way to get a magma-like, deliciously gooey sauce. Adding salsa verde and milk to the cheeses helps even out the hot spots in the microwave, steaming the cheese rather than scorching it.

16	ounces American cheese, shredded (4 cups)
16	ounces pepper Jack cheese, shredded (4 cups)
1	(16-ounce) jar salsa verde
2	cups whole milk

Combine all ingredients in large bowl. Microwave until cheese begins to melt around edges of dish, 2 to 5 minutes. Stir and continue to microwave until cheese is completely melted and just beginning to bubble around edges of dish, 4 to 7 minutes longer, whisking often. Serve immediately.

MORGAN'S TIP
› You want to use a big bowl here to prevent any risk of the cheese bubbling over.

CANDIED BACON S'MORES

Serves 10 to 12

Total Time: 45 minutes

WHY I LOVE THIS RECIPE It's really fun to present a big platter with all sorts of different s'mores ingredients and let guests assemble their own. And people get psyched about the porky addition of crispy candied bacon. The salty-sweet contrast is delightful. Using brown sugar (rather than a liquid sugar like maple) gives the bacon a great crunch that holds up in a s'more (or even just as a snack). You'll need enough 12-inch metal or wooden skewers so that everyone gets one.

CANDIED BACON

12	ounces center-cut bacon
¼	cup packed light brown sugar

S'MORES

1	(14-ounce box) graham crackers
6	(1½-ounce) bars milk chocolate, broken into pieces
6	(1½-ounce) packages regular-size peanut butter cups
1	(1-pound bag) marshmallows

1 FOR THE BACON Adjust oven racks to upper-middle and lower-middle positions and heat oven to 350 degrees. Line 2 rimmed baking sheets with aluminum foil. Cut bacon slices in half crosswise and arrange in single layer on prepared sheets.

2 Sprinkle sugar evenly over bacon (do not flip and sprinkle on second side). Use your fingers to spread sugar evenly over each piece.

3 Bake until bacon is dark brown and sugar is bubbling, 20 to 25 minutes, switching and rotating sheets halfway through baking (if bacon on 1 sheet finishes cooking sooner, it's OK to remove this sheet from oven first). Transfer bacon to wire rack and let cool for at least 5 minutes. (Bacon can be refrigerated for up to 2 days; bring to room temperature before serving).

4 FOR THE S'MORES Arrange graham crackers, bacon, chocolate, peanut butter cups, and marshmallows on platter. Have skewers and a fire for your guests and allow them to serve themselves!

MORGAN'S TIPS

> I use thick, center-cut bacon for a supreme sweet-and-savory experience. Traditional bacon also can be used; make sure to use uniform slices and reduce the cooking time accordingly.

> Don't use dark brown sugar here.

> Feel free to mix it up with what you include. I love Hershey's bars and Reese's peanut butter cups, but you can add dark chocolate bars or chocolate graham crackers—have fun with it!

Camila Chaparro's
BAO BAR

SERVES 6 TO 8

» **BAO BAR**

» **STAR ANISE– AND GINGER-BRAISED PORK**

» **CRISPY SESAME CHICKEN**
Crispy Sesame Tofu

» **DRIZZLING SAUCES**
Hoisin-Lime Sauce
Sriracha Mayo

» **SWEET AND SPICY QUICK PICKLED CARROTS**

» **GUAVA SORBET WITH FRESH FRUIT**

Camila
Chaparro

This mix-and-match DIY spread using steamed lotus leaf bao with an array of fillings and sauces is one of my favorite ways to entertain. "Bao" in Chinese refers to many types of yeasted wheat-flour buns that are most often steamed, then stuffed with a savory filling. Lotus leaf buns, which have become especially popular in the West, are made from oval pieces of dough that are folded in half and steamed, creating a fluffy clamshell shape perfect for fillings. In Taiwan, these buns are often filled with pork belly, pickled mustard greens, cilantro, and ground peanuts, but it's become common to see these buns on menus worldwide, filled with an array of global flavors, oftentimes combined in the same bite. I love how the pillowy, faintly sweet bao are a perfect contrast to a savory, meaty chunk of braised pork or a crispy piece of chicken or tofu. Topped with a spicy dollop of sriracha mayo or a drizzle of sweet-sour hoisin and lime, plus a handful of fresh or pickled crunchy vegetables and aromatic herbs, it's a riot of flavors and textures in every bite. So, how a-bao-t we have a party?

MY GAME PLAN

UP TO 1 WEEK AHEAD
> Make the Sweet and Spicy Quick Pickled Carrots.
> Make the Guava Sorbet.

UP TO 3 DAYS AHEAD
> Make the Hoisin-Lime Sauce and the Sriracha Mayo.

UP TO 2 DAYS AHEAD
> Braise the pork for the Star Anise– and Ginger-Braised Pork (through step 2).

UP TO SEVERAL HOURS AHEAD
> Marinate the chicken for the Crispy Sesame Chicken and dredge it in cornstarch (through step 3).
> Prep whatever fresh fruit you plan to serve with the sorbet.
> Prep fresh garnishes for the bao.

STREAMLINE
> It doesn't take a lot of filling to fill a bao, so you could easily make just the pork butt or the chicken, rather than both, if you'd like to simplify things. Just note that the tofu on its own won't be enough to serve 6 to 8.

BAO BAR

WHY I LOVE THIS RECIPE Look for pre-steamed lotus leaf buns in the freezer section of Asian grocery stores. They are also frequently called Taiwanese burger/sandwich buns, gua bao, gwa pao, or cut buns. Make sure they are packaged well and don't look cracked, dried out, or freezer burned. Most packages will include instructions for steaming and microwaving; however, if there aren't any, you can use the instructions below. You can use a bamboo steamer, collapsible steamer basket, or steamer insert for a large pot. Depending on the size of your setup, you may need to steam the buns in batches.

START WITH

- 24 (1-ounce) frozen lotus leaf bao
- 1 recipe Star Anise and Ginger Braised Pork (page 74)
- 1 recipe Crispy Sesame Chicken (page 75)
- 1 recipe Hoisin-Lime Sauce (page 76)
- 1 recipe Sriracha Mayo (page 76)
- 1 recipe Sweet and Spicy Quick Pickled Carrots (page 76)

  Fresh garnishes (cilantro sprigs, thinly sliced cucumber, thinly sliced scallions, shredded cabbage)

IF YOU WANT, ADD

Crispy Sesame Tofu (page 75)

Extra sauces (such as sriracha or chili crisp)

Everyday Long-Grain White Rice (page 24)

TO STEAM BUNS Cut piece of parchment paper slightly smaller than diameter of bamboo or collapsible steamer basket; place parchment in basket. Poke about 20 small holes in parchment and lightly spray with vegetable oil spray. Place frozen bao on parchment liner, making sure they are not touching. Set steamer basket over simmering water (match skillet size to steamer basket) and steam, covered, until puffed and heated through, 4 to 6 minutes. Carefully remove bao from basket and place on platter.

TO SET UP BAO BAR Arrange braised pork on platter or in large bowl and arrange chicken on platter. Place sauces, pickled carrots, and other garnishes in bowls that can be passed around.

CAMILA'S TIP

› If you don't have a steamer basket, you can also microwave the buns, although they will be less fluffy. Wrap the frozen buns in a damp dish towel (you may need to do this in batches to make sure they are not touching). Place the buns on a large plate and microwave for about 1 minute, flipping them halfway through microwaving.

STAR ANISE– AND GINGER-BRAISED PORK

Serves 6 to 8

Total Time: 3 hours

WHY I LOVE THIS RECIPE Chunks of rich pork shoulder get braised until tender with lots of aromatics—ginger, garlic, and star anise—plus umami-rich soy sauce and brown sugar. The flavorful braising liquid is then reduced and coats the pork pieces after crisping them up under the broiler. Drizzle with Hoisin-Lime Sauce for an irresistible bao.

1	(2½- to 3-pound) boneless pork butt roast, trimmed and cut into 2-inch pieces
2½	cups water
1	(3-inch) piece ginger, unpeeled, sliced into ¼-inch-thick rounds
4	scallions, cut into 2-inch lengths
2	tablespoons soy sauce
6	garlic cloves, lightly crushed and peeled
2	tablespoons packed brown sugar
2	whole star anise pods
¼	teaspoon red pepper flakes

1 Adjust oven rack to lower-middle position and heat oven to 300 degrees. Combine pork, water, ginger, scallions, soy sauce, garlic, sugar, star anise, and pepper flakes in Dutch oven. Bring to simmer over medium-high heat. Cover, transfer pot to oven, and cook until pork is tender and easily breaks apart when prodded with fork, 2 to 2½ hours, turning pork halfway through cooking.

2 Remove pot from oven and, using slotted spoon, transfer pork to bowl. Strain braising liquid into large bowl, discarding solids, and let settle for 10 minutes. Using wide, shallow spoon, skim fat from surface of liquid. Return defatted liquid to now-empty pot, bring to simmer, and cook until reduced to about ½ cup, 8 to 12 minutes. (Pork and reduced braising liquid can be refrigerated separately for up to 2 days. Bring liquid to brief simmer before proceeding.)

3 Adjust oven rack 6 inches from broiler element and heat broiler. Set wire rack in aluminum foil–lined rimmed baking sheet. Pull each piece of pork into 3 or 4 pieces, discarding any large pieces of fat. Arrange pork in even layer on wire rack and broil until spotty brown on top and edges begin to crisp, 4 to 8 minutes. Transfer pork to pot with liquid and toss gently to coat. Serve.

CAMILA'S TIPS

› Pork butt roast (which is actually a cut from the shoulder of the pig) is often labeled Boston butt in the supermarket.

› If you braise the pork ahead of time, you can break it into pieces and broil it straight from the fridge when it's time to serve.

› If you have pork left over, it keeps for up to 5 days.

CRISPY SESAME CHICKEN

Serves 6 to 8

Total Time: 50 minutes

WHY I LOVE THIS RECIPE I rarely deep fry at home (it's messy and involves so much oil), but this recipe is worth it, several times over. It's based on my colleague Lan Lam's incredible recipe for Japanese karaage chicken, by far the simplest, and tastiest, fried chicken I've ever made or eaten: Strips of skinless thighs marinate in a potent combination of soy sauce, ginger, garlic, and, in this version, toasted sesame oil before being tossed in cornstarch and fried. Sesame seeds added to the cornstarch heighten the sesame flavor for a crispy, nutty coating. The chicken is so flavorful and moist on the inside and crispy on the outside that it will elicit delighted groans at your table (I guarantee) when drizzled with Sriracha Mayo in a bao.

3	tablespoons soy sauce
2	tablespoons water
1	tablespoon grated fresh ginger
2	garlic cloves, minced
1	teaspoon toasted sesame oil
¾	teaspoon sugar
1½	pounds boneless, skinless chicken thighs, trimmed and cut crosswise into 1-inch-wide strips
1¼	cups cornstarch
3	tablespoons sesame seeds
2	quarts vegetable oil, for frying

1 Combine soy sauce, water, ginger, garlic, sesame oil, and sugar in medium bowl. Add chicken and toss to coat. Let sit at room temperature for 30 minutes.

2 Line rimmed baking sheet with parchment paper. Set wire rack in second rimmed baking sheet and line rack with triple layer of paper towels. Combine cornstarch and sesame seeds in shallow bowl.

3 Working with 1 piece of chicken at a time, lift chicken from marinade, allowing excess to drip back into bowl. Coat chicken with cornstarch mixture, shake off excess, and place on parchment-lined sheet. (Chicken can be coated in cornstarch, covered lightly with plastic wrap, and refrigerated for up to 6 hours.)

4 Add oil to large Dutch oven until it measures about 1½ inches deep and heat over medium-high heat to 325 degrees. Using tongs, add half of chicken, 1 piece at a time, to hot oil. Cook, stirring occasionally, until chicken is golden brown and crispy, 4 to 5 minutes. Adjust burner, if necessary, to maintain oil temperature between 300 and 325 degrees. Using spider skimmer or slotted spoon, transfer chicken to paper towel–lined rack. Return oil to 325 degrees and repeat with remaining chicken. Serve.

VARIATION

CRISPY SESAME TOFU

This is a great option to include for any friends with plant-based eating preferences. Since tofu is more delicate than chicken, marinate the fingers in a single layer in a shallow dish and use a spider skimmer or slotted spoon to place them in the hot oil. I don't recommend coating the tofu in advance. Prepare second batch of marinade and cornstarch mixture. Cut 14 ounces firm or extra-firm tofu into 3 by ½-inch fingers. Drain tofu on paper towels for 20 minutes, then marinate, coat tofu, and fry as directed.

CAMILA'S TIPS

> Use a Dutch oven that holds 6 quarts or more.

> Don't substitute chicken breasts for the thighs; they will dry out during frying.

> The chicken will be cooked through by the time it's golden brown and crispy, so you don't need to take its temperature.

HOISIN-LIME SAUCE

Makes about 1 cup

Total Time: 5 minutes

WHY I LOVE THIS RECIPE   This sauce is savory, sweet, salty, and tangy all at once. To offset hoisin sauce's sweetness and provide a counterpoint to the warm spices of fennel and star anise it usually contains, I add lime zest and juice, plus a boost of garlic and ginger.

- 2   tablespoons vegetable oil
- 3   garlic cloves, minced
- 1   tablespoon grated fresh ginger
- ¾   cup hoisin sauce
- 2   teaspoons soy sauce
- 2   teaspoons grated lime zest plus 3 tablespoons juice

Combine oil, garlic, and ginger in medium bowl. Microwave until bubbling and fragrant, 30 seconds to 1 minute. Stir in hoisin, soy sauce, and lime zest and juice. Serve. (Sauce can be refrigerated for up to 3 days.)

SRIRACHA MAYO

Makes about 1 cup

Total Time: 5 minutes

WHY I LOVE THIS RECIPE   When I first tasted this sauce on a chicken bao, it was so good that I did a little dance in my kitchen, and I hope you'll do a little dance too. Spicy mayo is the best form of mayo, IMO, and sriracha mayo is one of my favorites. The spicy acidity of the hot sauce boosted by a bit of lemon juice offsets mayo's richness, while sesame oil adds nuttiness.

- ¾   cup mayonnaise
- 3   tablespoons sriracha
- 1   tablespoon lemon juice
- ¾   teaspoon toasted sesame oil
- ¾   teaspoon minced garlic, mashed to paste

Combine mayonnaise, sriracha, lemon juice, sesame oil, and garlic in bowl. Serve. (Sauce can be refrigerated for up to 3 days.)

SWEET AND SPICY QUICK PICKLED CARROTS

Makes about 3 cups

Total Time: 1¼ hours

WHY I LOVE THIS RECIPE   Pickled vegetables can liven up practically anything. The crunchy texture and piquant flavor of these carrots are great for cutting through the rich bao fillings of pork shoulder and fried chicken. They hit all the right notes for me: sweet, sour, salty, and spicy (but feel free to leave out the chile if that's more to your taste). Salting and sugaring the carrots before adding them to the brine removes some liquid, giving the pickles a crunchy snap.

- 4   carrots, peeled, halved lengthwise, and sliced thin on bias
- 1   teaspoon plus 2 tablespoons sugar, divided
- 2   teaspoons table salt, divided
- ½   cup distilled white vinegar
- ½   cup water
- 1   garlic clove, halved
- ½–1   Thai chile, sliced thin (optional)

1   Toss carrots with 1 teaspoon sugar and ½ teaspoon salt in colander and let sit until carrots release liquid and become flexible, about 30 minutes.

2   Whisk vinegar, water, remaining 2 tablespoons sugar, and remaining 1½ teaspoons salt in medium bowl until sugar and salt have dissolved. Rinse carrots and pat dry. Add carrots, garlic, and Thai chile to vinegar mixture and toss to combine. Press on carrots to submerge and let sit for 30 minutes. Serve. (Pickles can be refrigerated for up to 1 week.)

CAMILA'S TIPS

› For a fun pop of color, use rainbow carrots.

› If you don't have Thai chiles, use ⅛ to ¼ teaspoon red pepper flakes.

› If you don't have a microwave, you can heat the Hoisin-Lime Sauce in a small saucepan or skillet over low heat.

GUAVA SORBET WITH FRESH FRUIT

Makes about 1 quart

Total Time: 30 minutes, plus 6 hours chilling and freezing

WHY I LOVE THIS RECIPE Light, fruity sorbet served with fresh fruit is a just-right ending to this full-flavored dinner. The supersimple sorbet starts with luscious guava nectar, which is made from the pulp of the fruit, meaning no fruit prep is required (you do need an ice cream maker for this). Guavas are naturally high in pectin, which is helpful for making a smooth sorbet, and adding a bit of corn syrup helps the sorbet freeze without becoming icy. A little lime juice keeps the sweetness in check.

- 4 cups guava nectar
- ⅓ cup light corn syrup
- 4 teaspoons lime juice
  Fresh fruit, peeled, seeded, and sliced as needed

1 Whisk guava nectar, corn syrup, and lime juice together in large bowl until corn syrup has dissolved. Transfer 1 cup mixture to small bowl. Cover both bowls with plastic wrap. Place large bowl in refrigerator and small bowl in freezer and chill for at least 4 hours or up to 24 hours. (Small bowl of base will freeze solid.)

2 Remove mixtures from refrigerator and freezer. Scrape frozen base from small bowl into base in large bowl. Stir occasionally until frozen base has fully melted. Transfer mixture to ice cream maker and churn until mixture has consistency of thick milk shake and color lightens, 15 to 20 minutes.

3 Transfer sorbet to airtight container, pressing firmly to remove any air pockets, and freeze until firm, at least 2 hours or up to 1 week. Serve with sliced fruit.

CAMILA'S TIPS

> I recommend Goya brand guava nectar here.

> Stop churning when the mixture is still somewhat slushy, with the consistency of a thick milk shake. If you churn until the mixture is firm, it will result in a crumbly sorbet when frozen.

> I love serving this with tropical fruit such as mango, kiwi, pineapple, starfruit, and toasted coconut for an impressive presentation.

Stephanie Pixley's

VEGETARIAN DUMPLING PARTY

SERVES 4 TO 6

» **VEGETABLE DUMPLINGS**

» **DIPPING SAUCES**
Soy-Mirin Dipping Sauce
Chili Crisp

» **GAI LAN WITH OYSTER SAUCE**

» **NO-CHURN LIME-PINEAPPLE SWIRL ICE CREAM**

Stephanie Pixley

There's no party like a dumpling party. As someone who eats mostly vegetarian, I love introducing my friends and family to the delicious meat-free dumplings that are the centerpiece of this meal. They can be made well ahead and cooked from frozen, but it's also fun to make the filling and dough ahead and turn your dinner party into a dumpling-making bash! For dipping sauces, I always include the basics (vinegar and chili oil), but for even more variety, I like to offer chili crisp and a sweet-savory sauce. I love Chinese broccoli and how quickly it cooks: This is the only element that really needs to be cooked à la minute, but it's so fast that it won't feel like an inconvenience. If you're serving 6, I recommend including a batch of Everyday Long-Grain White Rice (page 24). As a bonus, the rice also soaks up all the delicious juices left behind on your plate. To finish, impress your guests with a from-scratch ice cream that allows for your own flavor spin and doesn't even require an ice cream maker.

MY GAME PLAN

UP TO 3 MONTHS AHEAD
› Make the Chili Crisp. (Note that this needs to be made at least 12 hours ahead.)

UP TO 1 MONTH AHEAD
› Make and freeze the Vegetable Dumplings. (Whether you're planning to pan-fry or boil, you can do it direct from frozen!)

UP TO 1 WEEK AHEAD
› Make the No-Churn Lime-Pineapple Swirl Ice Cream.

UP TO 2 DAYS AHEAD
› Make the Soy-Mirin Dipping Sauce.

UP TO 1 DAY AHEAD
› Wash and trim the gai lan for the Gai Lan with Oyster Sauce.

UP TO 2 HOURS AHEAD
› Make the garlic mixture and broth mixture for the gai lan (leave at room temperature).

NOTE
› For a DIY dumpling-making party, make the filling 2 days ahead and the dough 1 hour ahead. Let everyone shape their own dumplings according to the photos on page 83.

STREAMLINE
› I enjoy making the dumpling dough from scratch, but you can use store-bought gyoza wrappers instead.
› Feel free to use store-bought chili crisp instead of making it from scratch!

VEGETABLE DUMPLINGS

Makes 40 dumplings

Total Time: 2½ hours

WHY I LOVE THIS RECIPE Here's proof positive that vegetarian dumplings don't take a back seat to pork dumplings. I could easily eat a dozen myself. The flavor is rich and complex, the combination of vegetables is stunningly pretty (trust me on the purple cabbage!), and the dough is super forgiving. I'm no professional when it comes to folding, but this method makes it easy. If your knife skills aren't up to the task, you can cut the cabbage into 1-inch pieces and pulse them in the food processor.

FILLING

- 8 ounces cremini mushrooms, trimmed and quartered
- 3 tablespoons vegetable oil; plus 2 tablespoons for pan-frying (optional)
- 2 cups thinly sliced purple cabbage
- 3 carrots, shredded (1 cup)
- 1 cup finely chopped garlic chives
- 1 tablespoon grated fresh ginger
- 3 tablespoons Shaoxing wine or dry sherry
- 2 tablespoons soy sauce, plus extra for serving
- 1 tablespoon hoisin sauce
- 2 teaspoons toasted sesame oil

DOUGH

- 2½ cups (12½ ounces) all-purpose flour
- 1 cup boiling water

  Black or rice vinegar
  Chili oil

1 FOR THE FILLING Pulse mushrooms in food processor until finely chopped, about 6 pulses, scraping down sides of bowl as needed; transfer to large bowl and wipe out food processor bowl. Heat 3 tablespoons vegetable oil in 12-inch nonstick skillet over medium heat until shimmering. Add mushrooms and cook until moisture has evaporated, about 5 minutes. Add cabbage, carrots, and garlic chives and cook until vegetables are softened, about 5 minutes. Stir in ginger and cook until fragrant, about 30 seconds. Transfer vegetable mixture to large bowl. Add Shaoxing wine, soy sauce, hoisin, and sesame oil and stir to combine. Set aside to cool completely, about 20 minutes. (Vegetable mixture can be refrigerated for up to 2 days.)

2 **FOR THE DOUGH** Place flour in now-empty processor. With processor running, add boiling water. Continue to process until dough forms ball and clears sides of bowl, 30 to 45 seconds longer. Transfer dough to counter and knead with your hands until smooth, about 3 minutes. Wrap dough in plastic wrap and let rest for 30 minutes. (The dough can rest for up to 1 hour, though it may stick to the plastic the longer it sits.)

3 Line 2 rimmed baking sheets with parchment paper and dust lightly with flour; set aside. Unwrap dough and roll into 12-inch cylinder on lightly floured counter, then cut cylinder into 4 equal pieces. Set 3 pieces aside on lightly floured counter, sprinkle lightly with flour, and cover loosely with plastic. Roll remaining piece into 8-inch cylinder. Cut cylinder in half and cut each half into 5 equal pieces. Place dough pieces on 1 cut side on lightly floured counter and lightly dust with flour. Press each dough piece into 2-inch disk. Cover disks with damp towel.

4 Roll 1 disk into 3½-inch round (wrappers needn't be perfectly round) and re-cover round with damp towel. Repeat with remaining disks. (Do not overlap rounds.) Divide filling into 4 equal portions; transfer 1 portion to small bowl and set aside remaining filling. Working with 1 wrapper at a time (keep remaining wrappers covered), place scant 1 tablespoon filling in center of wrapper. Brush away any flour clinging to surface of wrapper. Lift side of wrapper closest to you and side farthest away and pinch together to form 1½-inch-wide seam in center of dumpling. (When viewed from above, dumpling will have rectangular shape with rounded open ends.) Lift left corner farthest away from you and bring to center of seam. Pinch to seal. Pinch together remaining dough on left side to seal. Repeat pinching on right side. Gently press dumpling into crescent shape and transfer to prepared sheet. Repeat with remaining wrappers and filling in bowl. Repeat dumpling-making process with remaining 3 pieces dough and remaining 3 portions filling. (Dumplings can be frozen on rimmed baking sheet until solid, then transferred to zipper-lock bag and stored in freezer for up to 1 month. Do not thaw before cooking.)

5A **TO PAN FRY** Brush 12-inch nonstick skillet with 1 tablespoon vegetable oil. Evenly space 16 dumplings, flat sides down, around edge of skillet and place 4 in center. Cook over medium heat until bottoms begin to turn spotty brown, 3 to 4 minutes. Off heat, carefully add ½ cup water

(water will sputter). Return skillet to heat and bring water to boil. Cover and reduce heat to medium-low. Cook for 6 minutes. Uncover, increase heat to medium-high, and cook until water has evaporated and bottoms of dumplings are crispy and browned, 1 to 3 minutes. Transfer dumplings to platter, crispy sides up. To cook second batch of dumplings, let skillet cool for 10 minutes. Rinse skillet under cool water and wipe dry with paper towels. Repeat cooking process with 1 tablespoon vegetable oil and remaining dumplings. (To pan fry from frozen, increase water to ⅔ cup and covered cooking time to 8 minutes.)

5B **TO BOIL** Bring 4 quarts water to boil in large Dutch oven over high heat. Add 20 dumplings, a few at a time, stirring gently to prevent them from sticking. Return to simmer, adjusting heat as necessary to maintain simmer. Cook dumplings for 7 minutes. Drain well. (To boil from frozen, increase cooking time to 8 minutes.)

6 Serve dumplings hot, passing vinegar, chili oil, and extra soy sauce separately for dipping.

> **STEPHANIE'S TIPS**
> › When making the dough, weigh the flour and measure the water by bringing a full kettle to a boil and then measuring out the desired amount.
>
> › To ensure that the dumplings seal completely, use minimal flour when kneading, rolling, and shaping so that the dough remains slightly tacky.
>
> › If you have one, a shorter, smaller-diameter rolling pin works well here.
>
> › Garlic chives add amazing flavor and are worth seeking out (if you've got extra, may I suggest scrambling them with eggs, making a pesto, or adding them to a stir-fry?), but if you must skip them, use scallions in their place.
>
> › Shaoxing wine is used in lots of Chinese dishes and is a great shelf-stable ingredient to keep on hand. If you can't find it locally, purchase a bottle online!
>
> › If you're short on counter space, fill and shape each dough round immediately after rolling it out.

SHAPING VEGETABLE DUMPLINGS

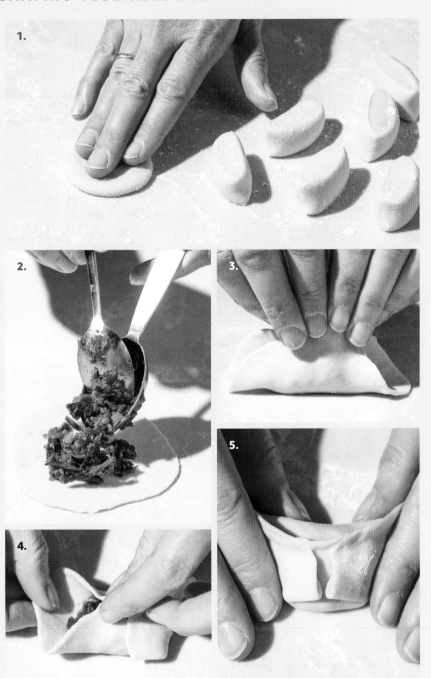

1. After rolling dough into 8-inch cylinder, halving cylinder, and cutting each half into 5 pieces, press each dough piece into 2-inch disk.

2. Roll disk into 3½-inch round and place scant 1 tablespoon filling in center of wrapper. Brush away any flour clinging to surface of wrapper.

3. Lift side of wrapper closest to you and side farthest away and pinch together to form 1½-inch-wide seam in center of dumpling. (When viewed from above, dumpling will have rectangular shape with rounded open ends.)

4. Lift left corner farthest away from you and bring to center of seam. Pinch to seal. Pinch together remaining dough on left side to seal. Repeat pinching on right side.

5. Gently press dumpling into crescent shape.

SOY-MIRIN DIPPING SAUCE

Makes about ½ cup

Total Time: 5 minutes

WHY I LOVE THIS RECIPE   I haven't come across anyone who would say no to an interesting dipping sauce! My favorite combines sweet, sour, bitter, salty, and umami, with a little heat for good measure.

- ¼   cup soy sauce
- 2   tablespoons seasoned rice vinegar
- 2   tablespoons mirin
- 1   teaspoon chili-garlic sauce (optional)

Mix all ingredients together in bowl and serve. (Sauce can be refrigerated for up to 2 days.)

CHILI CRISP

Makes about 1½ cups

Total Time: 45 minutes, plus 12 hours resting

WHY I LOVE THIS RECIPE   Chili crisp, aka lao gan ma, or "godmother sauce," is a spicy and versatile Chinese condiment. For this version, I fry shallots and garlic until crisp, which imparts their flavor to the oil, before removing them and adding cinnamon sticks, cardamom and star anise pods, and ginger. After straining the oil, I pour it over Sichuan chile powder, chopped peanuts, Sichuan peppercorns, salt, and a small but effective amount of MSG for a savory boost. Finally, in go the fried shallots and garlic along with some toasted sesame oil.

- ½   cup Sichuan chile powder
- ½   cup salted dry-roasted peanuts, chopped
- 2   tablespoons Sichuan peppercorns, crushed
- 1½   teaspoons kosher salt
- ¼   teaspoon monosodium glutamate (optional)
- 1   cup vegetable oil
- 2   large shallots, sliced thin

- 4   large garlic cloves, sliced thin
- 1   (1-inch) piece ginger, unpeeled, sliced into ¼-inch-thick rounds and smashed
- 3   star anise pods
- 10   green cardamom pods, crushed
- 2   cinnamon sticks
- 2   tablespoons toasted sesame oil

1   Combine chile powder; peanuts; peppercorns; salt; and monosodium glutamate, if using, in heat-proof bowl and set fine-mesh strainer over bowl. Cook vegetable oil and shallots in medium saucepan over medium-high heat, stirring frequently, until shallots are deep golden brown, 10 to 14 minutes. Using slotted spoon, transfer shallots to second bowl. Add garlic to vegetable oil and cook, stirring constantly, until golden brown, 2 to 3 minutes. Using slotted spoon, transfer garlic to bowl with shallots.

2   Add ginger, star anise, cardamom, and cinnamon sticks to vegetable oil. Reduce heat to medium and cook, stirring occasionally, until ginger looks dried out and mixture is very fragrant, 15 to 20 minutes. Strain oil through strainer into bowl with chili powder mixture (mixture may bubble slightly); discard solids in strainer. Stir well to combine, and let cool.

3   Stir shallots, garlic, and sesame oil into mixture. Transfer to airtight container and let sit for at least 12 hours before using. (Chili crisp can be refrigerated for up to 3 months.)

> **STEPHANIE'S TIPS**
>
> › Sichuan chile powder is milder and more finely ground than red pepper flakes, but Aleppo pepper or gochugaru (Korean red pepper flakes) is a good alternative.
>
> › You'll find monosodium glutamate (MSG) in the spice aisle under the brand name Ac'cent.

GAI LAN WITH OYSTER SAUCE

Serves 4 to 6

Total Time: 30 minutes

WHY I LOVE THIS RECIPE For perfectly crisp-tender gai lan, I favor a combination of two cooking methods—steaming and sautéing. The stalks often can be tough, so first I steam them to a vibrant green and then I sauté the tops and leaves for a little char, adding the stalks back at the end. The flavorful combination of oyster sauce, chicken broth, Shaoxing wine, brown sugar, and toasted sesame oil, thickened with cornstarch, clings to the vegetables. Garlic and a Sichuan chile add a welcome kick of heat.

5	teaspoons vegetable oil, divided
1	garlic clove, minced
1	dried Sichuan chile (about 3 inches long), stemmed and chopped fine
¼	cup chicken broth
¼	cup oyster sauce
4	teaspoons Shaoxing wine or dry sherry
1¼	teaspoons toasted sesame oil
1¼	teaspoons packed brown sugar
1¼	teaspoons cornstarch
2	pounds gai lan
5	tablespoons water

1 Combine 1 teaspoon vegetable oil, garlic, and chile in small bowl; set aside. Whisk broth, oyster sauce, wine, sesame oil, sugar, and cornstarch in second small bowl until sugar has dissolved; set aside.

2 Trim leaves from bottom 3 inches of gai lan stalks and reserve. Cut tops (leaves and florets) from stalks. Quarter stalks lengthwise if more than 1 inch in diameter; halve stalks if less than 1 inch in diameter. Keep leaves and tops separate from stalks.

3 Heat 2 teaspoons vegetable oil in 14-inch flat-bottomed wok or 12-inch nonstick skillet over medium heat until just smoking. Add stalks and water (water will sputter), cover, and cook until gai lan is bright green, about 5 minutes. Uncover, increase heat to high, and continue to cook, tossing slowly but constantly, until all water has evaporated and stalks are crisp-tender, 1 to 3 minutes; transfer to separate bowl.

4 Heat remaining 2 teaspoons vegetable oil in now-empty pan over high heat until just smoking. Add half of reserved gai lan tops and leaves and cook, tossing slowly but constantly, until beginning to wilt, 1 to 3 minutes. Add remaining gai lan tops and reserved leaves and continue to cook, tossing slowly but constantly, until completely wilted, about 3 minutes.

5 Push gai lan to 1 side of pan. Add reserved garlic mixture to clearing and cook, mashing mixture into pan, until fragrant, about 30 seconds. Stir garlic mixture into gai lan. Whisk reserved broth mixture to recombine, then add to pan with stalks and any accumulated juices and cook, tossing constantly, until sauce has thickened and coats gai lan, about 30 seconds. Serve.

> **STEPHANIE'S TIPS**
>
> › If you can't find gai lan (sometimes called Chinese broccoli), broccolini is a good substitute. Trim the broccolini stems and cut the tops (leaves and florets) from the stems, keeping them separate. Halve any stems thicker than ½ inch.
>
> › You can substitute ½ teaspoon Sichuan chile powder for the Sichuan chile.

NO-CHURN LIME-PINEAPPLE SWIRL ICE CREAM

Makes about 1 quart
Total Time: 10 minutes, plus 6 hours freezing

WHY I LOVE THIS RECIPE This is the easiest ice cream you'll ever make, and your guests will think you're some kind of wizard for making it from scratch. I have an ever-present sweet tooth, and this supersimple method allows for endless flavor customization. I often like to end a meal with a bright and fruity dessert like this one, but you could just as easily add chopped chocolate or nuts, candy pieces, crushed cookies, a caramel swirl, and so on. . .

2	cups heavy cream
¾	cup sweetened condensed milk
¼	cup whole milk
¼	cup light corn syrup
2	teaspoons grated lime zest
1	teaspoon vanilla extract
¼	teaspoon table salt
⅓	cup pineapple jam

1 Process cream in blender until soft peaks form, 20 to 30 seconds. Scrape down sides of blender jar and continue to process until stiff peaks form, about 10 seconds longer. Using rubber spatula, stir in condensed milk, whole milk, corn syrup, lime zest, vanilla, and salt. Process until thoroughly combined, about 20 seconds, scraping down sides of blender jar as needed.

2 Pour cream mixture into 8½ by 4½-inch loaf pan. Dollop jam over top and swirl it into cream mixture using tines of fork. Press plastic wrap flush against surface of cream mixture. Freeze until firm, at least 6 hours. Serve.

STEPHANIE'S TIPS

› The cream mixture freezes more quickly in a loaf pan than in a taller, narrower container. If you don't have a loaf pan, use an 8-inch square baking pan.

› You can freeze the ice cream in an airtight container for up to 1 week (though I doubt it will last that long). Just be sure to press plastic wrap flush to the surface of the ice cream to prevent freezer burn.

Dan Zuccarello's

SUMMERTIME AND THE GRILLING IS EASY

SERVES 4

» **CREAMY HERB DIP**

» **GRILLED LEMON-GARLIC CHICKEN WITH NEW POTATOES**

» **SUMMER TOMATO SALAD**

» **GRILLED PEACHES WITH BUTTER COOKIES AND ICE CREAM**

Dan
Zuccarello

During the summer, I make as many trips to my local farm stand as I possibly can, and often the meals I make for myself and my friends are a reflection of the incredible produce I find while I'm there. This menu lets the season's best produce shape your meal by taking advantage of summer's readily available fresh herbs, vegetables, and fruit in every recipe. To get started, a creamy dip loaded with fresh herbs accompanies just-harvested carrots, snap peas, and radishes. Grilled new potatoes and a juicy, farm-fresh tomato salad (with more herbs!) pair well with the impressive but easy main course of grill-roasted whole chicken. Lightly grilled pick-your-own peaches and a scoop of ice cream finish things off in simple but sophisticated style. Now that's my idea of summer eating.

MY GAME PLAN

UP TO 2 DAYS AHEAD

› Whip up the Creamy Herb Dip. The further ahead you make it, the better, as the flavors will have more time to meld.

› Grill the peaches for the Grilled Peaches with Butter Cookies and Ice Cream (this is especially easy if you're using a gas grill).

› Crumble the cookies for dessert and store in an airtight container.

UP TO 1 DAY AHEAD

› Butterfly, skewer, and marinate the chicken for the Grilled Lemon-Garlic Chicken with New Potatoes.

UP TO SEVERAL HOURS AHEAD

› Prep your chosen vegetables to serve with the dip. If you have a gas grill, it's easy to grill some bread ahead of the main cooking event too.

› Wash the parsley and slice the shallot for the Summer Tomato Salad. (But hold off on slicing the tomatoes until just before serving to capture all their fresh juice.)

› If you didn't grill the peaches ahead, halve and pit them and brush with butter.

CREAMY HERB DIP

Makes about 1½ cups

Total Time: 20 minutes

WHY I LOVE THIS RECIPE This dip is all about the fresh herbs, so I pack in as many as possible: Basil, dill, parsley, and tarragon all work well in any combination. Greek yogurt is my easy, one-stop source for tangy richness and full body. The flavor of this dip will continue to develop over the chilling and storage time, so it actually benefits from being made ahead. Set out the dip with a platter of crudités and slices of crusty bread that you've quickly grilled over the fire.

1½	cups plain Greek yogurt
½	cup fresh basil, dill, parsley, and/or tarragon
2	scallions, chopped
1	tablespoon lemon juice
⅛	teaspoon kosher salt
⅛	teaspoon pepper

Process all ingredients in food processor until smooth, about 30 seconds, scraping down sides of bowl as needed. Transfer dip to serving bowl, cover, and refrigerate until flavors meld, at least 15 minutes or up to 2 days. Season with salt and pepper to taste before serving.

DAN'S TIPS

› Got leftovers? Thin out the dip with a little water and use as a salad dressing. It will keep it in the fridge for up to 1 week.

› Buy whatever vegetables look best to you at the farmer's market. I like radishes, snap peas, bell peppers, carrots, and celery.

› I grill plenty of bread and keep it on the table throughout this meal. Look for a crusty French country-style loaf. Slice it on the diagonal into ¾-inch-thick slices, brush both sides with olive oil, and grill over the fire until toasted on both sides, 2 to 4 minutes.

GRILLED LEMON-GARLIC CHICKEN WITH NEW POTATOES

Serves 4

Total Time: 2½ hours

WHY I LOVE THIS RECIPE Grill-roasted chicken is a perennial favorite of mine for entertaining during the warmer months. It's relatively hands-off, receptive to all manner of seasonings, and impresses everybody. Butterflying the chicken accomplishes a lot: It makes the seasoning more effective, it speeds up the cooking process and ensures even cooking, and it maximizes contact with the cooking grate for perfectly crisp skin. I usually keep the seasonings simple, but you can get as creative as you want with herbs and spices. I arrange whole small potatoes around the chicken while it cooks—the indirect heat turns them supercreamy and subtly smoky.

6	garlic cloves, minced
2	tablespoons extra-virgin olive oil
4	teaspoons kosher salt
1	tablespoon sugar
2	teaspoons grated lemon zest, plus lemon wedges for serving
1½	teaspoons ground coriander
1	teaspoon pepper
1	(3½- to 4-pound) whole chicken, giblets discarded
2	(12-inch) wooden skewers
1	pound small Yukon gold potatoes, unpeeled

1 Combine garlic, oil, salt, sugar, lemon zest, coriander, and pepper in bowl until paste forms.

2 With chicken breast side down, use kitchen shears to cut along both sides of backbone. Discard backbone and trim any excess fat or skin at neck. Flip chicken over and use heel of your hand to flatten breastbone. Tuck wingtips behind back. Poke holes all over chicken with skewer. Insert 1 skewer down length of chicken through thickest part of breast and into and through drumstick. Repeat with second skewer on other half of chicken.

3 Rub paste evenly over skin side of chicken. Transfer chicken, skin side up, to plate and refrigerate, uncovered, for at least 1 hour or up to 24 hours.

4A **FOR A CHARCOAL GRILL** Open bottom vent completely. Light large chimney starter mounded with charcoal briquettes (7 quarts). When top coals are partially covered with ash, pour evenly over half of grill. Set cooking grate in place, cover, and open lid vent completely. Heat grill until hot, about 5 minutes.

4B **FOR A GAS GRILL** Turn all burners to high, cover, and heat grill until hot, about 15 minutes. Leave primary burner on high and turn off other burner(s). (Adjust primary burner or, if using three-burner grill, primary burner and second burner, as needed to maintain grill temperature around 400 degrees.)

5 Clean and oil cooking grate. Place chicken, skin side up, on cooler side of grill with skewers parallel to fire. Arrange potatoes around chicken on cooler side of grill. Cover (position lid vent over chicken if using charcoal) and cook until potatoes are tender and chicken breasts register 160 degrees and thighs register 175 degrees, about 1 hour, rotating chicken halfway through cooking.

6 Transfer potatoes to plate and chicken to carving board. Tent chicken with aluminum foil and let rest for 15 minutes. Carve chicken and serve with potatoes and lemon wedges.

DAN'S TIPS

› Look for potatoes that measure 1 to 2 inches in diameter. If your potatoes are a little larger, cut them in half.

› Instead of serving lemon wedges, you can halve the lemons and char them on the grill grates for a few minutes, for a lightly caramelized flavor.

› Threading two wooden skewers through the breasts and drumsticks helps keep the chicken intact during cooking.

› The two-level fire (with the coals piled on one side of the grill to concentrate the heat) prevents flare-ups and helps control the cooking rate.

SUMMER TOMATO SALAD

Serves 4

Total Time: 10 minutes

WHY I LOVE THIS RECIPE Tomato salad doesn't need to be complicated, particularly when the bright jewels are at their best. My favorite part of this salad is the dressing that forms from the mingling of tomato juices, shallot, oil, and vinegar. I always encourage people to scoop up the dressing and drizzle it over their chicken. And leave that platter of grilled bread from the dip on the table for soaking up every last drop.

1	pound mixed ripe tomatoes, cored
¼	teaspoon kosher salt
¼	teaspoon pepper
¼	cup fresh parsley leaves
1	shallot, sliced thin
2	tablespoons extra-virgin olive oil
1	tablespoon red wine vinegar

Halve or quarter small tomatoes; cut medium tomatoes into ½-inch wedges; slice large tomatoes ¼ inch thick. Arrange tomatoes attractively on serving platter and sprinkle with salt and pepper. Top with parsley and shallot and drizzle with oil and vinegar. Serve.

GRILLED PEACHES WITH BUTTER COOKIES AND ICE CREAM

Serves 4

Total Time: 45 minutes

WHY I LOVE THIS RECIPE Whenever I grill dinner, I inevitably start to think of ways to keep right on using the fire for dessert. Grilling fruit enhances its natural sweetness, and I especially enjoy gently grilling fragrant, in-season summer peaches while people linger at the table. Store-bought butter cookies and ice cream are a no-fuss complement.

1½	pounds ripe but slightly firm peaches or nectarines, halved and pitted
2	tablespoons unsalted butter, melted
2	cups crumbled butter cookies
1	pint vanilla ice cream

1A FOR A CHARCOAL GRILL Open bottom vent completely. Light large chimney starter half filled with charcoal briquettes (3 quarts). When top coals are partially covered with ash, pour evenly over half of grill. Set cooking grate in place, cover, and open lid vent completely. Heat grill until hot, about 5 minutes.

1B FOR A GAS GRILL Turn all burners to high, cover, and heat grill until hot, about 15 minutes. Turn primary burner to medium and turn off other burner(s).

2 Clean and oil cooking grate. Brush cut sides of peaches with melted butter. Arrange peaches cut side down on hotter side of grill and cook until grill marks have formed, 5 to 7 minutes, moving fruit as needed to ensure even cooking.

3 Transfer peaches cut side up to 13 by 9-inch baking pan and cover loosely with aluminum foil. Place pan on cooler side of grill and cook until fruit is very tender and paring knife slips in and out with little resistance, about 15 minutes. Remove pan from grill, uncover, and set peaches aside until ready to serve.

4 Cut peaches into wedges and divide evenly among serving bowls. Sprinkle with cookies and top with scoops of ice cream. Serve.

DAN'S TIPS

› You'll want to make this a lot, so I wrote it to stand alone. If making it with the grilled chicken, skip step 1 and grill the peaches over the remaining hot charcoal (for a gas grill, leave the primary burner on medium and turn off the other burners).

› Using a metal baking pan on the cooler side of the grill won't harm the pan; you can also use a disposable aluminum pan, but don't use any type of glass dish.

› You can grill the peaches up to 2 days in advance; bring them to room temperature before serving.

Joe Gitter's

THE GREAT BRITISH PICNIC

SERVES 6 TO 8

» **ENGLISH 75**

» **SAGE AND SCALLION SCOTCH EGGS**

» **BROWN BUTTER–POACHED POTTED SHRIMP**

» **CORONATION CHICKEN**

» **CUCUMBER AND ASPARAGUS SALAD**

» **NECTARINES AND BERRIES IN ELDERFLOWER AND SPARKLING WINE**

Joe Gitter

There's no British meal better at evoking feelings of warm nostalgia than a picnic. From *The Wind in the Willows* through Enid Blyton to Harry Potter, British literature is full of overflowing picnic hampers, tartan rugs, and choice morsels to while away long, sunny days on some patch (however small) of green grass. Here, I bring together some of my all-time favorite picnic treats. I'm a firm believer that a host should do as little cooking as possible after guests arrive so that they can devote their full attention to filling people's glasses, proffering another plate of food, and fully partaking in the moments of a joyous get-together. A picnic is by definition make-ahead, and all this food can be enjoyed at room temperature, further reducing any pre-party angst. While my perfect party involves a portable picnic, these treats work equally well in your backyard or simply on a sunny balcony.

MY GAME PLAN

UP TO 3 DAYS AHEAD

> Boil the eggs for the Sage and Scallion Scotch Eggs.
> Make the Brown Butter–Poached Potted Shrimp.
> Poach the chicken for the Coronation Chicken.

UP TO 2 DAYS AHEAD

> Make the Coronation Chicken.
> Blanch the asparagus for the Cucumber and Asparagus Salad.

UP TO 1 DAY AHEAD

> Coat the cooked eggs in their sausage and panko blankets for the Scotch eggs.

UP TO SEVERAL HOURS AHEAD

> Assemble the English 75 in its thermos.
> Fry the Scotch eggs.
> Make the salad.
> Prepare the fruits for the Nectarines and Berries in Elderflower and Sparkling Wine.

NOTES

> I suggest dividing and conquering the Sage and Scallion Scotch Eggs as above, but if you like, you can make them in their entirety up to 2 days ahead.

STREAMLINE

> These are fairly rich dishes, and it would require appetites of Hungry Caterpillian proportions for six people alone to eat their way through this entire menu. Feel free to skip something!

ENGLISH 75

Makes 8 cocktails

Total Time: 10 minutes

WHY I LOVE THIS RECIPE   Throwing away good food really gnaws at me, but this can easily happen when a recipe calls for a portion of a whole ingredient. Here's an elegant way to use up the leftover cucumber (from the cucumber salad) and lemon (from the potted shrimp and the fruit salad). It's a riff on the classic French 75 cocktail, but I cut the amount of lemon and sugar so the cucumber can really shine against the aromatic gin and lovely prickly bubbles of the wine.

½   cup thinly sliced English cucumber

3   ounces lemon juice

2   tablespoons sugar

8   ounces London dry gin

24   ounces chilled dry sparkling wine, divided

1   Add cucumber, lemon juice, and sugar to insulated thermos and muddle until cucumber is broken down and all juice has been expressed, about 30 seconds. Add gin, seal thermos, and shake vigorously until well combined and sugar has dissolved, about 30 seconds. Fill with ice and seal until ready to serve, up to 6 hours.

2   To serve, shake gin mixture until well combined, about 5 seconds. Strain 1½ ounces gin mixture into each glass and top with 3 ounces sparkling wine.

JOE'S TIPS

> If you have any lime juice left over from the Coronation Chicken, you can substitute up to 1½ ounces for an equal amount of the lemon juice.

> Any 16-ounce thermal carafe will work to keep the muddled gin mixture cold.

> If you don't have a muddler, you can use the end of a rolling pin or a potato masher in a large shallow bowl.

SAGE AND SCALLION SCOTCH EGGS

Makes 6 eggs

Total Time: 1 hour

WHY I LOVE THIS RECIPE A good Scotch egg is a thing of beauty: a not quite fully set yolk with a tender white surrounded by highly seasoned sausage meat in golden bread crumbs that yield with an audible crunch. To the uninitiated, it seems like an act of true cooking alchemy. However, with the right tools (and a little exactitude with a timer), it's well within the grasp of the home cook. I make my own sausage meat using sage (the ultimate pork herb) and scallions (in a nod to traditional British pork and leek sausages). Branston Pickle or English mustard makes the best companion, but piccalilli or another plucky sweet-and-sour pickle or chutney will perform admirably in their absence.

10	large eggs, divided
1	pound ground pork
4	scallions, sliced thin
1	tablespoon minced fresh sage
1	teaspoon table salt
½	teaspoon pepper
⅛	teaspoon ground mace or nutmeg
1½	cups panko bread crumbs
½	cup all-purpose flour
1	tablespoon water
6	cups vegetable oil for frying
	Branston Pickle or English mustard for serving

1 Bring 8 cups water to boil in large saucepan over high heat. Fill large bowl halfway with ice and water. Using slotted spoon, gently lower 7 eggs into boiling water and cook for 8 minutes (for a jammy center) or 10 minutes (for a fully set center). Using slotted spoon, transfer eggs to ice bath and let cool for 5 minutes. Peel eggs. (Eggs can be refrigerated for up 3 days.)

2 Mix pork, scallions, sage, salt, pepper, and mace in bowl with hands until well combined. Divide sausage mixture into 6 balls.

3 Lay sheet of plastic wrap on counter and flour generously. Place one sausage ball on plastic wrap, top with second layer of plastic wrap, and gently press into 6-inch circle; remove top layer of plastic. Place one peeled egg in center of circle and use edges of plastic to wrap egg in sausage. Remove plastic and pinch seams to seal. Using hands, roll egg into even shape. Repeat with remaining pork balls and eggs.

4   Spread panko in shallow dish. Spread flour in second shallow dish. Beat remaining 3 eggs with water in third shallow dish. Working with one sausage-wrapped egg at a time, dredge in flour, dip in egg, letting excess drip off, then coat with panko, pressing gently to adhere. Repeat coating process 1 more time, then transfer egg to plate. (Coated Scotch eggs can be refrigerated for up to 24 hours.)

5   Line large plate with triple layer of paper towels. Add oil to large pot and heat over medium-high heat to 350 degrees. Using slotted spoon, add 3 Scotch eggs to hot oil and fry until well browned, about 7 minutes, turning eggs occasionally. Adjust burner, if necessary, to maintain oil temperature between 325 and 350 degrees.

6   Using slotted spoon, transfer Scotch eggs to prepared plate. Return oil to 350 degrees and repeat with remaining 3 Scotch eggs. Serve warm or at room temperature, whole or sliced in half, with Branston Pickle. (Cooked Scotch eggs can be refrigerated for up 2 days. Bring to room temperature or reheat in a 400-degree oven for 10 to 12 minutes before serving.)

JOE'S TIPS

›   Eggs sometimes burst during boiling, so I call for a seventh egg as insurance. The stuffing and breading makes only enough for six Scotch eggs.

›   Working with sausage can be a sticky business. I like to wear disposable gloves or keep a small bowl of water nearby so that I can keep my hands damp to prevent sticking.

›   The double dip in the flour, egg, and panko gives the eggs a sturdier coating and helps them keep their crunch during transport in a picnic hamper.

›   The thought of frying at home used to terrify me. This changed when I started using a clip-on probe thermometer, which removes the need for guesswork, experience, or constant checking with an instant-read thermometer.

BROWN BUTTER–POACHED POTTED SHRIMP

Serves 6

Total Time: 1½ hours

WHY I LOVE THIS RECIPE   Three of my favorite things are butter-poached shrimp, brown butter, and potted shrimp, and this recipe unites them. Making potted foods—tongue, crab, shrimp, beef, and pork—was a medieval preserving method: Covering foods in fat prevents their exposure to air, so they stay fresher longer. Traditionally, boiled shrimp would be coated in clarified butter (since milk solids are more prone to oxidation), but my goal here is simply to serve beautifully cooked shrimp with oodles of brown butter to be smeared on crusty bread. It's customary to use small brown shrimp, but as these aren't widely available in the U.S., any size shrimp will do, as long as they are cut into small pieces.

1	pound shrimp, peeled, deveined, tails removed, and cut into ½-inch pieces
½	teaspoon table salt
16	tablespoons unsalted butter
1	teaspoon grated lemon zest, plus lemon wedges for serving
½	teaspoon ground coriander
¼	teaspoon ground white or black pepper
¼	teaspoon ground mace or nutmeg
	Pinch cayenne pepper
	Crusty bread or toast for serving

1 Toss shrimp with salt in bowl. Melt butter in small saucepan over medium heat. Continue cooking, swirling saucepan constantly, until butter is golden brown and has nutty aroma, 3 to 5 minutes.

2 Off heat, carefully and quickly stir in shrimp. Press on shrimp to submerge, then cover and let sit for 2 minutes. Stir in lemon zest, coriander, pepper, mace, and cayenne. Return shrimp to medium-low heat and cook, stirring constantly, until shrimp are opaque throughout, about 1 minute.

3 Using slotted spoon, divide shrimp among six 6-ounce ramekins. Pour butter over shrimp and let cool to room temperature, about 30 minutes. Cover and refrigerate until shrimp mixture is firm, about 30 minutes. (Shrimp can be refrigerated for up to 3 days; bring to room temperature before serving.) Serve with bread and lemon wedges.

JOE'S TIPS

› The butter will go from blond to brown to burnt quickly, so keep a cool head and your shrimp on hand to quickly stir in and halt the butter's cooking.

› You can purchase ramekin lids for secure transport; or look for 6-ounce mason jars.

› When served hot, before the butter solidifies, the shrimp are also an amazing topping for steak or fish. At the end of step 2, simply pour the contents of the saucepan over your protein.

CORONATION CHICKEN

Serves 6 to 8

Total Time: 1½ hours

WHY I LOVE THIS RECIPE The first version of this dish was prepared for the coronation of Queen Elizabeth II in 1953 and used whole chickens, which were poached in wine, with apricot puree, curry powder, mayonnaise, and cream. My picnic homage combines poached and shredded chicken breasts in a gingery, fruity mayonnaise that is punched up with bloomed curry powder, mango chutney, and lime juice. Cutting the sauce with a little Greek yogurt adds tang and keeps the chicken abundantly coated without overloading it with richness. Apple, celery, and romaine lettuce are decidedly nontraditional, but I love their refreshing sweet and savory crunch against the creamy spiced chicken.

4	(6- to 8-ounce) boneless, skinless chicken breasts, trimmed
	Table salt for poaching chicken
1	tablespoon vegetable oil
1	tablespoon curry powder
½	cup mayonnaise
¼	cup plain Greek yogurt
2	tablespoons mango chutney
2	tablespoons lime juice
1	teaspoon grated fresh ginger
1	Honeycrisp, Fuji, or Braeburn apple, cored and cut into ½-inch pieces
2	celery ribs, minced
1	shallot, minced
1	head romaine lettuce (12 ounces), sliced ½ inch thick
½	cup sliced almonds, toasted

1 Cover chicken breasts with plastic wrap and pound thick ends gently with meat pounder until 1 inch thick. Dissolve 2 tablespoons salt in 6 cups cold water in Dutch oven. Submerge chicken in water. Heat pot over medium heat until water registers 170 degrees. Turn off heat, cover pot, and let stand until chicken registers 165 degrees, 15 to 17 minutes. Transfer chicken to plate and refrigerate until cool, about 30 minutes. (Chicken can be refrigerated for up to 3 days.)

2 Microwave oil and curry powder in large bowl until fragrant, 30 to 60 seconds. Whisk in mayonnaise, yogurt, chutney, lime juice, and ginger.

3 Pat chicken dry with paper towels. Using 2 forks, shred chicken into bite-size pieces. Transfer chicken, apple, celery, and shallot to bowl with dressing and toss to coat. Season with salt and pepper to taste. (Salad can be refrigerated for up to 2 days.) Scatter lettuce on serving platter or individual plates, top with chicken, and sprinkle with almonds. Serve.

JOE'S TIPS

> To ensure that the chicken cooks through, start with cold water in step 1 and don't use breasts that weigh more than 8 ounces.

> This also makes for an amazing sandwich filling between buttered slices of a soft, seeded loaf.

CUCUMBER AND ASPARAGUS SALAD

Serves 6 to 8

Total Time: 45 minutes

WHY I LOVE THIS RECIPE There is something so clean about the English cucumber—I think it's down to its crispness and distinct aroma. Pairing it with blanched asparagus and giving it an herby, mustardy yogurt-based dressing makes for delicious picnic food that's a refreshing foil to the rest of the menu. Salting and draining the cucumber first means liquid won't leach out while you're waiting to eat it.

JOE'S TIP

> Use the remaining ½ cucumber in the English 75 (page 101).

1½	English cucumbers, halved lengthwise and sliced thin
½	teaspoon table salt, plus salt for cooking asparagus
1	pound asparagus, trimmed and cut on the bias into 2-inch lengths
⅓	cup plain Greek yogurt
4	teaspoons white wine vinegar
1	tablespoon extra-virgin olive oil
2	teaspoons Dijon mustard
1	large shallot, halved and sliced thin
2	tablespoons chopped fresh dill or tarragon

1 Place cucumbers in colander and toss with salt. Set colander in sink and let sit for 30 minutes.

2 Meanwhile, bring 2 quarts water to boil in large saucepan over high heat. Fill large bowl halfway with ice and water. Add ¼ cup salt and asparagus to boiling water, return to boil, and cook until bright green and crisp-tender, 2 to 3 minutes. Using slotted spoon, transfer asparagus to ice bath and let sit for 5 minutes. Drain and blot dry with paper towels. (Asparagus can be refrigerated for up to 2 days.)

3 Whisk yogurt, vinegar, oil, and mustard together in large bowl. Gently shake colander to drain excess liquid, then blot cucumbers dry with paper towels. Add cucumbers, asparagus, shallot, and dill to bowl with dressing and toss gently to combine. Season with salt and pepper to taste. Serve. (Salad can be refrigerated for up to 6 hours.)

NECTARINES AND BERRIES IN ELDERFLOWER AND SPARKLING WINE

Serves 6 to 8

Total Time: 10 minutes

WHY I LOVE THIS RECIPE I'm not one for making elaborate desserts; if I'm going to ingest sugar, I'd rather imbibe it. So, in that spirit, this dish draws inspiration from the sour family of cocktails—spirit-forward drinks punched up by citrus and balanced out with sweetness. To coax out the summer fruits' essential character, I macerate them in sugar, lemon juice, and elderflower liqueur. Elder trees are widespread across Great Britain, and their blossoms are beloved by foragers who turn them into elderflower wines, cordials, and liqueurs. Their floweriness strongly summons British summer for me. Dousing everything in a few bubbles only makes it all better.

1½   pounds nectarines, halved, pitted, and cut into ¼-inch wedges

1   pound strawberries, hulled and quartered (2 cups)

10   ounces (2 cups) blackberries and/or raspberries

¼   cup elderflower liqueur

2   tablespoons sugar

1   teaspoon grated lemon zest plus 1 teaspoon juice

1   cup chilled dry sparkling wine

1   cup torn fresh mint leaves

Gently toss nectarines, strawberries, blackberries, liqueur, sugar, and lemon zest and juice together in large bowl until sugar has dissolved. (Fruit mixture can be refrigerated for up to 8 hours; toss to recombine before serving.) Just before serving, pour wine over fruit and top with mint.

JOE'S TIPS

› For a nonalcoholic version, substitute elderflower cordial for the liqueur (Belvoir Farm is a good brand) and omit the sugar and sparkling wine.

› English sparkling wine and Italian prosecco are great candidates, but I'm particularly partial to the creamy, complex texture of Spanish cava.

Christie Morrison's

TAKE ME BACK TO TUSCANY

SERVES 4 TO 6

» **ANTIPASTI WITH SCHIACCIATA**

» **BROTHY WHITE BEANS WITH SUN-DRIED TOMATOES AND GARLIC**

» **FARRO AND KALE SALAD WITH FENNEL, OLIVES, AND PECORINO**

» **BISTECCA ALLA FIORENTINA WITH PORTOBELLOS AND GRILLED BREAD**

» **GELATO WITH OLIVE OIL, SEA SALT, AND AMARETTI CRUMBLE**

Christie Morrison

When I'm entertaining, the last thing I want is to be chained to the stove, monitoring a finicky recipe one-handed. (The other hand is balancing my wine glass; I'm not a heathen.) Putting together a menu with make-ahead options as well as dishes that are great served either warm or at room temperature is how I'm able to enjoy myself as I entertain others. This menu is wonderful at any time of year, but the vision board in my brain pictures it in late summer or early fall, so that we can sit outside where the smell of grilled steak, rosemary, and toasted bread will lure friends like moths to a flame. It's also a priority for me to offer hearty plant-based salads and sides. The inspiration for it all? A trip I took to Italy that culminated in some halcyon October days surrounded by olive trees and vineyards in the Tuscan countryside. The rustic dishes of the region resonated with me while I was there; now they evoke a sense of place, peace, and good times that I am happy to share with others.

MY GAME PLAN

UP TO 3 DAYS AHEAD
> Make the Brothy White Beans with Sun-Dried Tomatoes and Garlic.

UP TO 2 DAYS AHEAD
> Cook the farro for the Farro and Kale Salad with Fennel, Olives, and Pecorino.

UP TO 1 DAY AHEAD
> Make the schiacciata dough for the Antipasti with Schiacciata and refrigerate overnight to rise. (Note that this must be done at least 8 hours ahead of baking.)
> Make the farro and kale salad.
> If not making the white beans entirely ahead of time, brine them for at least 8 hours or up to 24 hours ahead.
> Salt the steak for the Bistecca alla Fiorentina with Portobellos and Grilled Bread.

UP TO SEVERAL HOURS AHEAD
> Bake the schiacciata.

STREAMLINE
> No one will judge you if you purchase plenty of focaccia from a bakery and serve that with the whole meal instead of making the Schiacciata and grilling Italian bread.

ANTIPASTI WITH SCHIACCIATA

Serves 4 to 6

Total Time: 1½ hours, plus 9½ hours rising and 30 minutes cooling

WHY I LOVE THIS RECIPE Schiacciata is often served as part of an antipasti spread in Tuscany. (The name means "pressed," referring to the method of dimpling the dough into the baking pan.) Unlike its cousin focaccia, which can have an open crumb and a higher rise, schiacciata often has a tighter crumb and lower profile—and a reputation for being a pretty unfussy dough. It gets richness from olive oil or lard, and it's best when it achieves a crunchy bottom. To build flavor, I mix and knead the dough in a stand mixer before transferring it to a baking pan for an overnight refrigerator rise. A final rise at room temperature before baking lets you focus on assembling the antipasti.

SCHIACCIATA

- 3 cups (15 ounces) all-purpose flour
- 1 tablespoon kosher salt, divided
- 1 teaspoon instant or rapid-rise yeast
- 1 cup plus 2 tablespoons water, room temperature
- 5 tablespoons extra-virgin olive oil, divided
- 1 tablespoon sugar

ANTIPASTI

- 8–16 ounces thinly sliced meats (finocchiona, prosciutto, mortadella, soppressata, Genoa salami)
- 8–16 ounces cheese (Pecorino, fresh mozzarella, Gorgonzola)
- Dried fruit (apricots, dates, figs)
- Assorted olives
- Nuts (almonds and walnuts)
- Extra-virgin olive oil
- Aged balsamic vinegar

CHRISTIE'S TIPS

> Be sure to use a metal baking pan to achieve that crunchy bottom.

> I've offered plenty of suggestions for the meats and cheeses, but don't feel like you need to include them all. Make it simpler if that works better for you!

1 **FOR THE SCHIACCIATA** Whisk flour, 2 teaspoons salt, and yeast together in bowl of stand mixer. Whisk water, 2 tablespoons oil, and sugar in 2-cup liquid measuring cup until sugar has dissolved.

2 Using dough hook on low speed, slowly add water mixture to flour mixture and mix until cohesive dough starts to form and no dry flour remains, about 2 minutes, scraping down sides of bowl as needed. Increase speed to medium-low and knead until dough is smooth and elastic and clears sides of bowl, about 4 minutes.

3 Coat 13 by 9-inch baking pan with remaining 3 tablespoons oil and sprinkle bottom of pan with ½ teaspoon salt. Place dough in pan and slide around to coat bottom and sides with oil, then flip. Using fingertips, gently press dough all over into even layer (it won't stretch to fill pan). Let dough rest, covered with greased plastic, until slightly puffed, about 30 minutes. Press dough into corners of pan (if dough resists stretching, let it relax for 5 to 10 minutes before trying again). Sprinkle with remaining ½ teaspoon salt, cover loosely with greased plastic, and refrigerate for at least 8 hours or up to 24 hours.

4 Adjust oven rack to middle position and heat oven to 450 degrees. Transfer pan to counter and let dough rest, covered, until puffed and nearly doubled, 1 to 2 hours. Using your fingertips, gently press dough into corners of pan. Bake until top is golden brown, about 20 minutes, rotating pan halfway through baking. Let cool in pan for 5 minutes. Remove loaf from pan, transfer to wire rack, and let cool for 30 minutes.

5 **FOR THE ANTIPASTI** Assemble meats, cheeses, dried fruit, olives, and nuts attractively on serving platter. Cut schiacciata into wedges or tear into large pieces and serve warm or at room temperature with plenty of oil and vinegar for dipping.

SALUTE

Most Italians wouldn't think of having a dinner party without aperitivi and wine. I like to serve Campari and soda or Aperol spritzes with the antipasti spread. I'll put out both a red and a white wine with dinner: Chianti is a classic pairing with the bistecca, and Vernaccia is a top Tuscan white that plays really well with the farro salad.

BROTHY WHITE BEANS WITH SUN-DRIED TOMATOES AND GARLIC

Serves 4 to 6

Total Time: 1½ hours, plus 8 hours soaking

WHY I LOVE THIS RECIPE Tuscans are known throughout Italy for their abundance of bean-forward dishes. I recently got into cooking my own beans, and I'm not sure why I waited so long. Canned beans are a great weeknight time-saver, but the flavor and texture of dried beans cooked with garlic and sun-dried tomatoes is really special. These beans are pretty hands-off and will make your home smell amazing. Soak up every last drop of that broth with a piece of schiacciata or grilled bread.

Table salt for brining

8 ounces dried cannellini beans, picked over and rinsed

1 onion, peeled and halved

1 garlic head, outer papery skins removed and top third of head cut off and discarded

3 sprigs fresh rosemary, thyme, and/or sage

¼ cup extra-virgin olive oil, divided

¼–½ teaspoon red pepper flakes

¼ cup oil-packed sun-dried tomatoes, patted dry and chopped coarse

1 Dissolve 1½ tablespoons salt in 2 quarts cold water in large container. Add beans and soak at room temperature for at least 8 hours or up to 24 hours.

2 Drain beans in colander and rinse well. Combine 6 cups water, beans, onion, garlic, rosemary sprigs, 2 tablespoons oil, and pepper flakes in Dutch oven and bring to boil. Reduce heat to gentle simmer (bubbles should just break surface of water) and cook until beans are barely al dente, 40 to 50 minutes. Off heat, stir in tomatoes, cover, and let beans sit until fully tender, 20 to 30 minutes.

3 Discard onion and rosemary sprigs. Remove garlic and squeeze head from root end to extrude garlic; discard skins. Stir garlic into beans and season with salt to taste. (Beans can be refrigerated for up to 3 days or transferred to zipper-lock bag and frozen for up to 1 month; bring to brief simmer before serving and adjust consistency with extra water as needed.) Transfer beans to shallow bowl and drizzle with remaining 2 tablespoons oil. Serve.

CHRISTIE'S TIP

> For a thicker consistency, remove 1 cup of the bean mixture after step 2 and mash it; then return the mash to the pot.

FARRO AND KALE SALAD WITH FENNEL, OLIVES, AND PECORINO

Serves 4 to 6

Total Time: 45 minutes

WHY I LOVE THIS RECIPE This salad is fantastic warm, at room temperature, or chilled, so it's perfect for entertaining. It's a great example of a dish being more than the sum of its parts, but I am an unabashed lover of each and every part. The nutty flavor and chewy texture of farro really work with the earthiness of Tuscan kale, and crisp fennel adds a faint licorice flavor. I incorporate a sharp lemon-shallot vinaigrette and briny olives (tearing rather than chopping them gives them more presence). I suppose that Pecorino Toscano is the correct sheep's milk cheese to use (so if you can find it, go for it), but Pecorino Romano is an excellent substitute: The funky, salty shreds bring everything together.

1½	cups whole farro, rinsed
½	teaspoon table salt, plus salt for cooking farro
5	ounces Tuscan kale, stemmed and sliced crosswise ¼ inch thick
3	tablespoons extra-virgin olive oil
2	tablespoons lemon juice
1	small shallot, minced
¼	teaspoon pepper
1	fennel bulb, fronds minced, stalks discarded, bulb halved, cored, and sliced thin
⅓	cup pitted Castelvetrano olives, torn in half
¼	cup slivered almonds, toasted, divided
1	ounce Pecorino Romano cheese, shaved thin

1 Bring 2 quarts water to boil in large saucepan. Stir in farro and 1 tablespoon salt, reduce to simmer, and cook until tender, 15 to 20 minutes. Drain well. Spread farro on rimmed baking sheet and let cool for 15 minutes. (Farro can be cooked up to 2 days ahead and refrigerated.)

2 Vigorously squeeze and massage kale with hands until leaves are uniformly darkened and slightly wilted, about 1 minute. Whisk oil, lemon juice, shallot, salt, and pepper together in large bowl. Add cooled farro and kale, sliced fennel, olives, and 2 tablespoons almonds and toss to combine. (Salad can be refrigerated for up to 24 hours; bring to room temperature before serving.) Season with salt and pepper to taste. Sprinkle with Pecorino Romano, fennel fronds, and remaining 2 tablespoons almonds. Serve.

CHRISTIE'S TIPS

› It's best to use whole-grain farro here. You can use pearled farro, but cooking times vary, so start checking for doneness after 10 minutes. Don't substitute quick-cooking farro.

› Tuscan kale (also known as dinosaur or Lacinato kale) is more tender than curly-leaf or red kale; if you need to substitute curly-leaf or red kale, increase the massaging time to 5 minutes. Don't use baby kale.

› You can use any type of brined olives, but I love the meaty texture of Castelvetrano olives.

BISTECCA ALLA FIORENTINA WITH PORTOBELLOS AND GRILLED BREAD

Serves 4 to 6

Total Time: 1¼ hours, plus 1 hour chilling

WHY I LOVE THIS RECIPE   A Tuscan-themed dinner doesn't feel complete without a thick, grilled porterhouse steak. This cut is expensive, but the grilling method is foolproof; your guests will raise glasses of Chianti to your grilling prowess. While I like to cook steak for others, I don't particularly enjoy eating it, so I also include a meatless option: portobello mushrooms. My favorite part of this recipe is its easy and logical flow. The lemons, mushrooms, and bread all grill while the steak rests, and you can sip a glass of wine as you move the elements around the grill. The grilled lemons give the steak and mushrooms a fresh blast of acidity, and everything is better with a final glug of olive oil.

1	(2½- to 3-pound) porterhouse steak, 2 inches thick, fat trimmed to ¼ inch
4	teaspoons kosher salt, divided
6	portobello mushrooms (4 to 5 inches in diameter), stems and gills removed
¾	cup plus 2 teaspoons extra-virgin olive oil, divided, plus extra for serving
3	tablespoons red wine vinegar
1	teaspoon minced fresh rosemary, plus 2 sprigs fresh rosemary
2	garlic cloves (1 minced, 1 peeled and halved)
1½	teaspoons pepper, divided
2	lemons, halved
1	loaf rustic Italian bread, cut into ¾-inch-thick slices
	Flake sea salt (optional)

1 Pat steak dry with paper towels and sprinkle each side with 1 teaspoon salt. Transfer to large plate and refrigerate, uncovered, for at least 1 hour or up to 24 hours.

2 Using tip of paring knife, cut ½-inch crosshatch pattern on tops of mushroom caps, 1/16 inch deep. Combine ½ cup oil, vinegar, minced rosemary, minced garlic, ½ teaspoon pepper, and remaining 2 teaspoons salt in 1-gallon zipper-lock bag. Add mushrooms, seal bag, turn to coat, and let sit for at least 30 minutes or up to 1 hour.

3A **FOR A CHARCOAL GRILL** Open bottom vent completely. Light large chimney starter filled with charcoal briquettes (6 quarts). When top coals are partially covered with ash, pour evenly over half of grill. Set cooking grate in place, cover, and open lid vent completely. Heat grill until hot, about 5 minutes.

3B **FOR A GAS GRILL** Turn all burners to high, cover, and heat grill until hot, about 15 minutes. Leave primary burner on high and turn off other burner(s). (Adjust primary burner [or, if using three-burner grill, primary burner and second burner] as needed to maintain grill temperature of 450 degrees.)

4 Pat steak dry with paper towels. Brush each side with 1 teaspoon oil and sprinkle with remaining 1 teaspoon pepper. Clean and oil cooking grate. Place steak on hotter side of grill, with tenderloin facing cooler side. Cook (covered if using gas) until evenly charred on first side, 6 to 8 minutes. Flip steak and position so tenderloin is still facing cooler side of grill. Continue to cook (covered if using gas) until evenly charred on second side, 6 to 8 minutes.

5 Flip steak and transfer to cooler side of grill, with bone side facing fire. Cover and cook until thermometer inserted 3 inches from tip of strip side of steak registers 115 to 120 degrees (for medium-rare), 8 to 12 minutes, flipping halfway through cooking. Transfer steak to wire rack set in rimmed baking sheet, tent with aluminum foil, and let rest while preparing mushrooms, lemons, and bread.

6 Remove mushrooms from marinade; discard marinade. Place lemons, cut side down, and mushrooms, gill side up, on hotter side of grill. Cook lemons and mushrooms (covered if using gas) until lemons are well charred on cut side, 6 to 8 minutes, and mushrooms have released their liquid and are charred on first side, about 6 minutes. Transfer lemons to bowl. Flip mushrooms and continue to cook until charred on second side, about 4 minutes. Transfer mushrooms to platter and tent with foil.

7 Brush bread with remaining ¼ cup oil. Place on hotter side of grill and cook, turning as needed, until lightly toasted, about 4 minutes. Transfer to separate platter and rub with cut sides of halved garlic clove.

8 Transfer steak to carving board. Carve strip and tenderloin from bone. Place bone on separate platter. Slice steak thin against grain, then reassemble sliced steak around bone. Brush steak and mushrooms with rosemary sprigs and set to sides of platters. Squeeze lemon over steak and mushrooms to taste, drizzle with extra oil, and sprinkle with sea salt, if using. Serve steak and mushrooms with bread, passing remaining lemon halves separately.

CHRISTIE'S TIPS

› A thick porterhouse steak like this might require a special order at your supermarket. Ask your butcher for the first or second cut; the first gives you the biggest piece of tenderloin, but the second gives you the best cut of the strip steak.

› Salting the steak ahead of time is clutch—it's just about the only seasoning you do on the meat, so don't skip this step.

GELATO WITH OLIVE OIL, SEA SALT, AND AMARETTI CRUMBLE

Serves 4 to 6

Total Time: 10 minutes

WHY I LOVE THIS RECIPE   Keep the casual vibes going with this dessert. I experienced the amazing combination of gelato and extra-virgin olive oil during my visit to Tuscany, and I still can't get the sensation out of my head. The sharp, grassy flavors of high-quality olive oil are a gorgeous counterpoint to the sweetness of gelato, and their rich textures complement each other beautifully. A sprinkle of crunchy flake sea salt enhances the flavors and adds more texture. You could stop there, but the extra crunch and bitter almond flavor from crushed amaretti cookies take this dessert home.

2	pints gelato
1	cup crushed amaretti cookies
4–6	tablespoons extra-virgin olive oil
	Flake sea salt

Scoop gelato into individual serving bowls. Top with cookies, drizzle with oil, and sprinkle with salt. Serve.

CHRISTIE'S TIPS

› You can use any flavor gelato you prefer, but I think the flavor of the olive oil works best with a subtly sweet flavor like vanilla or strawberry.

› A green, sharp, extra-virgin olive oil from a late summer or early fall harvest will give you the best contrast with the sweet gelato. Look for the harvest date on the bottle.

Sam Block's

POLENTA AND PALOMAS

SERVES 6

» **PALOMAS FOR A CROWD**

» **CREAMY BAKED POLENTA**

» **GRILLED SHRIMP WITH CALABRIAN CHILES, LEMON, AND PARMESAN**

» **GRILLED RATATOUILLE**

» **GRILLED CORN "CAPRESE" SALAD**

» **GRILLED POUND CAKE WITH PINEAPPLE AND HONEY MASCARPONE**

Sam
Block

The grill is one of my favorite cooking methods, so I designed this grill-forward party to highlight the advantages of summer produce while also keeping guest engagement in mind. (And if you don't have a grill? Don't sweat it: A grill pan on your stovetop will do the job just fine.) Hands-off baked polenta acts as the canvas for an assortment of goodies that your guests can pile on top or alongside. And with plenty of make-ahead options, you'll be able to entertain stress-free. Other than the polenta, these dishes are awesome hot, warm, room temperature, or even chilled, so there's no fuss when it comes to multiple dishes needing to be finished at a specific time. There are no rules! Just sip on a refreshing Paloma and≈relax. When it's time for dessert, grilled pound cake with pineapple comes together in minutes and is the perfect sweet ending to a perfect summer day.

MY GAME PLAN

UP TO 2 DAYS AHEAD

> Make the Grilled Ratatouille.

> Grill the corn for the Grilled Corn "Caprese" Salad.

UP TO 1 DAY AHEAD

> Combine the juices and tequila for Palomas for a Crowd and refrigerate.

> If using frozen shrimp for the Grilled Shrimp with Calabrian Chiles, Lemon, and Parmesan, transfer them to the refrigerator to thaw.

> Make the dressing for the caprese salad.

> Make the honey-mascarpone mixture for the Grilled Pound Cake with Pineapple and Honey Mascarpone.

UP TO 1 HOUR AHEAD

> Marinate the shrimp.

> Assemble the caprese salad.

NOTE

> I wrote these recipes to be freestanding so that you have make-ahead options (and so you can easily omit a dish if you don't want to make everything). If you're planning to grill everything all at once on a charcoal grill, here is my recommendation for setup:

1 Open bottom vent completely and arrange 3 quarts unlit charcoal briquettes evenly over grill. Light large chimney starter filled with charcoal briquettes (6 quarts). When top coals are partially covered with ash, pour evenly over unlit briquettes.

2 Begin by grilling the corn for the caprese salad, then cook the vegetables for the ratatouille.

3 Before grilling the shrimp, spread additional 3 quarts of unlit charcoal evenly over hot coals and let sit until partially covered with ash.

4 Grill pineapple and cake over remaining fire.

PALOMAS FOR A CROWD

Makes 8 cocktails

Total Time: 20 minutes, plus 1 hour chilling

WHY I LOVE THIS RECIPE   This cocktail is incredibly refreshing while also packing a punch. It's like a pretty-in-pink, less boozy margarita, perfect for sipping with your friends al fresco. Grapefruit's slightly sweet and bitter taste plays really well with the intensity of tequila, while the lime juice adds an additional burst of flavor. The salted rim is optional, but I think it makes the flavors more robust. This recipe makes a little extra, for those who want seconds!

32	ounces grapefruit juice, plus grapefruit slices for garnishing
12	ounces blanco or reposado tequila
4	ounces lime juice
3	tablespoons honey
½	cup kosher salt (optional)
16	ounces chilled seltzer, divided

1   Combine grapefruit juice, tequila, lime juice, and honey in serving pitcher or storage container until honey has dissolved. Refrigerate until flavors meld and mixture is well chilled, at least 1 hour or up to 1 day. Stir well before serving.

2   Spread salt, if using, into even layer in shallow bowl. Moisten about ½ inch of rims of chilled collins glasses by running grapefruit slice around outer edges; dry any excess juice with paper towel. Roll moistened rims in salt to coat. Remove any excess salt that falls into glasses.

3   Fill prepared glasses halfway with ice, then add 6 ounces grapefruit mixture. Top each glass with 2 ounces seltzer and, using bar spoon, gently lift grapefruit mixture from bottom of glass to top to combine. Top with additional ice and garnish with grapefruit slices. Serve.

SAM'S TIPS

> Be sure to use fresh grapefruit and lime juices, not a shelf-stable variety. If you want to juice the fruits yourself, you'll need about 4 grapefruits and 4 limes.

> Make sure to allow at least an hour of refrigeration time so the flavors can mingle and mellow.

CREAMY BAKED POLENTA

Serves 6

Total Time: 1¼ hours

WHY I LOVE THIS RECIPE Cooking polenta on the stovetop means up to a half-hour of nonstop stirring, but transferring it to the oven (while using the same 1:4 ratio of polenta to water) miraculously makes this version totally hands-off. You just need to whisk in butter and Parm at the end!

8	cups water
2	cups medium-grind polenta
2	teaspoons table salt
⅛	teaspoon pepper
4	ounces Parmesan cheese, grated (2 cups)
4	tablespoons unsalted butter, cut into 6 pieces

1 Adjust oven rack to middle position and heat oven to 375 degrees. Combine water, polenta, salt, and pepper in 13 by 9-inch baking dish. Transfer dish to oven and bake, uncovered, until water is absorbed and polenta has thickened, about 1 hour.

2 Remove dish from oven and whisk in Parmesan and butter until polenta is smooth and creamy. Serve hot.

> **SAM'S TIP**
> › You can use medium-grind cornmeal in place of the polenta; they are different names for the same thing. Don't use instant polenta, though.

GRILLED SHRIMP WITH CALABRIAN CHILES, LEMON, AND PARMESAN

Serves 6

Total Time: 1¼ hours

WHY I LOVE THIS RECIPE Slightly sweet shrimp makes an ideal vessel for the uber-Mediterranean combo of Calabrian chile, lemon, and Parmesan. Just a few spoonfuls of Calabrian chile paste is all you need; it's not overtly spicy but provides a little kick at the end to perk up your senses. Adding lemon zest and juice to the marinade and tossing the shrimp with more zest after grilling gives it an extra-citrusy punch. And I love the way that the Parmesan clings to the warm shrimp when you toss everything together, giving it a little umami hug. You'll need four 12-inch metal skewers.

- 2 pounds jumbo shrimp (16 to 20 per pound), peeled, deveined, and tails removed
- ¼ cup extra-virgin olive oil, divided
- 1 tablespoon grated lemon zest, divided, plus 1 tablespoon juice, plus lemon wedges for serving
- 4 teaspoons Calabrian chile paste
- ½ teaspoon table salt
- ¼ teaspoon pepper
- 6 tablespoons grated Parmesan cheese, divided
- 3 tablespoons chopped fresh parsley

1   Toss shrimp with 2 tablespoons oil, 2 teaspoons lemon zest, lemon juice, chile paste, salt, and pepper in bowl. Cover and refrigerate for at least 30 minutes or up to 1 hour.

2   Whisk remaining 2 tablespoons oil, remaining 1 teaspoon lemon zest, and ¼ cup Parmesan together in large bowl; set aside. Thread shrimp tightly onto four 12-inch metal skewers, alternating direction of heads and tails.

3A   **FOR A CHARCOAL GRILL** Open bottom vent completely. Light large chimney starter filled with charcoal briquettes (6 quarts). When top coals are partially covered with ash, pour evenly over grill. Set cooking grate in place, cover, and open lid vent completely. Heat grill until hot, about 5 minutes.

3B   **FOR A GAS GRILL** Turn all burners to high, cover, and heat grill until hot, about 15 minutes. Leave all burners on high.

4   Clean and oil cooking grate. Grill shrimp (covered if using gas) until lightly charred on first side, 3 to 4 minutes. Flip skewers, cover, and continue to cook until shrimp are opaque throughout, 1 to 2 minutes.

5   Using fork, push shrimp off skewers into bowl of reserved oil mixture and toss to coat. Transfer shrimp to platter and sprinkle with parsley and remaining 2 tablespoons Parmesan. Serve warm or at room temperature with lemon wedges.

SAM'S TIPS

> Since shrimp are frozen at their peak freshness, I prefer to buy frozen shrimp and thaw them the day before cooking.

> You can substitute extra-large shrimp; they will cook slightly faster.

> Threading the shrimp tightly onto the skewers prevents the shrimp from overcooking.

> Try to keep your face away from the shrimp while they're grilling. The smoke from the chile oil could make you start coughing!

GRILLED RATATOUILLE

Serves 6

Total Time: 45 minutes

WHY I LOVE THIS RECIPE The sturdy components of ratatouille make it a perfect match for grilling. The char and smoke from the fire deepens the flavors of the vegetables, and tossing the chopped grilled vegetables in an herbal sherry vinaigrette at the end brightens all their flavors. Plus, since ratatouille is best served at room temperature, it's a wonderful make-ahead dish. I could eat this day after day!

1	red onion, quartered
2	pounds eggplant, cut into ½-inch-thick rounds
1½	pounds zucchini or summer squash, halved lengthwise
2	red or green bell peppers, stemmed, seeded, and cut into quarters
1	pound plum tomatoes, cored and halved lengthwise
6	tablespoons extra-virgin olive oil, divided
½	teaspoon table salt
¼	teaspoon pepper
3	tablespoons sherry vinegar
½	cup chopped fresh parsley
1	tablespoon minced fresh thyme
1	garlic clove, minced

1 Brush vegetables with 2 tablespoons oil and sprinkle with salt and pepper. Whisk remaining ¼ cup oil, vinegar, parsley, thyme, and garlic together in large bowl; set vinaigrette aside.

2A **FOR A CHARCOAL GRILL** Open bottom vent completely. Light large chimney starter filled with charcoal briquettes (6 quarts). When top coals are partially covered with ash, pour evenly over grill. Set cooking grate in place, cover, and open lid vent completely. Heat grill until hot, about 5 minutes.

2B **FOR A GAS GRILL** Turn all burners to high, cover, and heat grill until hot, about 15 minutes. Leave all burners on high.

3 Clean and oil cooking grate. Working in batches, grill vegetables (covered if using gas), turning as needed, until tender and lightly charred, 10 to 20 minutes. Transfer vegetables to cutting board as they finish cooking and let cool slightly. Cut vegetables into ½-inch pieces, add to vinaigrette, and toss to coat. Season with salt and pepper to taste. Serve warm or at room temperature (or refrigerate for up to 2 days).

SAM'S TIPS

› Should you have any leftovers, they are delicious in the morning on top of your eggs or over toast.

› Don't be afraid of the char! That's your flavor bomb. Try to develop strong grill marks on your vegetables to make their flavors really shine.

GRILLED CORN "CAPRESE" SALAD

Serves 6

Total Time: 1 hour

WHY I LOVE THIS RECIPE Corn salads typically go down the bean route, but here I take the road less traveled by instead building off the classic components of a tomato, mozzarella, and basil caprese salad. The sweet char of the grilled corn and the heartiness of baby kale meld wonderfully with these ingredients, and a Dijon-balsamic vinaigrette adds a bold finish.

2	tablespoons balsamic vinegar
1	teaspoon mayonnaise
1	teaspoon Dijon mustard
½	teaspoon table salt
½	teaspoon pepper
6	tablespoons extra-virgin olive oil
12	ounces cherry tomatoes, halved
8	ounces fresh mozzarella pearls
4	ears corn, husks and silk removed
¼	cup chopped fresh basil
2	ounces (2 cups) baby kale

1 Whisk vinegar, mayonnaise, mustard, salt, and pepper together in large serving bowl until smooth. Whisking constantly, drizzle in oil until emulsified. Add tomatoes and≈mozzarella and toss to coat; set aside (or refrigerate for up to 1 day).

2A **FOR A CHARCOAL GRILL** Open bottom vent completely. Light large chimney starter filled with charcoal briquettes (6 quarts). When top coals are partially covered with ash, pour evenly over grill. Set cooking grate in place, cover, and open lid vent completely. Heat grill until hot, about 5 minutes.

2B **FOR A GAS GRILL** Turn all burners to high, cover, and heat grill until hot, about 15 minutes. Leave all burners on high.

3 Grill corn (covered if using gas), turning as needed, until well charred, 10 to 13 minutes. Transfer to plate and let cool to room temperature (or refrigerate for up to 2 days).

4 Cut corn from cobs and add to bowl with tomatoes and mozzarella. Add basil and kale and toss gently to combine. Season with salt and pepper to taste. Serve.

SAM'S TIPS

› Make sure to let the corn cool—you don't want to add it warm to your salad or it will wilt the greens and melt the cheese.

› If it's not fresh corn season, use 3 cups thawed frozen corn kernels and sear them in a skillet over medium-high heat with 2 tablespoons olive oil until they get charry.

› If mozzarella pearls are unavailable, use baby mozzarella balls (ciliegine). Larger balls of fresh mozzarella also can be used, although you'll need to cut them into ¾-inch pieces.

GRILLED POUND CAKE WITH PINEAPPLE AND HONEY MASCARPONE

Serves 6

Total Time: 35 minutes

WHY I LOVE THIS RECIPE After a big feast, the last thing I want is to eat a superrich, heavy dessert. For this simple offering, I love that the grill really does the talking: Pineapple turns sweetly caramelized, and pound cake becomes roasty and toasty. Slightly sweetened mascarpone for dolloping brings the whole thing together in fancy style.

- 8   ounces (1 cup) mascarpone cheese, room temperature
- 2   tablespoons honey, plus extra for drizzling
- ¼   teaspoon vanilla extract
- 1   pineapple, peeled, quartered lengthwise, cored, and each quarter halved lengthwise
- 2   tablespoons vegetable oil, divided
- 1   (1-pound) store-bought pound cake, ends trimmed, cut into 1-inch-thick slices
- ¼   cup chopped fresh mint

1 Whisk mascarpone, honey, and vanilla in small bowl until smooth; set aside (or refrigerate for up to 1 day).

2A **FOR A CHARCOAL GRILL** Open bottom vent completely. Light large chimney starter filled with charcoal briquettes (6 quarts). When top coals are partially covered with ash, pour evenly over grill. Set cooking grate in place, cover, and open lid vent completely. Heat grill until hot, about 5 minutes.

2B **FOR A GAS GRILL** Turn all burners to high, cover, and heat grill until hot, about 15 minutes. Leave all burners on high.

3 Brush pineapple with 1 tablespoon oil. Grill pineapple (covered if using gas) until well charred on all sides, 4 to 8 minutes; transfer to plate.

4 Brush one cut side of pound cake slices with remaining 1 tablespoon oil. Grill, oiled side down, until slightly charred, about 30 seconds. Arrange pound cake and pineapple attractively on platter. Sprinkle with mint and drizzle with extra honey. Serve, passing mascarpone mixture separately.

SAM'S TIP

› Stay close to the grill once you add the pound cake, as it takes less than a minute to develop grill marks!

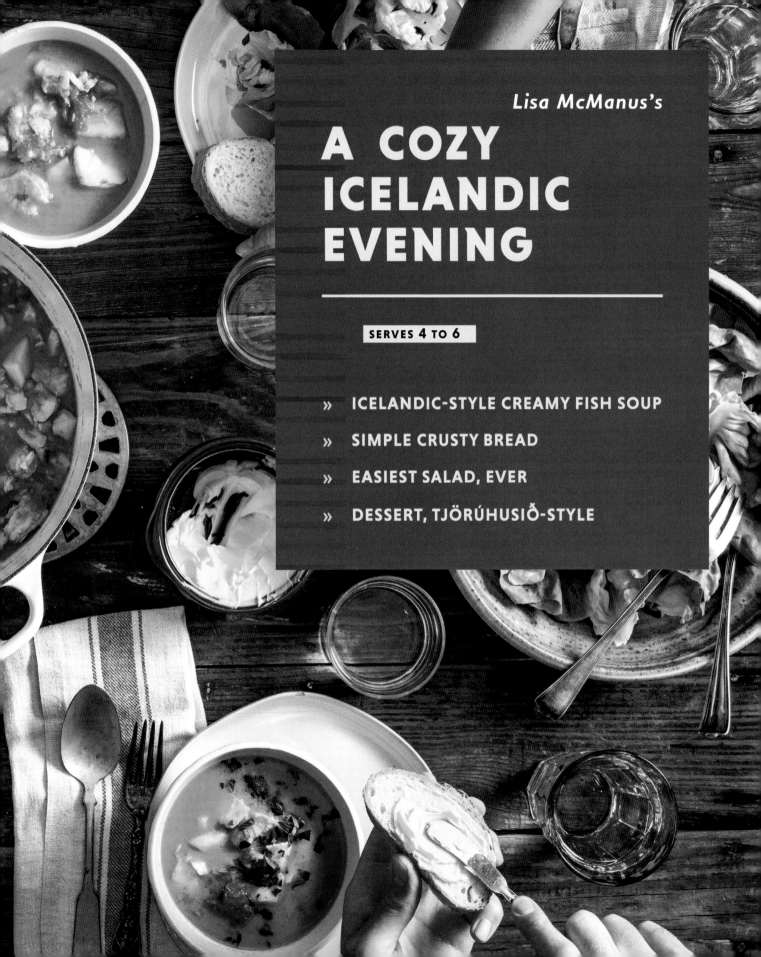

Lisa McManus's

A COZY ICELANDIC EVENING

SERVES 4 TO 6

» ICELANDIC-STYLE CREAMY FISH SOUP

» SIMPLE CRUSTY BREAD

» EASIEST SALAD, EVER

» DESSERT, TJÖRÚHUSIÐ-STYLE

Lisa McManus

I love seafood. And despite living in New England, I had the best fish dinner of my life—and one of the coziest meals I've ever experienced—at a restaurant called Tjöruhusið in Ísafjörður, Iceland. An 18th-century wooden shed with beamed ceilings, long wooden tables and benches, and a pile of colorful cushions near the door to make yourself comfortable, this rustic restaurant serves nothing but fish, cooked in enormous cast-iron skillets and set on the counter as soon as they're done. The selection is dictated by the day's catch—and you just help yourself. The one constant is a sideboard with a cauldron of stunningly delicious fish soup, a huge basket of freshly baked bread, thick pats of salted butter, a pot of strong coffee next to a rack of assorted mugs so you can pick your favorite, and a plate with squares of excellent chocolate, the only dessert offering. We ate to our hearts' content. Since I can't fly back to Iceland on demand, I like to invite friends to share this experience. So, light candles, gather soft cushions and throw blankets, and wear your coziest sweaters and socks, then pour big glasses of wine (like Albariño or Vinho Verde), ladle out deep bowls of soup, and dig in.

MY GAME PLAN

UP TO 1 DAY AHEAD

> The Icelandic-Style Creamy Fish Soup comes together fairly quickly, but you could prepare the broth (step 2) and refrigerate it overnight. Reheat it gently but thoroughly before adding the fish and cream.

UP TO SEVERAL HOURS AHEAD

> Bake the Simple Crusty Bread (and try not to eat it before your guests arrive!). It takes about 3 hours start to finish, assuming 1½ hours of rising time.

ICELANDIC-STYLE CREAMY FISH SOUP

Serves 4 to 6

Total Time: 1½ hours

WHY I LOVE THIS RECIPE This rich, deeply flavorful soup will warm you down to your toes. It's brimming with seafood, with 3 pounds of cod and shrimp, plus potatoes, so every spoonful is chock-full. Even though the result seems like you've been cooking for days, it's fast and easy. Use a Pedro Ximénez sherry, if available; its raisiny sweetness and full body complement the flavor of the soup.

2	pounds cod fillets, 1 to 1½ inches thick, cut in 1½-inch pieces
1	pound jumbo shrimp (16 to 20 per pound), peeled, deveined, and tails removed
1½	teaspoons table salt, divided
2	tablespoons unsalted butter
2	onions, finely chopped
1	leek, white and light-green parts only, halved lengthwise, sliced thin, and washed thoroughly (1 cup)
2	tablespoons tomato paste
2	tablespoons sweet sherry
4	cups chicken or vegetable broth
12	ounces russet potatoes, peeled and cut into ¾-inch pieces
2	tomatoes, cored and cut into ½-inch pieces
¼	cup heavy cream
¼	cup chopped fresh parsley or chives (optional)

1 Pat cod and shrimp dry with paper towels and sprinkle with ½ teaspoon salt; set aside.

2 Melt butter in Dutch oven over medium heat. Add onions and leek and cook, stirring occasionally, until softened, 12 to 15 minutes. Adjust heat as needed to prevent browning. Stir in tomato paste and remaining 1 teaspoon salt and cook until fragrant, about 30 seconds. Stir in sherry and simmer for 1 minute. Stir in broth and potatoes and bring to a boil. Reduce heat to medium-low, partially cover, and simmer, stirring occasionally, until potatoes are tender, 15 to 20 minutes. Stir in tomatoes, partially cover, and simmer for 5 minutes.

3 Stir cod and shrimp into soup and bring to gentle simmer. Partially cover and cook for about 5 minutes, until cod and shrimp are opaque throughout, taking care not to stir vigorously or break up the fish. Off heat, gently stir in cream and let sit until heated through, about 2 minutes. Sprinkle individual portions with parsley, if using, and serve.

LISA'S TIPS

› Peeled shrimp make this soup easier to eat, but I also like to use shell-on shrimp for their flavor and texture. Don't use precooked shrimp. If you can't find jumbo shrimp, you can use extra-large (21 to 25 per pound).

› Haddock or halibut are good substitutes for the cod; don't substitute skinny fillets like sole, because they'll break up and disappear.

› If you have homemade fish stock on hand, feel free to use it in place of the chicken broth.

› If you're feeling fancy, add lobster meat in addition to or in place of some of the shrimp.

SIMPLE CRUSTY BREAD

Serves 4 to 6

Total Time: 1¼ hours, plus 1½ hours rising

WHY I LOVE THIS RECIPE While you can simply grab a good baguette at the store, baking your own bread makes this meal extra-special (and your house will smell so good!). You don't need much in the way of special equipment; however, a baking stone will help your loaf develop a better crust. This bread is surprisingly easy to make—even for beginners. It has a gently crunchy exterior, a soft interior, and a lightly buttery flavor.

3¼	cups (17¾ ounces) bread flour
1¾	teaspoons table salt
1	tablespoon instant or rapid-rise yeast
1⅓	cups warm water (110 degrees)
2	tablespoons unsalted butter, softened, plus 1 teaspoon softened butter for bowl

1 Whisk flour, salt, and yeast together in large bowl. Make well in center of flour mixture and add warm water and butter. Using wooden spoon or dough whisk, stir water and butter into flour mixture until loose dough forms. Using hands, bring dough together in bowl and knead until all the dry ingredients are incorporated.

2 Transfer dough to lightly floured counter and knead by hand to form smooth, round ball, 3 to 5 minutes. Grease clean, dry large bowl with 1 teaspoon softened butter. Place dough seam side up in prepared bowl and flip to coat with butter. Cover tightly with plastic wrap and let rise until doubled in size, 1 to 3 hours depending on the warmth of your kitchen.

3 When dough has doubled in volume, adjust oven rack to middle position, place baking stone on rack, and heat oven to 450 degrees. Remove and reserve plastic wrap from dough. Punch down dough and turn out onto a lightly floured surface. Press and stretch dough into 15 by 7-inch rectangle. Roll up dough away from you into cylinder. Pinch seam closed, then roll loaf seam side down. Place loaf seam side down on large sheet of parchment paper. Reshape loaf as needed, tucking edges under to form torpedo shape. Cover loaf very loosely with reserved plastic wrap (to prevent drying out; check occasionally that plastic doesn't get tight as the loaf rises). Let rise until loaf doubles in size and dough springs back minimally when poked gently with your knuckle, 30 minutes to 1 hour.

4 Using sharp paring knife or single-edge razor blade, slash loaf diagonally at 3- to 4-inch intervals across its top surface. Mist loaf and parchment thoroughly with water. Using pizza peel (or back of rimmed baking sheet or cookie sheet), slide parchment paper with loaf onto peel or pan and carefully transfer bread and parchment onto hot baking stone. Bake until crust is golden brown and loaf registers 205 to 210 degrees, 30 to 35 minutes, rotating loaf halfway through baking. About 10 minutes before bread is done, use tongs to slide parchment out from under loaf, so bottom crust will crisp and brown more deeply. Transfer loaf to wire rack and let cool slightly, about 15 minutes, before serving.

LISA'S TIPS

› You can microwave the butter for a few seconds to start it softening if it's very hard and cold, but be careful not to melt it.

› If you don't have a pizza peel, a cookie sheet or inverted rimmed baking sheet also works well. If you don't have a baking stone, preheat the oven, transfer the loaf to a parchment paper–lined baking sheet, and bake as directed.

› If you don't have a spray bottle of water to mist the dough before baking, which helps the dough develop a crisper crust, just wet your hands with cool water and flick your fingers over the dough.

› This recipe produces a loaf with a semifirm crust. For a crunchier crust, bake the loaf until the crust is deep brown, 45 to 50 minutes.

› Invest in a great salted butter to serve with this bread, such as Smjör from Iceland or Lurpak from Denmark.

EASIEST SALAD, EVER

Serves 4 to 6

Total Time: 5 minutes

WHY I LOVE THIS RECIPE My favorite salad starts with a stripped-down vinaigrette (made right in the bowl) that depends on good ingredients. I think people fuss too much about emulsifying dressing; if the components are practically good enough to drink on their own, an emulsion doesn't matter. Next, I pile bitter and sweet greens into the bowl (toughest greens on the bottom, touching the dressing; delicate ones on top) and add a big pinch of sea salt and lots of freshly ground pepper. I set the bowl aside until I'm ready to serve, then I toss everything thoroughly.

Extra-virgin olive oil

Balsamic vinegar

8   ounces (8 cups) lettuce or other greens, torn into bite-size pieces if necessary

Flake sea salt

In bottom of large salad bowl, add generous splash of oil and smaller splash of vinegar and mix together with back of large spoon (mixture does not need to emulsify). Add lettuce (toughest greens first so they touch the dressing; delicate greens on top), large pinch of sea salt, and freshly ground pepper. Just before serving, toss greens thoroughly to coat with dressing.

LISA'S TIPS

> Bitter greens to consider include watercress, escarole, frisée, arugula, and radicchio. More delicate greens to add include baby spinach and Bibb and red or green leaf lettuce.

> I'm a big fan of California Olive Ranch Extra-Virgin Olive Oil and Oliviers & Co Premium Balsamic Vinegar, but any high-quality oil and vinegar will work.

> I'm also a big fan of Maldon salt for salad.

DESSERT, TJÖRÚHUSIÐ-STYLE

The strong, hot coffee and squares of high-quality dark chocolate set out at the restaurant hit the spot after the warming stew and bread. Even though I rarely have coffee after dinner, the combination was terrific. So, if someone offers to bring dessert, let them, but the beauty of offering just these two simple things is its simplicity. For the coffee, I recommend using a French press and grinding the best coffee beans you can get. Set out heavy cream and sugar with the coffee pot and mugs, and let guests help themselves. Buy a bar or two of good chocolate—or buy a few different bars and let guests enjoy comparing them. Break into squares and set on pretty plates to pass around. Don't knock it 'til you've tried it. Dare to do less!

Becky Hays's

MIDWESTERN BRUNCH

SERVES 8 TO 10

» **FRESH JUICE BAR**
Simple Green Juice
Carrot-Pineapple-Ginger Juice

» **GOETTA**
Pressure-Cooker Goetta

» **BRUNCH SALAD WITH CREAMY PARMESAN DRESSING**

» **BLUEBERRY SWIRL BUNS WITH LEMONY CREAM CHEESE ICING**

Becky Hays

Brunch has always been one of my favorite ways to entertain. A morning party feels more casual than an evening one, and a daytime finish eliminates loading the dishwasher and scrubbing pots and pans into the wee hours. I've centered my menu around goetta, a homemade sausage that's a Midwestern favorite (my mom and dad are Hoosiers). It's satisfying and utterly delicious, and many people haven't tried it, so it's a fun way to introduce friends to something new. I like to balance the rich goetta with a big brunch salad. (Yes, you can eat salad before noon!) To round out the meal and make guests very happy, I bake blueberry swirl buns. When I'm hosting, I often include some type of conversation-starting "bar." (A pickle bar at my son's 8th birthday party was a huge hit.) Here, it's a colorful DIY juice bar. Set it up as a place to congregate outside the kitchen so that it keeps your guests occupied while you put the finishing touches on the rest of the meal.

MY GAME PLAN

UP TO 2 MONTHS AHEAD
> Make and freeze the loaves for the Goetta.

UP TO 3 DAYS AHEAD
> Make the filling and icing for the Blueberry Swirl Buns with Lemony Cream Cheese Icing.
> Hard-boil the eggs (and peel them), prep the artichoke hearts, crumble the bagel chips, shave the Parmesan, and mix the dressing for the Brunch Salad; store in separate airtight containers.

UP TO 2 DAYS AHEAD
> If not making and freezing the goetta loaves ahead, make and refrigerate them (note that they must be made at least 8 hours ahead of frying).

UP TO 1 DAY AHEAD
> Wash and dry all of the produce for the Fresh Juice Bar.
> If frozen, transfer the Goetta loaves to the refrigerator to thaw.
> Prepare the blueberry buns through the end of step 8 and refrigerate. (Remove the buns and icing from the refrigerator 2 hours before baking.)

UP TO 30 MINUTES AHEAD
> Arrange the chilled fruits and vegetables for the juice bar in attractive bowls near the juicer along with glasses and straws. Set out a cutting board, chef's knife, and scraps bowl at the juice bar.

FRESH JUICE BAR

Total Time: 10 minutes per serving

WHY I LOVE THIS RECIPE Years ago, I sprang for an electric juicer as a way to introduce my young son to lots of different fruits and vegetables. It was a great purchase: We had fun chopping up the produce together and experimenting with flavor combinations, and now that he's a teenager, we still juice all the time as a quick way to enjoy a healthful drink. (Juicing is also a terrific option for using up any produce that's on the verge of going bad.) In addition to the fruits and vegetables required for these recipes, consider supplementing your juice bar with pears, cranberries, celery, grapes, and beets.

BECKY'S TIPS

› Write the recipes for the two juices on a chalkboard (or tack up a sheet of paper with the recipes), but encourage your guests to experiment.

› Maximize your yield of juice by cutting your produce the least amount necessary to fit through the juicer's feeding tube. In general, bigger is better and the less "prep" you do for a juicer, the better.

› I have had great success using my Breville centrifugal juicer. If using a masticating juicer, ignore the speed level and process the ingredients in the order listed. Your yield may vary slightly depending on what brand of juicer you have.

› You can adjust the sweetness of your juice by adding the juice of half an apple. Or, if your juice is too sweet, try adding a little lemon juice.

› Enjoy the juice as soon as you make it because it will quickly start to separate.

› If you don't own a juicer, don't let that stop you from setting up a juice bar. Offer store-bought choices such as pomegranate, pineapple, grapefruit, orange, apple, and carrot juice (you can even find little bottles of ginger juice in many supermarkets) and encourage guests to come up with their own blends. Offer mint leaves and lemon slices for garnishes.

SIMPLE GREEN JUICE

Serves 1

1	cucumber, unpeeled
1	ounce (1 cup) baby spinach
10–12	fresh mint leaves (optional)
2	apples, cored and cut into quarters
½	lemon, peeled

On high speed and in order listed, process ingredients through juicer into serving glass. Stir to combine before serving.

CARROT-PINEAPPLE-GINGER JUICE

Serves 1

2	large carrots, unpeeled
1	(½-inch) piece fresh ginger, unpeeled
¼	fresh pineapple, peeled

On high speed and in order listed, process ingredients through juicer into serving glass. Stir to combine before serving.

GOETTA

Serves 8 to 10

Total Time: 4½ hours, plus 8 hours chilling

WHY I LOVE THIS RECIPE If you're not familiar, goetta is pork shoulder slowly simmered with onion, herbs, and spices; shredded and mixed with steel-cut oats; formed into a loaf; chilled; sliced; and fried in butter until it's crispy and golden brown. Whenever my mom comes to visit, she hands over one or two foil-wrapped loaves as she walks in the door. Her mother started making goetta as a treat for my grandfather when they were first married. He was raised in Cincinnati, where the hearty specialty was introduced by immigrants from northwest Germany. After my grandmother died, my mom and her siblings couldn't find her recipe, so they assembled this one from memory. Now we all carry on the tradition, enjoying big batches for holiday breakfasts and family get-togethers, each time oohing and ahhing over just how good and satisfying it is.

1	(5-pound) bone-in pork butt roast, trimmed
2½	teaspoons table salt, divided
½	teaspoon ground pepper, plus 1 teaspoon black peppercorns
1	tablespoon vegetable oil
5	cups water
1	large onion, quartered
1	teaspoon allspice berries
½	teaspoon dried thyme
2	bay leaves
2½	cups steel-cut oats
4	tablespoons unsalted butter, divided

1 Pat pork dry with paper towels and sprinkle with 1 teaspoon salt and ground pepper. Heat oil in Dutch oven over medium-high heat until just smoking. Brown roast on all sides, 7 to 10 minutes. Add water, onion, allspice berries, thyme, bay leaves, peppercorns, and remaining 1½ teaspoons salt. Bring to boil, then reduce heat to low, cover, and simmer until meat is tender and falls off bone, 3 to 3½ hours.

2 Transfer pork to carving board and let rest until cool enough to handle. Meanwhile, strain cooking liquid through fine-mesh strainer into large pot; discard solids. Do not discard rendered fat. Bring cooking liquid to boil, then stir in oats. Reduce heat to medium-low and simmer gently, stirring occasionally to avoid scorching, until mixture is creamy and oats are just tender, 25 to 30 minutes.

3 Using 2 forks, shred pork into bite-size pieces, discarding bones and any large pieces of fat or connective tissue. Stir pork and any accumulated juices into oats. Divide mixture between 2 greased 8½ by 4½-inch loaf pans. Smooth tops and tap firmly on counter to remove any air pockets. Let cool completely, then cover with plastic wrap and refrigerate until fully chilled and firm, at least 8 hours or up to 2 days. (Goetta can be wrapped tightly in plastic, then aluminum foil, and frozen for up to 2 months. Thaw goetta overnight before frying.)

4 Run thin knife around edges of each goetta and turn out onto cutting board. Cut each loaf crosswise into 12 slices (about ½ inch thick). Heat 1 tablespoon butter in 12-inch cast-iron skillet over medium heat until melted and foaming subsides. Add 6 slices goetta and cook until well browned and lightly crisp, 2 to 3 minutes per side (it's okay if goetta breaks apart while flipping); transfer to serving platter. Repeat browning remaining goetta in 3 batches, wiping skillet clean with paper towels and heating additional butter between each batch. Serve.

BECKY'S TIPS

> Steel-cut oats are essential; don't substitute rolled oats.

> If you can't find a skinless bone-in pork shoulder, buy one with the skin attached and use a chef's knife to remove the skin (and any fat that's beneath it) before proceeding.

> I like to fry the goetta in a cast-iron skillet because it retains heat well and browns the slices evenly and deeply, but if you don't own one, it's fine to use a nonstick skillet.

VARIATION

PRESSURE COOKER GOETTA

Depending on the size of your pressure cooker, you may need to cut the pork roast into two smaller pieces for easier browning.

FOR MULTICOOKER Using highest sauté or browning function, heat oil in multicooker until just smoking and brown pork as directed in step 1. Add water and spices, lock lid in place, and close pressure-release valve. Select high pressure-cook function and cook for 1½ hours. Turn off multicooker and let pressure release naturally for 15 minutes. Quick-release any remaining pressure, then carefully remove lid, allowing steam to escape away from you. Strain cooking liquid into large bowl or container in step 2, then return to now-empty multicooker. Use lowest sauté or browning function to cook oats.

FOR STOVETOP PRESSURE COOKER Heat oil and brown pork as directed in step 1. Add water and spices, lock lid in place, and close pressure-release valve. Bring cooker to high pressure over medium-high heat. As soon as indicator signals that pot has reached high pressure, reduce heat to medium-low and cook for 1½ hours, adjusting heat as needed to maintain high pressure. Remove cooker from heat and let pressure release naturally for 15 minutes. Quick-release any remaining pressure, then carefully remove lid, allowing steam to escape away from you. Strain cooking liquid into large bowl or container in step 2, then return to now-empty cooker. Cook oats as directed.

BRUNCH SALAD WITH CREAMY PARMESAN DRESSING

Serves 8 to 10

Total Time: 30 minutes

WHY I LOVE THIS RECIPE Spinach-artichoke dip is on my top-ten list of favorite foods, so I wanted to use some of the same ingredients to create a brunch-friendly salad. Baby spinach leaves and tender butter lettuce are tossed with marinated artichoke hearts and sliced red onion. Then, to bring the brunch element home, quartered hard-cooked eggs and bagel-chip croutons go on top. Lots of shaved Parmesan cheese and a creamy Parmesan dressing echo the flavors of the dip that inspired the salad.

CREAMY PARMESAN DRESSING

¼	cup buttermilk, plus extra if needed
¼	cup mayonnaise
¼	cup sour cream
¼	cup grated Parmesan cheese
1	tablespoon lemon juice
1	teaspoon Dijon mustard
1	teaspoon minced shallot
½	teaspoon pepper
¼	teaspoon table salt

SALAD

⅓	cup thinly sliced red onion
5	ounces (5 cups) baby spinach
1	head Bibb or Boston leaf lettuce (8 ounces), leaves separated and torn
1	(12-ounce) jar marinated artichoke hearts, drained, patted dry, and chopped coarse
6	hard-cooked eggs, quartered
2	ounces Parmesan cheese, shaved
¾	cup lightly crumbled plain bagel chips

1 FOR THE DRESSING Stir all ingredients together until smooth. Dressing should have consistency of heavy cream; adjust consistency with extra buttermilk as needed. Season with salt and pepper to taste. (Dressing can be refrigerated for up to 3 days.)

2 FOR THE SALAD Soak onion in ice water for 15 minutes; drain and thoroughly pat dry with paper towels.

3 Toss spinach, lettuce, artichoke hearts, and onion together in large bowl. Season with salt and pepper to taste and transfer to large serving platter or bowl. Arrange eggs over salad, followed by Parmesan. Sprinkle with crumbled bagel chips and serve, passing dressing separately.

BECKY'S TIPS

> The dressing relies on the viscosity of buttermilk. Don't use buttermilk powder. Low-fat sour cream and reduced-fat mayonnaise can be substituted for the full-fat versions.

> Use the best-quality marinated artichoke hearts you can find.

> Use a vegetable peeler to shave the Parmesan.

> If you have leftovers, add some canned chickpeas and you'll have a salad that's hearty enough to enjoy as lunch the next day.

EASY-PEEL HARD-COOKED EGGS

Here's a foolproof method for cooking up to 12 eggs at once. You can refrigerate them, peeled or unpeeled, for up to 3 days. Bring 1 inch water to rolling boil in medium saucepan over high heat. Place eggs in steamer basket and transfer basket to saucepan. Cover, reduce heat to medium-low, and steam eggs for 13 minutes. When eggs are almost finished cooking, combine 2 cups ice cubes and 2 cups cold water in bowl. Using tongs or slotted spoon, transfer eggs to ice bath and let sit for 15 minutes before peeling.

BLUEBERRY SWIRL BUNS WITH LEMONY CREAM CHEESE ICING

Makes 12 buns

Total Time: 1½ hours, plus 80 minutes rising

WHY I LOVE THIS RECIPE My husband is a cinnamon bun fanatic, and I'm all about treats made with berries. This recipe marries our two loves: Instead of cinnamon sugar, a simple homemade blueberry jam is spiraled inside a light, fluffy dough, and the baked buns are capped with a citrusy cream cheese frosting. To ensure tender buns, the dough uses the tangzhong technique, which originated in Japan and incorporates a cooked flour-and-water paste. The paste traps water, making the dough easy to work with, and the increased hydration converts to steam during baking, which makes the rolls fluffy. The added water also keeps the crumb moist for several days, if you happen to have any leftovers.

BLUEBERRY FILLING

12	ounces (2½ cups) frozen wild blueberries
¼	cup (1¾ ounces) sugar
⅛	teaspoon table salt
1½	teaspoons cornstarch
2	teaspoons water

BUNS

⅔	cup water
3	cups (16½ ounces) bread flour, divided
⅔	cup milk
1	large egg plus 1 large yolk
2	teaspoons instant or rapid-rise yeast
3	tablespoons sugar
1½	teaspoons table salt
6	tablespoons unsalted butter, softened
	Vegetable oil spray

CREAM CHEESE ICING

4	ounces cream cheese, softened
½	teaspoon grated lemon zest plus 1 tablespoon juice
1½	cups (6 ounces) confectioners' sugar

1 **FOR THE FILLING** Cook blueberries, sugar, and salt in small saucepan over medium heat, stirring occasionally, until berries break down and mixture thickens slightly and measures 1 cup, 8 to 10 minutes.

2 Stir cornstarch and water together in bowl, then stir into blueberry mixture. Cook until thickened and translucent, 30 to 60 seconds. Transfer filling to bowl and refrigerate, uncovered, until completely cool, at least 1 hour or up to 3 days.

3 **FOR THE BUNS** Whisk water and ¼ cup flour together in small bowl until no lumps remain. Microwave, whisking every 25 seconds, until mixture thickens to stiff, smooth, pudding-like consistency that forms mound when dropped from end of whisk into bowl, 50 to 75 seconds.

4 Whisk flour paste and milk together in bowl of stand mixer until smooth. Whisk in egg and yolk until incorporated. Add remaining flour and yeast. Fit stand mixer with dough hook and mix on low speed until all flour is moistened, 1 to 2 minutes. Let stand for 15 minutes.

5 Add sugar and salt and mix on medium-low speed for 5 minutes. Stop mixer and add butter. Mix dough on medium-low speed until butter is fully incorporated, about 5 minutes, scraping down dough hook and sides of bowl halfway through (dough will stick to bottom of bowl).

6 Transfer dough to lightly floured counter and knead by hand to form smooth, round ball, about 30 seconds. Place dough seam side down in lightly greased bowl or container. Lightly coat surface of dough with vegetable oil spray and cover bowl with plastic wrap. Let dough rise until just doubled in size, 40 minutes to 1 hour.

7 Turn out dough onto lightly floured counter. With floured hands, press dough gently but firmly to expel air. Working from center toward edge, pat and stretch dough to form 18 by 15-inch rectangle with long edge nearest you. Using offset spatula, spread filling into even layer over dough, leaving 1½-inch border along top edge and 1 inch border along sides.

8 Beginning with long edge nearest you, roll dough into cylinder, taking care not to roll too tightly. Pinch seam to seal and roll cylinder seam side down. Mark gently with knife to create 12 equal portions. To slice, hold strand of dental floss taut and slide underneath cylinder, stopping at first mark. Cross ends of floss over each other and pull. Slice cylinder into 12 portions and transfer, cut sides down, to greased 13 by 9-inch baking pan. Cover tightly with plastic and let rise until buns are puffy and touching one another, 40 minutes to 1 hour. (Buns may be refrigerated immediately after shaping for up to 24 hours. To bake, remove pan from refrigerator and let sit until buns are puffy and touching one another, 1 to 1½ hours.)

9 **FOR THE ICING** Adjust oven rack to lower-middle position and heat oven to 375 degrees. Whisk cream cheese, lemon zest and juice, and confectioners' sugar in medium bowl until smooth. (Icing can be refrigerated for up to 3 days; bring to room temperature before using.)

10 Discard plastic and bake buns until golden brown, about 20 minutes. Rotate pan, tent with aluminum foil, and continue to bake until center of dough registers at least 200 degrees, 10 to 15 minutes longer. Let buns cool in pan on wire rack for 10 minutes. Using offset spatula, spread icing evenly over buns. Serve warm.

BECKY'S TIPS

> I prefer wild blueberries in these buns, since the smaller berries roll up neatly in the dough. They are generally a great value when purchased frozen, and they perform just as well as fresh in this recipe.

> I developed this recipe using King Arthur bread flour; other bread flours can be used but may result in a slightly stickier dough.

> To avoid misshapen rolls, make sure not to roll the dough too tightly in step 8.

Amanda Luchtel's

NOT DOG PARTY

SERVES 8

» NOT DOG TABLE

» SPARKLING SPIKED LEMONADE

» SMOKY CARROT DOGS

» LENTIL CHILI DOG SAUCE

» SPICED CHEEZ SAUCE

» CHICAGO-STYLE NEON RELISH

» JALAPEÑO RELISH

» PEANUT BUTTER–CHOCOLATE CHUNK COOKIES

Amanda Luchtel

Let's be frank, this is not your ordinary chili dog party, but it's not the wurst! Do you have vegetarian friends and/or friends with kids? Do you like to have a little fun with your food? This "not dog" party is an exciting way to entertain a diverse crowd. The menu has so much flavor and fun going on that your guests won't even realize it is vegan unless you tell them. They can mix and match condiments (put out lots of them!) depending on their favorite style of hot dog, build a plate of nachos using the Lentil Chili Dog Sauce and Spiced Cheez Sauce, or just devour a bowl of chili and sip a cocktail. This menu feels very inclusive because you can easily add your favorite store-bought meat-based hot dogs if you have meat eaters in your bunch (or if you just aren't feeling ambitious enough to make the carrot dogs).

MY GAME PLAN

UP TO 1 MONTH AHEAD

❭ Make the lemon simple syrup for the Sparkling Spiked Lemonade.

❭ Make the Chicago-Style Neon Relish and the Jalapeño Relish.

❭ Make the dough for the Peanut Butter–Chocolate Chunk Cookies, shape into balls, and freeze.

UP TO 3 DAYS AHEAD

❭ Make the Lentil Chili Dog Sauce.

❭ Make the Spiced Cheez Sauce.

UP TO 1 DAY AHEAD

❭ Marinate the carrots for the Smoky Carrot Dogs. (The longer you marinate them, up to 24 hours, the smokier they will get.)

❭ Bake the cookies.

UP TO SEVERAL HOURS AHEAD

❭ Stir together the ingredients for the spiked lemonade.

STREAMLINE

❭ Homemade condiments like the two relishes here are easy to make and keep well, but of course you can substitute your favorite store-bought condiments to simplify things!

❭ Use your favorite store-bought vegan hot dogs or meat hot dogs instead of making the Smoky Carrot Dogs.

NOT DOG TABLE

WHY I LOVE THIS RECIPE There's just so much versatility to play around with here, between building different hot dog–topping combos, maybe having a side bowl of lentil chili, or even creating your very own single serving of nachos with tortilla chips and all the toppings.

START WITH
>   Smoky Carrot Dogs (page 148)
>   Hot dog buns
>   Lentil Chili Dog Sauce (page 149)
>   Spiced Cheez Sauce (page 150)
>   Basic hot dog condiments (ketchup, assorted mustards, diced onions)

IF YOU WANT, ADD
>   Chicago-Style Neon Relish (page 151)
>   Jalapeño Relish (page 152)
>   More hot dog condiments (tomato wedges, dill pickle spears, sauerkraut, sport peppers, shredded vegan cheese, hot sauce, celery salt)
>   Chips of choice (tortilla, Frito, or potato)

SPARKLING SPIKED LEMONADE

Makes 8 cocktails

Total Time: 20 minutes, plus 2 hours chilling

WHY I LOVE THIS RECIPE Add bubbles and vodka to homemade lemonade, and you've got yourself a party! This tart-sweet spiked lemonade is the perfect refreshing cocktail to cut through the decadent chili dog dinner.

LEMON SIMPLE SYRUP
>   1   cup sugar
>   1   cup water
>   2   tablespoons grated lemon zest
>   ¼   teaspoon table salt

SPIKED LEMONADE
>   16   ounces lemon juice, plus lemon slices for garnishing
>   16   ounces vodka
>   32   ounces seltzer, chilled

1 **FOR THE SIMPLE SYRUP** Heat sugar, water, lemon zest, and salt in small saucepan over medium-high heat, stirring occasionally, until sugar has dissolved, about 5 minutes. Let cool to room temperature. Strain mixture through fine-mesh strainer into bowl, pressing on solids to extract as much liquid as possible; discard solids. (Syrup can be refrigerated for up to 1 month.)

2 **FOR THE LEMONADE** Combine lemon juice, vodka, and simple syrup in serving pitcher or large container. Cover and refrigerate until flavors meld and mixture is well chilled, at least 2 hours or up to 8 hours. Just before serving, gently stir seltzer into lemonade mixture. Serve over ice, garnishing individual portions with lemon slices.

AMANDA'S TIP
> To make individual cocktails instead of a pitcher drink, skip adding seltzer to lemonade mixture. Pour 6 ounces lemonade mixture into collins glass filled halfway with ice. Top with 4 ounces seltzer and garnish with lemon slice.

SMOKY CARROT DOGS

Serves 8

Total Time: 50 minutes, plus 8 hours cooling and chilling

WHY I LOVE THIS RECIPE These umami-packed carrot dogs are every bit as versatile as "traditional" hot dogs, so have some fun serving them. For a chili dog, top with Jalapeño Relish, Lentil Chili Dog Sauce, and Spiced Cheez Sauce. For a Chicago-style dog, "drag it through the garden" on a poppy seed bun with yellow mustard, chopped white onion, Chicago-Style Neon Relish, sport peppers, sliced tomatoes, a kosher dill pickle spear, and a sprinkle of celery salt. Or go classic and top with chopped onion, sauerkraut, ketchup, mustard, or pickle relish.

16	carrots, peeled
4	cups water
½	cup soy sauce
¼	cup cider vinegar
1	tablespoon liquid smoke
1	tablespoon roasted vegetable bouillon paste
1	teaspoon red pepper flakes
1	teaspoon garlic powder
1	teaspoon onion powder
½	teaspoon pepper
¼	teaspoon nutmeg
¼	cup vegetable oil (if using skillet), divided

1 Cut each carrot into 6½-inch lengths, starting from thickest part of carrot; discard carrot tips or save for another use. Whisk water, soy sauce, vinegar, liquid smoke, bouillon paste, pepper flakes, garlic powder, onion powder, pepper, and nutmeg together in Dutch oven. Add carrots and bring to a boil over high heat. Reduce heat to medium-low and simmer until tender and tip of paring knife inserted into thickest carrot meets little resistance, about 15 minutes. Let carrots cool in their cooking liquid until both are at room temperature, about 2 hours.

2 Transfer carrots and cooking liquid to 1-gallon zipper-lock bag and refrigerate for at least 6 or up to 24 hours. Remove carrots from marinade and pat dry with paper towels; discard cooking liquid.

3A **FOR A STOVETOP** Heat 2 tablespoons oil in 12-inch nonstick skillet over medium heat until shimmering. Place 8 carrots in skillet and cook until brown on all sides, about 5 minutes. Transfer to platter and tent with aluminum foil. Wipe skillet clean with paper towels and repeat with remaining 2 tablespoons oil and remaining 8 carrots; transfer to platter. Serve.

3B **FOR A GRILL** Prepare hot, single-level fire in gas or charcoal grill. Set cooking grate in place and heat grill until hot, about 5 minutes. Grill carrots until well browned on all sides, about 5 minutes. Serve.

AMANDA'S TIP

› I have the best success using carrots that are about ¾ inch in diameter at their thickest point; picking through the bulk carrot bin at the grocery store ensures I get uniform carrots. Avoid carrots that are larger than 1 inch thick.

LENTIL CHILI DOG SAUCE

Makes about 8 cups
Total Time: 55 minutes

WHY I LOVE THIS RECIPE This "sauce" can just as easily be served as a bowl of chili for an entrée as it can be slathered on a hot dog as a topping. I love how the warm spices complement the sweet and smoky flavors of the carrot dogs, but the sauce also makes for a delicious chili dog using regular store-bought hot dogs. It's also really speedy to make and uses all pantry-friendly ingredients.

½	ounce dried shiitake mushrooms
1	tablespoon dried oregano
3	tablespoons chili powder
2	teaspoons ground cumin
1¾	teaspoons table salt, divided
1½	teaspoons ground cinnamon
¾	teaspoon pepper
¼	teaspoon allspice
⅓	cup extra-virgin olive oil
2	onions, chopped fine
1	(6-ounce) can tomato paste
6	garlic cloves, minced
1¾	quarts water, plus extra as needed
3	tablespoons soy sauce
1	cup dried brown lentils
1	cup medium-grind bulgur

1 Grind shiitakes and oregano in spice grinder until finely ground. Combine shiitake mixture, chili powder, cumin, 1 teaspoon salt, cinnamon, pepper, and allspice in small bowl; set aside.

2 Heat oil in Dutch oven over medium-high heat until shimmering. Add onion and remaining ¾ teaspoon salt and cook until softened and lightly browned, 3 to 5 minutes. Stir in tomato paste, garlic, and spice mixture and cook until fragrant and paste begins to darken, 1 to 2 minutes.

3 Whisk in water and soy sauce, scraping up any browned bits. Stir in lentils and bulgur and bring to simmer. Reduce heat to low, cover, and cook, stirring occasionally, until lentils are tender but still hold their shape, 20 to 25 minutes. Off heat, let sit for 10 minutes. Adjust consistency with extra hot water and season with salt to taste. (Chili can be refrigerated for up to 3 days; bring to brief simmer over medium-low heat and adjust consistency with extra water as needed.)

AMANDA'S TIP

> This chili thickens as it sits, so if you are reheating it, do so over medium-low heat and add a little water to reach the desired spoonable consistency.

SPICED CHEEZ SAUCE

Makes 2½ cups

Total Time: 40 minutes

WHY I LOVE THIS RECIPE With its familiar yellow-orange color, cheesy flavor, and ultra-creamy texture, you'll have a hard time believing that this sauce is vegan. It combines boiled potatoes for starchiness and a carrot for color (see how versatile carrots are?)—these are whirred in the blender at high speed to release as much sauce-building starch from the potatoes as possible. Nutritional yeast and mustard powder add funk, and a little vinegar adds tang. Plenty of spices pump things up.

1½	pounds russet potatoes, peeled and cut into 1-inch pieces
2	small carrots, peeled and cut into ½-inch pieces (⅔ cup)
¼	teaspoon table salt, plus salt for cooking potatoes
¼	cup extra-virgin olive oil
3	tablespoons nutritional yeast
1	tablespoon distilled white vinegar
1	teaspoon ground cumin
1	teaspoon garlic powder
½	teaspoon cayenne pepper
¼	teaspoon mustard powder

1 Place potatoes, carrots, and 1 tablespoon salt in large saucepan and cover with water by 1 inch. Bring to boil over high heat, then reduce heat to medium and simmer until potatoes are tender, about 13 minutes. Reserve ⅔ cup cooking water, then drain potatoes in colander.

2 Combine cooked vegetables, oil, nutritional yeast, vinegar, cumin, garlic powder, cayenne, mustard powder, salt, and reserved potato water in blender. Pulse until chopped and combined, about 10 pulses, scraping down sides of blender jar as needed. (You will need to stop processing to scrape down sides of blender jar several times for mixture to come together.) Begin processing mixture on low speed, then gradually increase speed to high and process until very smooth, about 2 minutes. (Sauce can be refrigerated in airtight container for up to 3 days; reheat in microwave, stirring every 30 seconds, until glossy and pourable. Adjust consistency with hot water as needed.) Serve.

AMANDA'S TIP

› You can substitute vegetable oil for the extra-virgin olive oil, if you like.

CHICAGO-STYLE NEON RELISH

Makes 1½ cups

Total Time: 30 minutes, plus 1 hour resting and 2 hours cooling

WHY I LOVE THIS RECIPE This recipe is a bright and colorful addition to any hot dog table. Its origins are unclear and debated, but its startling signature color comes from adding blue food coloring to green pickle relish. Chicago-style hot dog lovers and kids of all ages will be thrilled that this vivid relish is a topping option.

1	pound English or Kirby cucumbers, cut into 1-inch pieces
½	large bell pepper, stemmed, seeded, and cut into 1-inch pieces
1	small onion, cut into 1-inch pieces
1	garlic clove, minced
1	tablespoon kosher salt
1	cup distilled white vinegar
½	cup sugar
½	teaspoon ground turmeric
½	teaspoon yellow mustard seeds
⅛	teaspoon blue food coloring (optional)

1 Pulse cucumbers in food processor until pieces measure roughly ¼ inch, about 10 pulses, scraping down sides of bowl as needed; transfer to large bowl. Pulse bell pepper, onion, and garlic until pieces measure roughly ¼ inch, about 10 pulses; transfer to bowl with cucumbers. Stir in salt and let rest for 1 hour.

2 Place one-third of vegetable mixture in center of clean dish towel. Gather ends of towel and twist tightly to wring out excess moisture from vegetables. Transfer dried vegetables to large saucepan. Repeat 2 more times with remaining vegetables.

3 Stir vinegar, sugar, turmeric, and mustard seeds into vegetables and bring to boil over medium-high heat. Reduce heat to medium and simmer until vegetables are translucent and mixture has thickened slightly, 10 to 15 minutes. (Mixture will continue to thicken as it cools.) Off heat, stir in food coloring, if using. Let relish cool completely, about 2 hours. (Relish can be refrigerated for up to 1 month.) Serve.

AMANDA'S TIPS

› The food coloring gives this relish its iconic color; however, you can omit it.

› Depending on the brand of food coloring you use, you may need to add more to achieve the proper color. Add a few extra drops at a time and thoroughly mix until the desired color is achieved.

JALAPEÑO RELISH

Makes 1 cup

Total Time: 10 minutes, plus 1 hour cooling

WHY I LOVE THIS RECIPE Bright and acidic with a hint of spice, this relish is my go-to condiment. Besides hot dogs, I use it to top tacos, nachos, chili, and anything else that I think could use a spicy pop. As a bonus, it has minimal ingredients and comes together with just a few pulses in a food processor.

6	ounces jalapeños, sliced crosswise 1 inch thick
1	large garlic clove, chopped
½	cup distilled white vinegar
1	teaspoon kosher salt

1 Pulse jalapeños and garlic in food processor until pieces measure roughly ¼ inch, 8 to 10 pulses, scraping down sides of bowl as needed.

2 Bring vinegar and salt to boil in small saucepan over high heat. Off heat, stir in jalapeño mixture and let cool to room temperature, about 1 hour. (Relish can be refrigerated for up to 1 month.) Serve.

AMANDA'S TIP

› If your jalapeños are unusually spicy, you can remove the ribs and seeds from half or all of them. I suggest wearing food-handling gloves when working with chiles.

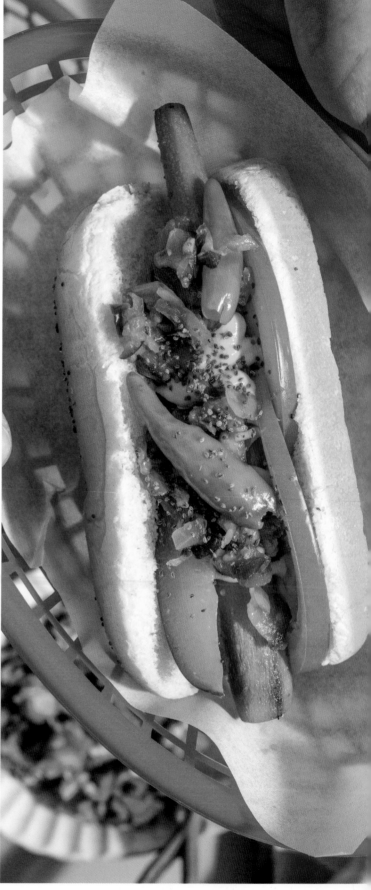

PEANUT BUTTER–CHOCOLATE CHUNK COOKIES

Makes 16 cookies
Total Time: 55 minutes, plus 2 hours chilling

WHY I LOVE THIS RECIPE Vegan cookies are the best cookies because they literally can be made using pantry ingredients, with nothing from the refrigerator. Processed peanut butter is the way to go here; the natural variety will make the cookies too dry. You can use either refined or unrefined coconut oil (just keep in mind that unrefined oil will give the cookies a stronger coconut flavor).

1½	cups (7½ ounces) all-purpose flour
1	teaspoon baking soda
½	teaspoon table salt
1¼	cups creamy peanut butter
1	cup packed (7 ounces) light brown sugar
½	cup maple syrup or light corn syrup
¼	cup coconut oil, melted and cooled
3	tablespoons water
1	teaspoon vanilla extract
1¼	cups (7½ ounces) semisweet chocolate chips or chunks

1   Whisk flour, baking soda, and salt together in bowl. Whisk peanut butter, sugar, maple syrup, melted oil, water, and vanilla in large bowl until well combined and smooth. Using rubber spatula, stir flour mixture into peanut butter mixture until just combined. Fold in chocolate chips. Cover and refrigerate until dough is firm, at least 2 hours or up to 24 hours. (If refrigerated overnight, allow to sit at room temp for 15 minutes before scooping.)

2   Adjust oven rack to middle position and heat oven to 350 degrees. Line 2 rimmed baking sheets with parchment paper. Divide dough into 16 portions, each about 3 tablespoons (or use #24 cookie scoop), and roll into balls. Arrange dough balls 2 inches apart on prepared baking sheets, 8 dough balls per sheet. Using bottom of a drinking glass, flatten dough balls until 2 inches in diameter.

3   Bake cookies, 1 sheet at a time, until puffed and edges have begun brown and set but centers are still soft, 12 to 18 minutes, rotating sheet halfway through baking. Let cookies cool on sheet for 5 minutes, then transfer to wire rack to cool completely before serving. (Cookies can be stored in airtight container at room temperature for up to 1 day.)

AMANDA'S TIPS

› This dough is quite soft, so keep it chilled until you are ready to form and bake the cookies.

› Not all semisweet chocolate chips are vegan, so check ingredient lists.

› If you like, after forming the dough into balls in step 2, you can freeze the dough balls for up to 1 month. Thaw them in the refrigerator overnight, and let them sit on the prepared sheet pans at room temperature while the oven is preheating so that they will flatten easily.

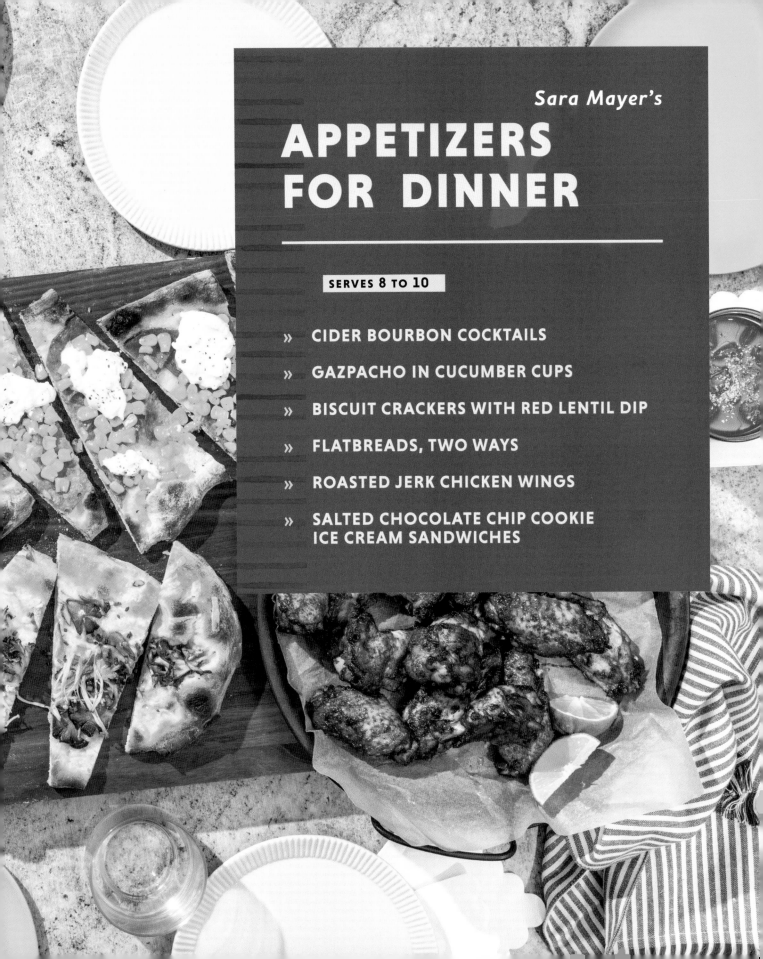

Sara Mayer's

APPETIZERS FOR DINNER

SERVES 8 TO 10

- » **CIDER BOURBON COCKTAILS**
- » **GAZPACHO IN CUCUMBER CUPS**
- » **BISCUIT CRACKERS WITH RED LENTIL DIP**
- » **FLATBREADS, TWO WAYS**
- » **ROASTED JERK CHICKEN WINGS**
- » **SALTED CHOCOLATE CHIP COOKIE ICE CREAM SANDWICHES**

Sara Mayer

When I have people over, I usually have to prepare foods for many diets and palates. It seems that no matter what the menu, someone has an allergy or an item they cannot or will not eat. So, why not make it easy and fun for myself? By putting together a variety of appetizers, I can make sure to include something for everyone. This menu serves 8 to 10 people overall, but since it's a safe bet that not everyone is going to eat everything, some of the recipes serve 6 to 8. (This also means there won't be excess leftovers.) And, while this concept started out for me as a sit-down dinner party, it's equally as fun to turn it into a cocktail party, as all the items are small and can be eaten with one hand. Many elements of this menu also can be made ahead of time, making the amount of last-minute work minimal. I think this menu is superfun and diverse and hope you agree!

MY GAME PLAN

UP TO 2 MONTHS AHEAD
› Make and freeze the Salted Chocolate Chip Cookie Ice Cream Sandwiches.

UP TO 1 MONTH AHEAD
› Make and freeze the dough for the Biscuit Crackers.

UP TO 3 DAYS AHEAD
› Make the Red Lentil Dip for the biscuit crackers.

UP TO 2 DAYS AHEAD
› Make the soup for the Gazpacho in Cucumber Cups.

UP TO 1 DAY AHEAD
› Stir together the ingredients for the Cider Bourbon Cocktails.
› Make the cucumber cups for the gazpacho.
› Bake the biscuit crackers.
› Marinate the chicken for the Roasted Jerk Chicken Wings.

UP TO A COUPLE OF HOURS AHEAD
› Roast the chicken wings. (They are great at room temperature, or you can reheat them in a 325-degree oven.)

STREAMLINE
› I love the multitude of flavors in this menu, but you can simplify things by making both flatbreads with the same topping.
› Though the homemade crackers are really worth it, feel free to serve the dip with store-bought water crackers instead.

CIDER BOURBON COCKTAILS

Makes 10 cocktails

Total Time: 5 minutes

WHY I LOVE THIS RECIPE Although there's always an opinionated debate over just how much bourbon to include, this has become the signature cocktail in my house no matter the occasion or time of year. I like to add a heavy grating of fresh nutmeg, for fragrance as well as flavor.

15	ounces bourbon
5	ounces ginger liqueur
5	cups apple cider, chilled
	Ground nutmeg

1 Combine bourbon, ginger liqueur, and cider in pitcher and stir gently. Refrigerate, covered, until ready to serve (up to 1 day).

2 Fill rocks glasses halfway with ice and pour cocktail into glasses. Sprinkle nutmeg over top of each serving.

SARA'S TIPS

› Feel free to add more bourbon if you like a stronger cocktail, but I don't recommend adding more ginger liqueur.

› I use Domaine de Canton for the ginger liqueur.

› I strongly recommend grating fresh nutmeg for the garnish.

GAZPACHO IN CUCUMBER CUPS

Serves 6 to 8

Total Time: 20 minutes, plus 1 hour chilling

WHY I LOVE THIS RECIPE This recipe is so old school that every time I think of serving it, I second-guess myself. Maybe it's too played out, or retro in a not-good way? But then I make it, and I remember exactly why I love it. The soup is zesty with spice and superbold. The cucumber cups calm and refresh the other flavors. Because this appetizer is served cold, it can come right out of the refrigerator to be served; in fact, it's at its best that way! This little dish hits every note and gets applause every time.

4	English cucumbers, ends trimmed and reserved, cut crosswise into 1½-inch lengths
½	cup tomato juice
1	small tomato (4 ounces), cored and chopped
½	small red bell pepper, chopped
1	small shallot, chopped
2	tablespoons extra-virgin olive oil, plus extra for serving
1½	tablespoons sherry vinegar, plus extra for seasoning
1	small garlic clove, minced
½	teaspoon table salt
½	teaspoon hot sauce (optional)
¼	teaspoon pepper

1 Using melon baller or small soup spoon, scoop out insides of cucumber pieces from one cut side, leaving ¼-inch border around walls and bottoms, to form cups. Arrange cups on serving platter, cover with damp paper towels, and refrigerate until ready to serve. (Cups can be wrapped in plastic and refrigerated for up to 24 hours.)

2 Process reserved cucumber ends; tomato juice; tomato; bell pepper; shallot; oil; vinegar; garlic; salt; hot sauce, if using; and pepper in blender until mostly smooth, about 1 minute. Transfer to 8-cup liquid measuring cup or bowl, cover, and refrigerate until completely chilled, at least 1 hour or up to 2 days. Stir gazpacho to recombine and season with extra vinegar, salt, and pepper to taste. Divide gazpacho among cucumber cups, drizzle with extra oil, and sprinkle with pepper. Serve.

SARA'S TIPS

› You can choose how smooth or chunky to make the soup, based on your taste.

› The food processor or immersion blender is your friend here.

› I love to serve this on a rectangular platter, lining up all the cups like soldiers, or on a circular platter, like a flower.

BISCUIT CRACKERS WITH RED LENTIL DIP

Serves 6 to 8

Total Time: 2 hours, plus 30 minutes chilling

WHY I LOVE THIS RECIPE I love the rich flavor and tender texture of biscuits, and both shine through when compacted into a crisp cracker form. The browning you get highlights their buttery qualities in a very satisfying way. The crackers nicely tame the spicy flavor of the hearty red lentil dip, which is great served either warm or at room temperature. (Its spiciness comes through more strongly when it's warm.)

BISCUIT CRACKERS

¾	cup (3¾ ounces) all-purpose flour
1½	teaspoons sugar
1	teaspoon baking powder
⅛	teaspoon baking soda
¼	teaspoon table salt
4	tablespoons unsalted butter, chilled, plus 1 tablespoon, melted
5	tablespoons buttermilk
2	teaspoons coarse sea salt

RED LENTIL DIP

2	tablespoons extra-virgin olive oil, divided
1	red bell pepper, stemmed, seeded, and chopped fine
½	onion, chopped fine
1	teaspoon table salt
2	tablespoons harissa
2	tablespoons tomato paste
¼	teaspoon cayenne pepper (optional)
2	cups water
⅔	cup dried red lentils, picked over and rinsed
2	tablespoons lemon juice
2	tablespoons plain yogurt
½	cup chopped fresh parsley

1 **FOR THE CRACKERS** Whisk flour, sugar, baking powder, baking soda, and salt together in large bowl. Grate 3½ tablespoons chilled butter on large holes of box grater; reserve excess chilled butter for another use. Add grated butter to flour mixture and toss gently to combine.

2 Add buttermilk to flour mixture and fold with spatula until just combined (dough will look dry). Transfer dough to liberally floured counter. Dust surface of dough with flour. Using your floured hands, knead dough until cohesive mass forms. Transfer dough to sheet of plastic wrap. Wrap in plastic and flatten to form 5-inch disk. Refrigerate dough for at least 30 minutes or up to 2 days. Let chilled dough sit on counter to soften slightly, about 10 minutes, before rolling. (Wrapped dough can be frozen for up to 1 month. If frozen, let dough thaw completely in refrigerator before rolling.)

3 Adjust oven rack to upper-middle position and heat oven to 375 degrees. Roll dough into 11-inch square on lightly floured counter. Using pizza cutter or chef's knife, cut dough into rough 2 by 1-inch pieces (you should have about 40 pieces). Arrange pieces at least ¼ inch apart on parchment paper–lined rimmed baking sheet. Prick dough pieces 1 or 2 times with fork. Brush tops with melted butter and sprinkle with sea salt. Cover crackers with second sheet of parchment, then second rimmed baking sheet.

4 Bake crackers until golden brown, about 30 minutes, rotating sheet halfway through cooking. Let crackers cool completely on wire rack between sheets. (Crackers can be stored in an airtight container for up to 24 hours.)

5 **FOR THE DIP** Heat 1 tablespoon oil in medium saucepan over medium heat until shimmering. Add bell pepper, onion, and salt and cook until softened, 5 to 7 minutes. Stir in harissa; tomato paste; and cayenne, if using; and cook, stirring frequently, until fragrant, about 1 minute. Stir in water, scraping up any browned bits. Stir in lentils and bring to simmer. Reduce heat to low, cover, and simmer, stirring occasionally, until lentils begin to break down, about 15 minutes.

6 Off heat, lay clean dish towel underneath lid and let lentil mixture sit for 10 minutes. Add lemon juice, yogurt, and remaining 1 tablespoon oil and stir vigorously until mixture is cohesive. Stir in parsley and season with salt and pepper to taste. Serve warm or at room temperature. (Dip can be refrigerated for up to 3 days; bring to room temperature and stir to recombine before serving.)

SARA'S TIPS

› Usually, you want to knead biscuit dough as little as possible to keep the dough crumbly and flaky, but for these crackers, more kneading is better to make it cohesive and easier to roll out thin.

› You can sub any kind of seeds or seed blend for the coarse salt topping. I particularly like everything bagel blend or sesame seeds.

› If you prefer a smoother dip, process the mixture using a food processor or immersion blender in step 6 before stirring in the parsley.

› Harissa spiciness varies by brand. If your harissa is spicy, omit the cayenne.

FLATBREADS, TWO WAYS

Makes two 12-inch flatbreads

Total Time: 1¾ hours

WHY I LOVE THIS RECIPE In my eyes, flatbread is basically pizza with more-fun toppings, and you cannot go wrong with pizza, ever. The beauty of these is that the toppings can be mixed up or interchanged for other ingredients you prefer or have on hand. For one flatbread, I pair fontina cheese with earthy mushrooms and fresh chives. The other flatbread is spicy from salami, creamy from burrata, and sweet from corn. I shape these into long ovals, making them easier to cut for a crowd and giving them an elegant look.

2	pounds store-bought pizza dough
2	ounces fontina, shredded (¾ cup)
4	ounces wild mushrooms, stemmed and roughly torn, if necessary
1	tablespoon minced fresh chives
1½	ounces thinly sliced salami or pepperoni
½	cup frozen corn, thawed and patted dry
3	ounces burrata, torn

SARA'S TIPS

› You can use your favorite homemade pizza dough, if you prefer.

› For the wild mushrooms, try shiitake, oyster, chanterelle, and/or maitake.

› Other great topping combos: pesto, peas, and baby arugula (add the arugula after baking); fig jam, Brie, and prosciutto (add the prosciutto after baking); cheddar, apples, chopped pancetta, and baby arugula (add the arugula after baking); and peaches and mozzarella with balsamic vinegar drizzled on after baking.

1 One hour before baking flatbreads, adjust oven rack to second highest position (rack should be 4 to 5 inches below broiler), set baking stone on rack, and heat oven to 500 degrees. Divide dough in half and shape each half into smooth, tight ball. Place balls on lightly oiled baking sheet, at least 3 inches apart. Cover loosely with greased plastic wrap and let sit at room temperature for 1 hour.

2 Generously coat 1 dough ball with flour and place on well-floured countertop. Using fingertips, gently flatten into 8-inch disk, leaving 1 inch of outer edge slightly thicker than center. Using your hands, continue stretching dough into 16 by 6-inch oval, working along edges and giving dough half turns as you stretch. Transfer dough oval to well-floured baking peel and reshape as needed. Sprinkle with fontina and mushrooms, leaving ½-inch border.

3 Slide flatbread carefully onto baking stone and bake until crust is well browned and fontina is bubbly and beginning to brown, 5 to 7 minutes, rotating flatbread halfway through baking. Transfer flatbread to wire rack, let cool for 5 minutes, then sprinkle with chives.

4 Meanwhile, repeat shaping remaining dough ball. Sprinkle with salami and corn, leaving ½-inch border, and bake until crust is well browned and salami is crispy, 5 to 7 minutes, rotating flatbread halfway through. Transfer flatbread to wire rack, let cool for 5 minutes, then sprinkle with burrata. Slice flatbreads into wedges and serve.

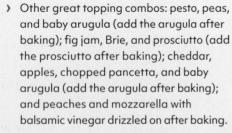

ROASTED JERK CHICKEN WINGS

Serves 6 to 8

Total Time: 1 hour, plus 1 hour marinating

WHY I LOVE THIS RECIPE This is my favorite way to make chicken wings. As someone who does not like Buffalo sauce, I get a lot of flack, but once I make these for guests, they understand why they're my favorite. The spiciness is just enough that even those with a spice aversion can enjoy them without being overwhelmed. The fact that you can marinate the wings for anywhere from 1 to 24 hours in advance gives you a huge window in which to cook them. (They also make great leftovers.)

4	scallions, chopped
¼	cup vegetable oil
¼	cup soy sauce
2	tablespoons cider vinegar
2	tablespoons packed brown sugar
1–2	habanero chiles, stemmed
10	sprigs fresh thyme
5	garlic cloves, peeled
2½	teaspoons ground allspice
1½	teaspoons table salt
½	teaspoon ground cinnamon
½	teaspoon ground ginger
3	pounds chicken wings, cut at joints, wingtips discarded
	Lime wedges, for serving

1 Process scallions, oil, soy sauce, vinegar, sugar, habanero(s), thyme sprigs, garlic, allspice, salt, cinnamon, and ginger in blender until smooth, about 30 seconds, scraping down sides of blender jar as needed.

2 Place chicken and marinade in 1-gallon zipper-lock bag. Press out air, seal bag, and turn to coat chicken in marinade. Refrigerate for at least 1 hour or up to 24 hours, turning occasionally.

3 Adjust oven rack to upper-middle position and heat oven to 450 degrees. Line rimmed baking sheet with aluminum foil and spray with vegetable oil spray. Remove wings from marinade and arrange in single layer, fatty side up, on prepared sheet; discard marinade. Roast until chicken registers 160 degrees, flipping wings halfway through cooking, 25 to 30 minutes. Transfer wings to serving platter and let rest for 5 minutes. Serve warm or at room temperature with lime wedges.

SARA'S TIPS

> I prefer to buy whole wings and split them myself because they tend to be larger than pre-split wings. Three pounds wings should ideally contain 12 wings to yield 24 pieces (12 drumettes and 12 flats). If you can find only split wings, look for larger ones.

> Use more or fewer habaneros depending on your preferred level of spiciness. You can remove the seeds and ribs or substitute jalapeños for less heat. For more heat, use Scotch bonnets.

> I recommend wearing food-handling gloves when prepping the chiles.

> Use thyme sprigs with plenty of leaves; there's no need to remove leaves from stems.

SALTED CHOCOLATE CHIP COOKIE ICE CREAM SANDWICHES

Makes 10 cookie sandwiches
Total Time: 45 minutes, plus 30 minutes cooling and 2 hours freezing

WHY I LOVE THIS RECIPE These ice cream sandwiches are a throwback to childhood that have been leveled up to make them a delightful way to finish any dinner party. The cookies themselves are a fan favorite in my house. To make them moist enough to hold up well to freezing, I replace some of the white sugar I usually use with brown sugar, since the molasses it contains is hygroscopic—that is, very effective at attracting moisture. It also adds appealing toffee-like notes to the cookies. In addition, I brown the butter, which further bolsters the toffee angle. Sprinkling them with smoked salt takes the flavor through the roof.

6	tablespoons unsalted butter, divided
½	cup (3½ ounces) packed light brown sugar
¼	cup (1¾ ounces) granulated sugar
1	teaspoon vanilla extract
½	teaspoon table salt
1	large egg
1	cup (5 ounces) plus 1 tablespoon all-purpose flour
¼	teaspoon baking soda
6	tablespoons bittersweet, milk, and/or white chocolate chips
½	teaspoon smoked sea salt
1¼	cups vanilla ice cream

SARA'S TIPS

> I especially like to use alder smoked salt in these cookies. You can use plain sea salt instead of smoked salt, if you prefer.

> I prefer plain old vanilla ice cream here, but the world is your oyster, so use any flavor that suits your fancy!

> If using a premium brand of ice cream, such as Ben & Jerry's or Häagen-Dazs, which tend to be harder when frozen, let the ice cream soften slightly in the refrigerator before scooping.

1 Adjust oven rack to middle position and heat oven to 325 degrees. Line baking sheet with parchment paper. Melt 5 tablespoons butter in 10-inch skillet over medium-high heat. Continue to cook, swirling skillet constantly, until butter is dark golden brown and has nutty aroma, 1 to 3 minutes. Transfer browned butter to large bowl and stir in remaining 1 tablespoon butter until melted. Whisk in brown sugar, granulated sugar, vanilla, and table salt until incorporated. Whisk in egg until smooth and well incorporated, about 30 seconds. Whisk in flour and baking soda until combined. Gently fold in chocolate chips.

2 Working with 1 rounded tablespoon dough at a time, roll into balls (you should have 20 balls). Space 1 inch apart on prepared sheet and sprinkle with sea salt. Bake until edges are light golden brown but centers are still soft and puffy, about 15 minutes. Let cookies cool on sheet for 5 minutes, then transfer to wire rack and let cool completely, about 30 minutes. Place sheet, still lined with parchment, in freezer.

3 Place 10 cookies upside down on counter. Quickly deposit 2-tablespoon portions ice cream in center of each cookie. Place 1 cookie from wire rack right side up on top of each scoop. Gently press and twist each sandwich between your hands until ice cream spreads to edges of cookies (this doesn't have to be perfect; ice cream can be neatened after chilling). Transfer sandwiches to sheet in freezer and freeze for at least 2 hours before serving. (Sandwiches can be individually wrapped tightly in plastic wrap, transferred to zipper-lock bag, and frozen for up to 2 months.)

Ashley Moore's

ROAD TRIP DINNER PARTY

SERVES 6 TO 8

» **STICKY SPICED NUTS WITH ORANGE, HONEY, AND ROSEMARY**

» **MEDITERRANEAN LAYERED DIP**

» **"THE ITALIAN" STROMBOLI**

» **BROWNED BUTTER RKTS**

Ashley
Moore

Dinner on the first night of vacation should be easy, delicious, and fun for everyone—a party, not a chore! There have been far too many times that my family and friends have road-tripped to our rental destination and either been too tired to go out to dinner or didn't have many available restaurant options to choose from. And the thought of both stocking the rental fridge *and* cooking on the first night is just too much. This menu fixes that problem! These recipes are so simple and will make you feel right at home. The sticky spiced nuts travel great in a container or zipper-lock bag; the stromboli can be assembled or made entirely ahead and transported in a cooler, along with the convenient ingredients for the layered dip. And if you can make it to your rental without snacking on some, my rice cereal treats will please all of your travelers. All you have to do is arrive, unpack, and assemble the dip while the stromboli are in the oven!

MY GAME PLAN

UP TO 1 MONTH AHEAD

› Assemble and freeze "The Italian" Stromboli. Thaw them overnight in the refrigerator (or in the cooler on your way to your destination) before baking them.

UP TO 3 WEEKS AHEAD

› Make the Sticky Spiced Nuts with Orange, Honey, and Rosemary.

UP TO 3 DAYS AHEAD

› Make the Browned Butter RKTs.

NOTE

› You have choices with the stromboli:

- Instead of freezing the assembled stromboli, you can refrigerate them for up to 24 hours before baking.

- Alternatively, you could assemble and bake the stromboli 1 day ahead and let them cool completely before wrapping and packing them in your cooler to reheat at your destination.

STICKY SPICED NUTS WITH ORANGE, HONEY, AND ROSEMARY

Makes about 4 cups

Total Time: 15 minutes (air fryer); 50 minutes (oven)

WHY I LOVE THIS RECIPE These are sticky and delicious! I love using my air fryer, especially for things that can take a while in the oven. Because it is essentially a convection oven, it quickly crisps and browns the nuts. Though the nuts take longer in an oven, they're still pretty hands-off, so I've given those instructions, too. This makes enough for your crew to snack on all week.

½	cup honey
1	tablespoon unsalted butter
2	teaspoons grated orange zest plus 1 tablespoon juice
2	teaspoons minced fresh rosemary
2	teaspoons kosher salt, divided
½	teaspoon pepper
1	large egg white
12	ounces raw whole nuts

1 Line rimmed baking sheet with parchment paper and lightly spray with vegetable oil spray; set aside. Microwave honey, butter, orange zest and juice, rosemary, 1½ teaspoons salt, and pepper in bowl until butter has melted, about 1 minute, stirring halfway through microwaving. Whisk egg white in large bowl until foamy. Add honey mixture and whisk to combine. Add nuts and toss to coat. Drain nuts in colander for 5 minutes.

2A **FOR AN AIR FRYER** Lightly spray base of 6-quart air-fryer basket with vegetable oil spray. Add nuts to prepared basket and spread into even layer. Place basket into air fryer and set temperature to 325 degrees. Cook until nuts are golden brown and crisp, 5 to 7 minutes, stirring nuts halfway through cooking.

2B **FOR AN OVEN** Adjust oven rack to middle position and heat oven to 300 degrees. Line second rimmed baking sheet with parchment. Spread nuts evenly on prepared sheets and bake until golden brown and crisp, 40 to 45 minutes, rotating sheets halfway through baking.

3 Transfer nuts to prepared sheet and let cool. Sprinkle with remaining ½ teaspoon salt. Break nuts apart and package in airtight containers or zipper-lock bags. (Nuts can be stored in airtight container for up to 3 weeks.)

ASHLEY'S TIPS

> My favorite combo is almonds and pistachios, but use any type or combination of unsalted nuts that you like.

> Save one of those little moisture-absorbing silica packets that come in some food packages and put it in the container with the nuts to keep them crisp (just be careful not to eat it, though!).

MEDITERRANEAN LAYERED DIP

Serves 6 to 8

Total Time: 15 minutes

WHY I LOVE THIS RECIPE This dip disappears really quickly! I like to assemble it in a wide, shallow bowl or on a platter so that there is lots of surface area to successfully load up your dipper of choice. Just layer two flavor-packed store-bought ingredients—hummus and tzatziki—then top them with a Mediterranean mix of roasted red peppers, olives, feta, and cucumbers. Serve with pita chips or sliced vegetables (carrots and bell peppers travel especially well).

2½	cups hummus
2½	cups tzatziki
½	English cucumber, cut into ½-inch pieces
½	cup jarred roasted red peppers, patted dry and chopped
⅓	cup pitted kalamata olives, chopped
3	tablespoons extra-virgin olive oil, plus extra for drizzling
1	tablespoon red wine vinegar
¼	teaspoon table salt
¼	teaspoon pepper
2	ounces feta cheese, crumbled (½ cup)

Spread hummus in single layer on large, shallow serving platter, then gently spread tzatziki evenly over top. Combine cucumber, red peppers, olives, oil, vinegar, salt, and pepper in bowl. Spoon vegetable mixture in even layer over tzatziki. Sprinkle with feta and drizzle with extra oil. Serve immediately.

ASHLEY'S TIPS

> 12-ounce containers of both hummus and tzatziki provide enough for this recipe. I go for store-bought for the greatest ease, but feel free to use your favorite homemade versions instead.

> I don't recommend making this ahead of time, so remember that you'll need to pack the ingredients for this dip to assemble it when you're ready to eat.

"THE ITALIAN" STROMBOLI

Makes two 11-inch stromboli; serves 6 to 8
Total Time: 1¼ hours

WHY I LOVE THIS RECIPE   There's just something awesome about an Italian grinder (aka a sub), with its hearty combination of meats, cheeses, and bread. Here I take all the elements of that pickle-y, spicy, meaty-cheesy goodness, wrap it in some store-bought pizza dough, and bake it. And because I love a spinach and cheese calzone, I add some spinach too! Salami goes solo here for the meat, but feel free to include another cured meat if you'd like.

2	tablespoons extra-virgin olive oil
4	garlic cloves, minced
20	ounces frozen spinach, thawed, squeezed dry, and chopped
¼	cup chopped pepperoncini or hot cherry peppers, plus 2 tablespoons brine
2	(1-pound) balls pizza dough, room temperature
8	ounces thinly sliced aged provolone cheese, divided
4	ounces thinly sliced salami, divided
8	ounces block mozzarella cheese, shredded (2 cups), divided
2	large eggs, lightly beaten
2	teaspoons sesame seeds
2	cups store-bought marinara sauce, warmed

1 Adjust oven rack to middle position and heat oven to 375 degrees. Line rimmed baking sheet with aluminum foil and grease foil. Heat oil in 12-inch nonstick skillet over medium heat until shimmering. Add garlic and cook until fragrant, about 30 seconds. Add spinach and pepperoncini and brine and cook until heated through, about 1 minute; transfer to bowl.

2 Roll 1 dough ball into 12 by 10-inch rectangle on lightly floured counter with long side parallel to counter edge. Shingle 4 ounces provolone evenly over dough, leaving ½-inch border along top and sides. Layer 2 ounces salami over provolone. Sprinkle 1 cup mozzarella and half of spinach mixture over salami.

3 Brush borders with beaten eggs. Fold bottom third of stromboli in toward middle. Fold top third of stromboli down to cover first fold, creating log. Pinch seam to seal. Transfer stromboli to one side of prepared sheet, seam side down. Pinch ends to seal and tuck underneath. Repeat with remaining dough ball, 4 ounces provolone, 2 ounces salami, 1 cup mozzarella, and spinach mixture; transfer to other side of sheet. (Assembled stromboli may be covered and refrigerated for up to 24 hours. Or freeze until firm, then wrap tightly in plastic wrap and aluminum foil and freeze for up to 1 month.)

4 Brush tops of stromboli with remaining beaten eggs. Using sharp knife, make 5 evenly spaced ½-inch-deep slashes, 2 inches long, on top of each stromboli. Sprinkle with sesame seeds. Bake until crust is golden and center registers 200 degrees, 35 to 45 minutes, rotating sheet halfway through baking. Transfer stromboli to wire rack and let cool for 10 minutes. Transfer to cutting board and cut into 2-inch-thick slices. Serve with marinara sauce.

ASHLEY'S TIPS

› Be sure to let the pizza dough come to room temperature before rolling it out.

› Assembling and baking these stromboli can sometimes be too much to tackle all in one day, especially if you're packing for a trip. Thankfully, the assembled stromboli can be refrigerated or frozen before baking. Thaw frozen stromboli overnight in the refrigerator before baking (or in the cooler while traveling). Increase the baking time to 45 to 55 minutes.

› If you're planning to bake the stromboli at your destination, you'll need to beat only one of the eggs (for step 3). Plan to bring along the remaining egg and the sesame seeds for brushing and sprinkling the stromboli before baking.

BROWNED BUTTER RKTS

Makes 12 bars

Total Time: 15 minutes, plus 1 hour setting

WHY I LOVE THIS RECIPE   There is only one thing that my entire family insists I bring for any get-together, and it's these RKTs. (In fact, I've even had to bring an extra batch for my sister, who may or may not have needed to hide some in her house just for herself . . . sorry, Mandy!) It takes only a minute to brown the butter, which is one of those things that sounds fancy and difficult, but rest assured, it's as easy as melting butter. You just need to watch so that it doesn't burn. But follow this recipe and that won't happen!

8	tablespoons unsalted butter
2	(10-ounce) packages large marshmallows
1	teaspoon vanilla extract
¼	teaspoon table salt
9	cups (9 ounces) crisped rice cereal
¾	teaspoon flake sea salt

1   Spray rubber spatula and 13 by 9-inch baking pan with vegetable oil spray. Melt butter in Dutch oven over medium heat. Continue cooking, stirring constantly with wooden spoon, until butter is dark golden brown and has nutty aroma, 1 to 3 minutes.

2   Add marshmallows, vanilla, and table salt and cook, stirring often with prepared spatula, until marshmallows are just melted, about 3 minutes (some marshmallows may not be fully melted; this is OK). Off heat, stir in cereal until fully combined.

3   Transfer cereal mixture to prepared pan. Using your damp hands, press mixture into even layer. Sprinkle with sea salt and let set for 1 hour. Run knife around edge of pan to loosen treats, then turn out onto cutting board. Flip treats right side up and cut into 12 equal-size bars. (Bars can be stored in airtight container for up to 3 days.) Serve.

RENTAL ROULETTE

Consider bringing along some backup equipment for this dinner (such as your favorite knife, dish soap and sponge, wine opener, serving platter), just in case your vacation rental isn't superstocked.

ASHLEY'S TIPS

› Avoid using mini marshmallows here.

› For the best results, weigh the cereal.

› Don't shy away from using damp hands to flatten the sticky mixture into the baking pan—it will save you from a sticky mess on your hands.

Mark Huxsoll's

OKTOBERFEST AT HOME

SERVES **8**

» **BEER-CARAWAY PRETZELS**
Bavarian-Inspired Mustard Sauce

» **SCHWEINEBRATEN**

» **BROWNED BUTTER SAUERKRAUT**

» **KÄSESPÄTZLE**

» **BLACK FOREST BROWNIES**

Mark Huxsoll

Though I didn't get the chance to meet most of them, my dad's family emigrated from Bavaria, Germany, and settled in Indiana and Ohio. As I think about passing traditions on to the next generation, it's becoming more important to me to look to my heritage and learn as much as I can about where I come from. One of the most well-known and celebrated traditions from Bavaria (Munich, specifically) is Oktoberfest, which originated in 1810 as a 2-week celebration leading up to the wedding of the crown prince and princess of Bavaria. A special beer, known as Festbier, was brewed just for the occasion. Today, this celebration has spread the world over and is beloved for lots of beer (of course), plus great food, live music, and a jovial atmosphere. This is my inspiration for a dinner party, not only to celebrate my heritage but also because it is a fun and festive time with lots of great energy, eating, drinking, and dancing—many of my favorite things to do.

MY GAME PLAN

UP TO 6 MONTHS AHEAD
› Make the Bavarian-Inspired Mustard Sauce.

UP TO 5 DAYS AHEAD
› Make the Black Forest Brownies; store them, uncut, in an airtight container at room temperature.

UP TO 2 DAYS AHEAD
› Make the Beer-Caraway Pretzels.
› Make the Browned Butter Sauerkraut.
› Make and boil the Käsespätzle and toss them with the butter and cheese (but wait to broil them until just before serving).

UP TO 1 DAY AHEAD
› Season pork shoulder for the Schweinebraten (note that you must do this at least 12 hours ahead).
› Make the gravy for the Schweinebraten.

STREAMLINE
› If you have access to a bakery that sells fresh pretzels, you can buy them instead of baking them from scratch. Although it's not traditional, you could also substitute large hard pretzels.

BEER-CARAWAY PRETZELS

Makes 8 pretzels

Total Time: 1¼ hours, plus 2 hours rising and resting

WHY I LOVE THIS RECIPE I've been a pretzel fan ever since I was a young boy. There is sheer magic in how they turn mahogany in the oven after being boiled in water with baking soda (or, more traditionally, when soaked in a lye solution). Using beer in the dough adds a yeasty, malty flavor. These pretzels are crisp yet chewy and have a lovely salty crunch. Baking is one of the main reasons I got into cooking, so I am always happy to do it. Baking fills my home with incredible aromas and a feeling of warmth.

3¾	cups (20⅔ ounces) bread flour
2	tablespoons packed dark brown sugar
2	teaspoons instant or rapid-rise yeast
1½	teaspoons table salt
1½	cups beer
2	tablespoons unsalted butter, melted
½	cup baking soda
2	teaspoons flake sea salt
1	teaspoon caraway seeds

MARK'S TIPS

> I use a beer with a robust flavor profile, such as a German Märzen or a darker ale. However, you can also use something lighter, such as a pilsner.

> Take care when removing the pretzels from the boiling water, as they can unravel and lose their shape.

> I prefer a good-quality flake sea salt such as Maldon for the topping; it's a little more refined than coarse pretzel salt.

> When I have the time, I prefer to make these the day I serve them, but they definitely can be made a couple of days ahead. If you do this, reheat them on a baking sheet in a 300-degree oven for 5 minutes.

> You can also freeze these pretzels, wrapped well in plastic wrap, for up to 1 month. Let thaw before reheating.

1   In bowl of stand mixer, whisk together flour, sugar, yeast, and table salt. Fit stand mixer with dough hook, add beer and butter, and knead on low speed until dough comes together and clears sides of bowl, 4 to 6 minutes.

2   Turn out dough onto lightly floured counter and knead by hand until smooth, about 1 minute. Transfer dough to lightly greased large bowl and cover with plastic wrap. Let dough rise at room temperature until almost doubled in size, about 1½ hours.

3   Gently press center of dough to deflate. Transfer dough to lightly greased counter, divide into 8 equal pieces, and cover with plastic.

4   Lightly flour 1 rimmed baking sheet. Working with 1 piece of dough at a time, roll into 24-inch-long rope, keeping center of ropes slightly thicker than ends (centers should have a 3-inch-long section that is 1 inch thick and ends should be just under ½ inch thick). Shape rope into U with 2-inch-wide bottom curve and ends facing away from you. Crisscross ropes 2 inches from ends and twist once more. Fold ends up and firmly press ends halfway into U to create classic pretzel shape. (Lightly grease counter as needed if dough begins to stick.) Transfer pretzels to prepared sheet, knot side up, and cover with plastic. Let rest at room temperature for 20 minutes.

5   Adjust oven rack to upper-middle position and heat oven to 425 degrees. Dissolve baking soda in 8 cups water in Dutch oven and bring to boil over high heat. Press ends of rope into pretzel once more. Use slotted spatula to carefully transfer 2 pretzels, knot side down, to boiling water and cook for 30 seconds, flipping halfway through cooking. Transfer pretzels to greased wire rack, knot side up, and quickly sprinkle with sea salt and caraway while still wet. Repeat with remaining 6 pretzels. Let pretzels rest for 5 minutes.

6   Wipe baking sheet clean and lightly oil. Using sharp knife, make 2-inch-long by ¼-inch-deep slash in bottom curve of each pretzel. Transfer pretzels to prepared sheet and bake until deep mahogany brown, about 20 minutes, rotating halfway through baking. Let cool for 10 minutes. Serve warm.

PROST!

In true Oktoberfest style, serve lots and lots of good German beer, preferably an official Oktoberfest Festbier (a light lager) or Märzen (a full-bodied lager). Only six breweries, all Munich-based, are allowed to serve their Festbier at Oktoberfest in Munich: Paulaner Brauerei, Spaten-Franziskaner-Bräu, Löwenbräu, Augustiner-Bräu, Staatliches Hofbräu-München, and Hacker-Pschorr-Bräu.

ACCOMPANIMENT

BAVARIAN-INSPIRED MUSTARD SAUCE

Makes about 1 cup

Total Time: 45 minutes, plus 1 hour resting

WHY I LOVE THIS RECIPE Inspired by the sweet mustard sauce that is served with pretzels and sausages throughout Bavaria, this is punchy from whole-grain mustard and vinegar, with a brown sugar–honey sweetness for balance. The spices are just enough to add sophistication.

- ¼ cup cider vinegar
- ¼ cup packed dark brown sugar
- ¼ cup honey
- 2 tablespoons water
- 2 teaspoons table salt
- 1 garlic clove, peeled and smashed
- 5 allspice berries, lightly crushed
- 5 juniper berries, lightly crushed
- 5 black peppercorns, lightly crushed
- 3 whole cloves
- ¼ cup mustard powder
- ¼ cup whole-grain mustard

1 Bring vinegar, sugar, honey, water, salt, garlic, allspice, juniper, peppercorns, and cloves to boil in small saucepan over medium heat, stirring occasionally. Off heat, cover and let steep for 30 minutes.

2 Strain mixture through fine-mesh strainer into medium bowl, pressing on solids to extract as much liquid as possible. Whisk in mustard powder and whole-grain mustard until smooth. Cover and let mustard sit at room temperature for at least 1 hour or up to 2 days. (Mustard will become spicier as it rests at room temperature, so refrigerate it once it has reached desired spice level. Once refrigerated, its flavor will continue to mature, but it will not become spicier. Sauce can be refrigerated for up to 6 months.)

SCHWEINEBRATEN

Serves 8

Total Time: 3½ hours, plus 12 hours chilling and 30 minutes resting

WHY I LOVE THIS RECIPE It's no secret that many Germans love pork. I, too, love pork, and the shoulder is my favorite cut. A traditional German Schweinebraten, usually flavored with cumin, caraway, and mustard, can be similar to an American pot roast; I've also incorporated some elements of a barbecue pork shoulder that I make often in the summer. Seasoning with salt, sugar, and spices ahead of time helps those flavors penetrate deep into the shoulder while helping to retain juiciness. The exterior gets very dark, developing a beautiful bark on the outside. I keep the seasoned gravy light and fresh by using white wine instead of the more typical red.

PORK

- 3 tablespoons kosher salt
- 3 tablespoons packed dark brown sugar
- 2 teaspoons caraway seeds, toasted and cracked
- 2 teaspoons pepper
- 2 teaspoons paprika
- 2 teaspoons mustard powder
- 1 teaspoon ground cumin
- 1 (4-pound) boneless pork butt roast

GRAVY

- 4 tablespoons unsalted butter
- 1 onion, chopped fine
- 1 carrot, peeled and chopped
- 1 celery rib, minced
- 1 tablespoon tomato paste
- 1 teaspoon caraway seeds
- 1 teaspoon pepper
- 1 teaspoon paprika
- 1 teaspoon mustard powder
- ½ teaspoon ground cumin
- 3 sprigs fresh thyme
- 2 bay leaves
- 3 tablespoons all-purpose flour
- 1 cup dry Riesling
- 4 cups beef broth, plus extra as needed

1 **FOR THE PORK** Combine salt, sugar, caraway, pepper, paprika, mustard powder, and cumin in bowl. Rub salt mixture over entire pork roast. Wrap roast tightly in double layer of plastic wrap, place on rimmed baking sheet, and refrigerate for at least 12 hours or up to 24 hours.

2 Set wire rack in rimmed baking sheet. Adjust oven rack to middle position and heat to 325 degrees. Unwrap roast and transfer to prepared rack. Roast until pork registers 190 degrees, 3¼ to 3¾ hours.

3 **FOR THE GRAVY** Meanwhile, melt butter in large saucepan over medium-high heat. Add onion, carrot, and celery and cook until beginning to soften, about 3 minutes. Stir in tomato paste, caraway, pepper, paprika, mustard powder, cumin, thyme sprigs, and bay leaves and cook until fragrant, about 1 minute. Stir in flour until well incorporated. Stir in wine, scraping up any browned bits. Stir in broth and bring to simmer. Cook, stirring occasionally, until reduced by about half, 30 to 35 minutes. Discard thyme sprigs and bay leaves and season with salt and pepper to taste. (Gravy can be refrigerated for up to 24 hours; bring to brief simmer over medium-low heat and adjust consistency with extra hot broth as needed.)

4 Remove pork from oven and let rest on rack for 30 minutes. Transfer pork to carving board and slice thin. Serve with gravy.

> **MARK'S TIPS**
> › The pork must rest for 30 minutes, but it can certainly rest longer if your guests are running late or you're having fun eating pretzels and catching up.
>
> › Pork butt roast is often labeled Boston butt in the supermarket. Go to your local butcher and get the best-quality pork shoulder you can. Look for a roast that has at least a ¼-inch-thick fat cap.
>
> › For the gravy, use a dry Riesling, from Germany if possible. Sweeter Rieslings might make the sauce too sweet.

BROWNED BUTTER SAUERKRAUT

Serves 8

Total Time: 15 minutes

 WHY I LOVE THIS RECIPE This fun and fancy spinoff of a centuries-old food takes just minutes to make. Start with store-bought sauerkraut, with all of its punchy flavor and lactic acidity from fermentation, and cook it with browning butter. The fat and the nutty flavor from the browned butter mellows the sharpness of the sauerkraut—but it still stays sharp enough to cut through the richness of the pork roast.

- 8 tablespoons unsalted butter
- 1½ pounds sauerkraut, drained thoroughly
- 1 tablespoon packed brown sugar
- 1 tablespoon whole-grain mustard

Melt butter in 12-inch nonstick skillet over medium-high heat. Continue to cook until foaming subsides and butter is beginning to brown, 3 to 5 minutes, swirling regularly. Stir in sauerkraut and sugar and cook until golden brown, about 5 minutes. Off heat, stir in mustard. (Sauerkraut can be made up to 2 days ahead and refrigerated in airtight container.) Serve warm.

> **MARK'S TIPS**
> › Look for good-quality sauerkraut packaged in a glass jar in the refrigerated section.
>
> › Drain the sauerkraut very well or it will spatter when added to the hot butter, which makes a mess and could also cause burns.

KÄSESPÄTZLE

Serves 8

Total Time: 45 minutes

WHY I LOVE THIS RECIPE I can still remember learning about spaetzle in culinary school. I had never seen them before and they were so fun to make. Käsespätzle is the German equivalent of macaroni and cheese—which means it's always a hit. These are dressed up with a sophisticated mix of Gruyère cheese, for its flavor, and fontina cheese, which melts well. They will catch juices from the pork as well as any gravy that drips onto them, which is divine.

3	cups (15 ounces) all-purpose flour
2	teaspoons table salt, plus salt for cooking spaetzle
1	teaspoon pepper
½	teaspoon ground nutmeg
1	cup whole milk
4	large eggs
1	(13 by 9-inch) disposable aluminum pan
4	tablespoons unsalted butter, melted
4	ounces Gruyère cheese, shredded (1 cup), divided
4	ounces fontina cheese, shredded (1 cup), divided

MARK'S TIPS

> If you have a spaetzle maker or a food mill with ¼-inch holes, you can use that instead of the disposable aluminum pan.

> You will need a 2-quart broiler-safe baking dish. A 10- or 12-inch broiler-safe skillet is also a good option.

 Whisk flour, salt, pepper, and nutmeg together in large bowl. Whisk milk and eggs together in second bowl until smooth. Slowly whisk milk mixture into flour mixture until smooth. Cover and let rest for 15 to 30 minutes.

2 Meanwhile, adjust oven rack 6 inches from broiler element and heat broiler. Bring 4 quarts water to boil in Dutch oven. Using scissors, poke about forty ¼-inch holes in bottom of disposable pan.

3 Add 1 tablespoon salt to boiling water and set prepared disposable pan on top of pot. Transfer half of batter to disposable pan. Use spatula to scrape batter across holes, letting batter fall into water. Boil until all spaetzle float, about 30 seconds. Using spider skimmer or slotted spoon, transfer spaetzle to colander set in large bowl to drain. Repeat with remaining batter.

4 Discard any accumulated water in bowl and transfer spaetzle to now-empty bowl. Add melted butter, ½ cup Gruyère, and ½ cup fontina and toss to combine. (Käsespätzle can be made up to 2 days ahead and refrigerated in airtight container. Let come to room temperature before broiling.) Spread spaetzle into even layer in 2-quart broiler-safe baking dish and sprinkle with remaining ½ cup Gruyère and ½ cup fontina. Broil until bubbling and browning in spots, about 5 minutes. Serve.

BLACK FOREST BROWNIES

Makes 16 brownies

Total Time: 1¼ hours, plus 2 hours cooling

WHY I LOVE THIS RECIPE   These incredible brownies have all the magic of the classic Black Forest layer cake of chocolate sponge cake, cherries, and whipped cream, but they are much easier to make. Dried cherries plumped up in the microwave with Kirsch flavor the dense, not-too-sweet brownies, and when the pan comes out of the oven, on goes a layer of tart cherry jam mixed with additional Kirsch to soak into the brownies as they cool. I love serving them with small glasses of chilled Kirsch as a digestif to end the night.

- 2 cups (8 ounces) dried tart cherries
- ¾ cup Kirsch, divided
- 5 ounces semisweet chocolate or bittersweet chocolate, chopped
- 2 ounces unsweetened chocolate, chopped
- 8 tablespoons unsalted butter, cut into quarters
- 3 tablespoons cocoa powder
- 3 large eggs
- 1¼ cups (8¾ ounces) granulated sugar
- 2 teaspoons vanilla extract
- ½ teaspoon table salt
- 1 cup (5 ounces) all-purpose flour
- ½ cup sour cherry jam
- Confectioners' sugar

MARK'S TIPS

> Dried tart cherries may also be called sour cherries. Don't use dried sweet cherries, and look for a sour or tart cherry jam that isn't too sweet.

> The glaze provides a strong kick; for a slightly less assertive glaze, substitute water for the Kirsch.

> If you make the brownies ahead, to preserve their texture, don't cut them into pieces until you're ready to serve them.

1   Adjust oven rack to lower-middle position and heat oven to 350 degrees. Make foil sling for 8-inch square baking pan by folding 2 long sheets of aluminum foil so each is 8 inches wide. Lay sheets of foil in pan perpendicular to each other, with extra foil hanging over edges of pan. Push foil into corners and up sides of pan, smoothing foil flush to pan. Grease foil.

2   Combine cherries and ½ cup Kirsch in microwave-safe bowl and microwave for 1 minute. Cover tightly with plastic wrap and set aside. In medium heatproof bowl set over a pan of almost-simmering water, melt semisweet chocolate, unsweetened chocolate, and butter, stirring occasionally, until mixture is smooth. Whisk in cocoa until smooth. Set aside to cool slightly.

3   Whisk together eggs, sugar, vanilla, and salt in medium bowl until combined. Whisk warm chocolate mixture into egg mixture, then stir in flour and cherries and their liquid with wooden spoon until just combined. Pour mixture into prepared pan, spread into corners, and level surface with rubber spatula. Bake until slightly puffed and toothpick inserted in center comes out with small amount of sticky crumbs clinging to it, 35 to 40 minutes.

4   Whisk jam and remaining ¼ cup Kirsch. Spread glaze evenly over warm brownies and let cool to room temperature on wire rack, about 2 hours. Using foil overhang, lift brownies out of pan and transfer to cutting board; discard foil. (Brownies can be made up to 5 days ahead and stored in airtight container at room temperature.) Dust brownies with confectioners' sugar and cut into 16 squares. Serve.

Morgan Bolling's

PORKADISE FOUND

SERVES 4 TO 6

» **THE SPIKED SWINE**

» **SALAMI GET THIS STRAIGHT SALAD**

» **PIGGY PEPPERS**

» **CRISPY, SPICY SWINEAPPLE RIBS**

» **STICKY SWEET SOW BARS**

Morgan Bolling

One of my lessons in culinary school was to butcher a whole hog and use as much of the animal as possible. The instructors weighed any pieces of the pig we didn't use and counted that weight as a deduction in our grade. So my classmates and I made stock with the bones, rendered the lard for fat, ground meat into sausages, and got creative in using that hog in as many delicious ways as we could. I assure you, I am not calling for you to start here with a whole pig (and there will be no grading). But I did have fun remembering that experience while building this menu that is an ode to all things pork. You'll use four different types here. If you want to push the limits, you can put out a charcuterie board with even more cured pork products. You can also fry the ribs in lard instead of vegetable oil. Have guests bring other dishes showcasing their own favorite type(s) of pork. I once made a homemade bacon-shaped piñata for a gathering and stuffed it with candy and slips of paper with pig puns. However you want to get your pig count up, what really matters is that you have fun while paying homage to this noble meat.

UP TO 1 WEEK AHEAD
› Make The Spiked Swine.

UP TO 3 DAYS AHEAD
› Make the Sticky Sweet Sow Bars.

UP TO 2 DAYS AHEAD
› Make the Piggy Peppers through step 2. Bring to room temperature before serving.

UP TO 1 DAY AHEAD
› Make the croutons for the Salami Get This Straight Salad.
› Braise the ribs and make the sauce for the Crispy, Spicy Swineapple Ribs and refrigerate separately.

STREAMLINE
› The more pork the better, as far as I'm concerned, but you'll still have plenty of food if you make either the Salami Get This Straight Salad or the Piggy Peppers rather than both.

THE SPIKED SWINE

Makes 6 cocktails

Total Time: 25 minutes, plus 2 hours chilling

WHY I LOVE THIS RECIPE There's something a little kitschy (in a fun way) about having bacon in a drink. This cocktail has a slight smokiness and a mild pork flavor from infusing bourbon with crumbled cooked bacon. A little maple syrup and some bitters balance the flavors, and half a strip of crispy bacon and a cocktail cherry dress it up in the glass.

5	slices thick-cut bacon, halved crosswise
12	ounces bourbon
8	ounces water
1½	tablespoons pure maple syrup
1	teaspoon old-fashioned aromatic bitters
	Cocktail cherries

1   Arrange bacon in single layer in 12-inch skillet and add just enough water to cover. Bring to simmer over medium heat and cook until water has completely evaporated, about 10 minutes. Reduce heat to medium-low and continue to cook until bacon is crispy and well browned, about 10 minutes. Transfer bacon to paper towel–lined plate. (Bacon can be refrigerated for up to 3 days.)

2   Crumble 4 pieces bacon into small bits. Stir crumbled bacon, bourbon, water, maple syrup, and bitters in serving pitcher or large container until maple syrup has dissolved. Cover and refrigerate until well chilled, at least 2 hours or up to 1 week.

3   Stir cocktail to recombine, then strain into chilled cocktail glasses. Garnish with remaining bacon pieces and cocktail cherries before serving.

MORGAN'S TIPS

› If you plan to refrigerate the cocktail for longer than 3 days, I recommend waiting to crisp up the 6 half-strips of bacon for the garnish until the day of serving.

› Experiment with using different bitters here, including orange bitters or maple bitters.

› If you want to lean into the saltiness of the bacon, you can add a salty-sweet rim to the cocktail glasses by combining ⅓ cup sugar and 2 teaspoons kosher salt. Spread into an even layer on a small saucer. Moisten about ½ inch of the glass rim by running an orange wedge around the outer edge. Roll the moistened rim in the sugar-salt mixture to coat.

SALAMI GET THIS STRAIGHT SALAD

Serves 4 to 6

Total Time: 30 minutes

WHY I LOVE THIS RECIPE Salads can be an afterthought at parties, but this salad is far, far above that bar. Between the garlicky dressing, tangy pickled cherry peppers, and aged provolone, this salad packs a ton of flavor. The crunchy, salty, spicy salami croutons lift it even higher.

SPICY SALAMI CROUTONS

2	tablespoons extra-virgin olive oil
4	ounces baguette, cut into 1-inch pieces (about 2 cups)
3	ounces link salami, cut into ½-inch pieces (about ¾ cup)
⅛	teaspoon table salt
⅛	teaspoon red pepper flakes

SALAD

2	tablespoons extra-virgin olive oil
1	tablespoon red wine vinegar
1	tablespoon mayonnaise
1	garlic clove, minced
¾	teaspoon table salt
½	teaspoon pepper
½	cup thinly sliced red onion
¼	cup thinly sliced pickled cherry peppers
1	head romaine lettuce (12 ounces), cored and torn into 2-inch pieces
2	ounces aged provolone cheese, shredded (½ cup)

1 FOR THE CROUTONS Heat oil in 12-inch nonstick skillet over medium heat until shimmering. Add baguette pieces, salami, and salt and cook, stirring occasionally, until bread is toasted and salami is rust-colored, about 10 minutes. Using slotted spoon, transfer croutons to paper towel–lined plate. Sprinkle with pepper flakes and let cool for 5 minutes. (Croutons can be stored in airtight container for up to 24 hours.)

2 FOR THE SALAD Whisk oil, vinegar, mayonnaise, garlic, salt, and pepper together in large bowl. Add onion and cherry peppers and let sit for 15 minutes.

3 Add romaine, provolone, and croutons to bowl with dressing and toss to combine. Season with salt and pepper to taste. Serve.

PIGGY PEPPERS

Serves 4 to 6

Total Time: 50 minutes

WHY I LOVE THIS RECIPE I love using charred bell peppers as a room-temperature salad base. They're meltingly tender and a touch bitter from the charring, and they play well with other textures. And there are lots of other textures here: chickpeas, shaved Parmesan, hazelnuts, golden raisins, and parsley. The pork component is capicola, which is similar to prosciutto but comes from the hog's neck or shoulder (rather than the hind quarters). Tossed with a smoked paprika and lemon vinaigrette, this salad feels like many flavors from an antipasti board happily fell together into a salad bowl.

5	tablespoons extra virgin olive oil, divided
1½	tablespoons lemon juice
1	teaspoon table salt, divided
½	teaspoon smoked paprika
⅛	teaspoon cayenne pepper
1	(15-ounce) can chickpeas, rinsed
3	red bell peppers, stemmed, seeded, and sliced ½ inch thick
4	ounces thinly sliced capicola, torn into bite-size pieces
1	ounce Parmesan cheese, shaved
¼	cup hazelnuts, toasted, skinned, and chopped
¼	cup golden raisins
¼	cup coarsely chopped fresh parsley

1 Whisk ¼ cup oil, lemon juice, ½ teaspoon salt, paprika, and cayenne together in large bowl. Add chickpeas and toss to combine.

2 Heat remaining 1 tablespoon oil in 12-inch nonstick skillet over medium-high heat until shimmering. Add peppers and remaining ½ teaspoon salt and cook, stirring once every 2 minutes, until tender and deep spotty brown, about 8 minutes. Transfer peppers to bowl with chickpeas and toss to combine. Let sit until flavors meld, about 30 minutes. (Chickpea-pepper mixture can be covered and refrigerated for up to 2 days; bring to room temperature before serving.)

3 Just before serving, add capicola, Parmesan, hazelnuts, raisins, and parsley to chickpea-pepper mixture and toss to combine. Season with salt and pepper to taste. Serve.

CRISPY, SPICY SWINEAPPLE RIBS

Serves 4 to 6

Total Time: 2¾ hours

WHY I LOVE THIS RECIPE For meltingly tender meat cloaked in a crispy crust, these ribs are oven-braised and then fried. The resulting texture is just so, so good. Yes, it takes some time, but you can braise them and make the sauce ahead so that all you have to do the day-of is fry them. They're finished with a sticky, glossy sauce made with pineapple juice, soy sauce, ginger, garlic, and jalapeños. Savory, sweet, and a touch sour—it's a party for your mouth.

MORGAN'S TIPS

> Use a fresh head of romaine for the Salami Get This Straight Salad rather than precut bagged lettuce.

> If you can't find aged provolone, use Parmesan or Pecorino.

> Play with the flavors in the Piggy Peppers by swapping in a different nut or dried fruit for the hazelnuts or raisins. And while capicola is awesome, any salty, boldly flavored cured meat will work.

2¾	cups pineapple juice, divided
2½	cups water
⅓	cup soy sauce
⅓	cup ketchup
¼	cup sugar
2	tablespoons fish sauce
2	(2-pound) racks baby back ribs, trimmed and halved crosswise
2	tablespoons vegetable oil
2	jalapeño chiles, stemmed and sliced into thin rings
2	garlic cloves, minced
1	teaspoon minced fresh ginger
½	cup plus 1½ tablespoons cornstarch, divided
½	cup all-purpose flour
½	teaspoon table salt
	Vegetable oil for frying
2	scallions, sliced thin

1   Adjust oven rack to lower-middle position and heat oven to 325 degrees. Whisk 2½ cups pineapple juice, water, soy sauce, ketchup, sugar, and fish sauce together in large Dutch oven. Nestle ribs into pot and spoon some of cooking liquid over top (ribs will not be fully submerged in cooking liquid). Bring sauce to boil over high heat. Cover, transfer pot to oven, and cook until ribs are tender and fork inserted into meat meets little resistance, 1½ to 2 hours, flipping and rotating ribs halfway through cooking.

2   Remove pot from oven. Transfer ribs to cutting board and let rest while preparing sauce. Measure out 2 cups cooking liquid; discard remaining liquid. Heat 2 tablespoons oil in large saucepan over medium-high heat until shimmering. Add jalapeños, garlic, and ginger and cook until fragrant, about 30 seconds. Stir in reserved cooking liquid, bring to boil, and cook until reduced by half, about 5 minutes.

3   Whisk 1½ tablespoons cornstarch and remaining ¼ cup pineapple juice together in small bowl, then stir mixture into sauce. Return to boil and cook, stirring occasionally, until thickened, about 2 minutes. Remove from heat and cover to keep warm. (Ribs and sauce can be refrigerated separately for up to 24 hours; return sauce to simmer before tossing with ribs in step 5.)

4   Combine flour, salt, and remaining ½ cup cornstarch in shallow dish. Cut ribs between bones into individual ribs. Set wire rack in rimmed baking sheet and line with triple layer of paper towels. Add oil to large clean Dutch oven until it measures about 1½ inches deep and heat over medium-high heat to 375 degrees. Toss 6 ribs in flour mixture, pat off excess, then add to hot oil. Fry until coating is crisp and golden brown, about 2 minutes. Adjust burner, if necessary, to maintain oil temperature between 350 and 375 degrees. Transfer ribs to prepared sheet. Return oil to 375 degrees and repeat with remaining ribs in 4 or 5 batches; transfer to sheet.

5   Toss ribs with sauce in large bowl until well coated. Transfer to serving platter and sprinkle with scallions. Serve.

MORGAN'S TIPS

› Use a Dutch oven that holds 6 quarts or more.

› If you want to up the count of pork products, you can use 2 pounds lard to fry the ribs instead of vegetable oil. While it does make the overall porky flavor a bit more robust, the sauce is so bold that it can be hard to tell.

STICKY SWEET SOW BARS

Makes 24 bars

Total Time: 1¼ hours, plus 2 hours cooling

WHY I LOVE THIS RECIPE   I love the buttery, brown sugar flavors of blondies. So for my porkadise dessert, I start there, adding chocolate chips to the batter. A gooey topping made from dulce de leche (a glossy, coffee-colored milk jam popular throughout Latin America), cashews, and crumbled crispy bacon makes these no ordinary blondies. Sprinkling the bars with flake salt enhances all the flavors. This makes a lot, yet they always seem to disappear.

2¼	cups (11¼ ounces) all-purpose flour
1¼	teaspoons table salt
½	teaspoon baking powder
10	tablespoons unsalted butter, melted
1¾	cups packed (12¼ ounces) light brown sugar
3	large eggs
½	cup corn syrup
2	tablespoons vanilla extract
½	cup (3 ounces) milk chocolate chips or chunks
6	slices bacon
5	ounces salted cashews, coarsely chopped
1	(13.4-ounce) can dulce de leche
1	tablespoon water
½	teaspoon flake sea salt (optional)

1   Adjust oven rack to middle position and heat oven to 350 degrees. Make foil sling for 13 by 9-inch baking pan by folding 2 long sheets of aluminum foil; first sheet should be 13 inches wide and second sheet should be 9 inches wide. Lay sheets of foil in pan perpendicular to each other, with extra foil hanging over edges of pan. Push foil into corners and up sides of pan, smoothing foil flush to pan. Lightly spray foil with vegetable oil spray.

2   Whisk flour, table salt, and baking powder in medium bowl. Whisk butter and sugar in large bowl until combined. Add eggs, corn syrup, and vanilla and whisk until smooth.

3   Using rubber spatula, stir flour mixture into egg mixture until fully incorporated. Stir in chocolate chips. Transfer batter to prepared pan. Using spatula, spread batter into corners of pan and smooth surface. Bake until top is deep golden brown and springs backs when lightly pressed, 35 to 40 minutes, rotating pan halfway through baking. Let cool on wire rack while preparing topping.

4   Arrange bacon in single layer in 12-inch skillet and add just enough water to cover. Bring to simmer over medium heat and cook until water has completely evaporated, about 5 minutes. Reduce heat to medium-low and continue to cook until bacon is crispy and well browned, about 5 minutes. Transfer bacon to paper towel–lined plate and let cool slightly. Coarsely chop bacon.

5   Combine bacon, cashews, dulce de leche, and water in large bowl and microwave until hot and dulce de leche has loosened, about 2 minutes, stirring frequently with rubber spatula. Pour evenly over bars and spread to edges of pan. Sprinkle with sea salt, if using, and let sit until fully cooled, about 2 hours.

6   Using foil overhang, lift bars out of pan and transfer to cutting board. Discard foil (use paring knife to separate foil from bars, if necessary). Cut into 24 squares and serve. (Bars can be stored in airtight container for up to 3 days.)

MORGAN'S TIPS

> I like milk chocolate chips in these bars, but feel free to use semisweet or bittersweet chocolate.

> To avoid overbaking, use a metal baking pan rather than a glass baking dish.

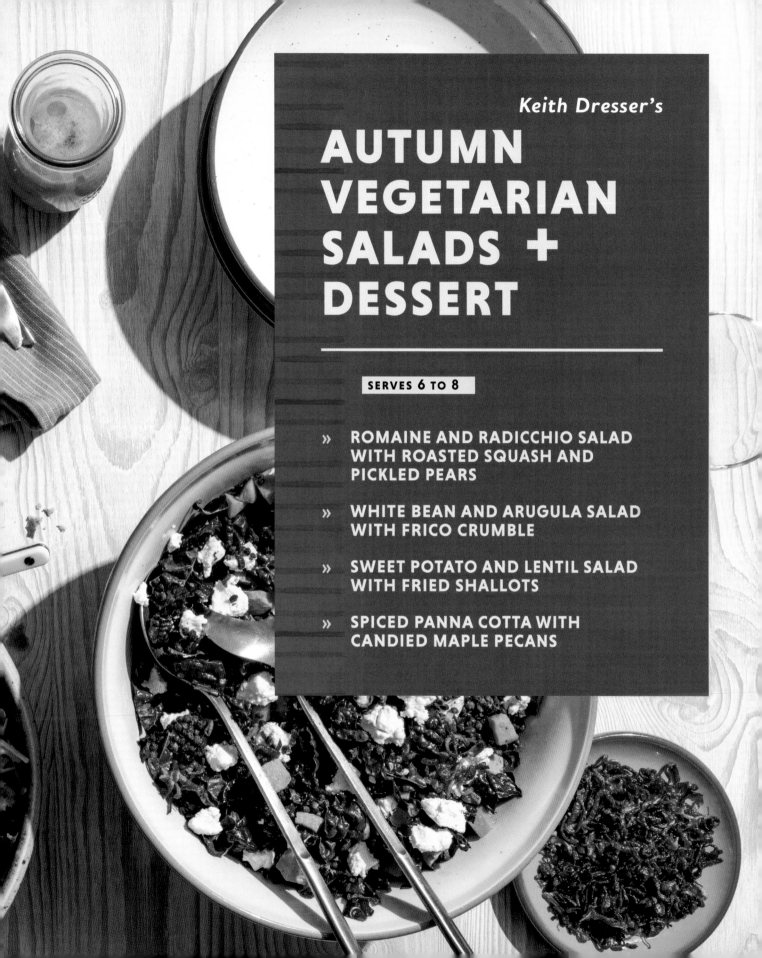

Keith Dresser's

AUTUMN VEGETARIAN SALADS + DESSERT

SERVES 6 TO 8

» **ROMAINE AND RADICCHIO SALAD WITH ROASTED SQUASH AND PICKLED PEARS**

» **WHITE BEAN AND ARUGULA SALAD WITH FRICO CRUMBLE**

» **SWEET POTATO AND LENTIL SALAD WITH FRIED SHALLOTS**

» **SPICED PANNA COTTA WITH CANDIED MAPLE PECANS**

Keith Dresser

Having spent many years working in restaurant kitchens, I used to approach dinner parties like I was still working in the hospitality business. After countless hours creating elegant multiple-course meals with intricate platings, it dawned on me that I was spending more time in the kitchen than I was with my guests. My approach now is almost the opposite, and I've embraced the informal family-style dinner party where most of the components can be made ahead of time and assembled with minimal effort. Now I can enjoy the dinner too. For this menu, I've focused on three hearty vegetarian salads, designed to be served at room temperature, that incorporate popular autumn produce along with contrasting flavors and textures. I finish things off with a favorite make-ahead dessert, also perfectly tailored for fall with warm spices and maple-glazed nuts.

MY GAME PLAN

UP TO 5 DAYS AHEAD

› Make the candied pecans for the Spiced Panna Cotta with Candied Maple Pecans.

› Make the frico for the White Bean and Arugula Salad with Frico Crumble.

UP TO 3 DAYS AHEAD

› Fry the shallots and make the dressing for the Sweet Potato and Lentil Salad with Fried Shallots.

› Make the panna cotta. (If you choose not to make it ahead, note that it must be made at least 6 hours in advance so that it sets properly.)

UP TO 2 DAYS AHEAD

› Pickle the pears, make the dressing, and toast the pepitas for the Romaine and Radicchio Salad with Roasted Squash and Pickled Pears.

UP TO 1 DAY AHEAD

› Roast the squash for the romaine and radicchio salad. Bring to room temperature before adding to salad.

› Roast the sweet potatoes and cook the lentils for the sweet potato and lentil salad. Bring to room temperature before adding to salad.

UP TO SEVERAL HOURS AHEAD

› Wash and dry all the greens for the salads and refrigerate, covered with a damp cloth.

› Make the beans and shallots for the white bean and arugula salad.

ROMAINE AND RADICCHIO SALAD WITH ROASTED SQUASH AND PICKLED PEARS

Serves 6 to 8

Total Time: 1¼ hours

WHY I LOVE THIS RECIPE   This salad boasts a great range of textures and flavors. Green leaf lettuce offers a sturdy base to support the hearty add-ins, with slightly bitter radicchio as a colorful partner. Quick pickled pears lend the salad a delicate crispness, while tender chunks of roasted butternut squash give it substance. A final sprinkle of pepitas adds crunchy richness and a fall flair.

PICKLED PEARS

2	Bosc pears, peeled, halved, cored, and sliced thin crosswise
¾	cup cider vinegar
¾	cup water
2	tablespoons sugar
1½	teaspoons table salt
1	star anise pod

DRESSING

1½	tablespoons white wine vinegar
1	tablespoon very finely minced shallot
¾	teaspoon mayonnaise
¾	teaspoon Dijon mustard
¼	teaspoon table salt
5½	tablespoons extra-virgin olive oil

SALAD

1½	pounds butternut squash, peeled, seeded, and cut into ½-inch pieces (5 cups)
2	tablespoons extra-virgin olive oil
½	teaspoon table salt
¼	teaspoon pepper
1	head green leaf lettuce (12 ounces), torn into bite-size pieces (8 cups)
½	head radicchio (5 ounces), torn into bite-size pieces (2 cups)
⅓	cup raw pepitas, toasted, divided

1   **FOR THE PEARS**   Place pears in medium bowl. Bring vinegar, water, sugar, salt, and star anise to boil in medium saucepan. Pour vinegar mixture over pears and let sit until room temperature, about 30 minutes. Cover and refrigerate until chilled, at least 1 hour or up to 2 days.

2   **FOR THE DRESSING**   Combine vinegar, shallot, mayonnaise, mustard, and salt in medium bowl and season with pepper to taste. Whisk until mixture is milky in appearance and no lumps of mayonnaise remain. Whisking constantly, very slowly drizzle oil into vinegar mixture until glossy and lightly thickened, with no pools of oil visible. (Dressing can be refrigerated for up to 2 days; whisk to recombine before serving.)

3   **FOR THE SALAD**   Adjust oven rack to lowest position and heat oven to 450 degrees. Toss squash with oil, salt, and pepper. Spread squash on rimmed baking sheet and roast until well browned and tender, 20 to 25 minutes, stirring halfway through roasting. Let cool slightly, about 5 minutes. (Squash can be roasted up to 1 day ahead. Bring to room temperature before using.)

4   Gently toss lettuce, radicchio, squash, drained pickled pears, and half of pepitas together in large bowl. Drizzle with dressing and toss until greens are evenly coated. Season with salt to taste. Transfer to serving platter and sprinkle with remaining pepitas. Serve immediately.

KEITH'S TIPS

> Feel free to vary the greens. For the best flavor, I recommend a ratio of 4 parts mild green (such as romaine or Bibb) to 1 part assertive green (think frisée or watercress). Mature lettuces offer a sturdier base for add-ins than baby lettuces do.

> I like the firm texture and spicy flavor of Bosc pears, but you can use other varieties.

WHITE BEAN AND ARUGULA SALAD WITH FRICO CRUMBLE

Serves 6 to 8

Total Time: 1½ hours

WHY I LOVE THIS RECIPE Canned beans make for an easy and customizable salad base, but without some embellishments they can taste, well, canned. To rectify this, I steep them in a garlic- and sage-infused broth. Spicy arugula and pickled shallots add texture and pleasingly sharp flavor to the creamy beans. But my favorite part of the salad is the frico. The crispy shards of fried cheese add a ton of savory flavor. I usually make a double batch because I end up snacking on most of it before I get a chance to top the salad.

FRICO CRUMBLE

- 2 ounces Manchego cheese, grated fine (1 cup)
- 2 ounces Parmesan cheese, grated fine (1 cup)

SALAD

- 5 tablespoons extra-virgin olive oil, divided
- 4 garlic cloves, peeled and smashed
- 1 sprig fresh sage, plus 2 tablespoons minced
  Table salt for steeping beans
- 3 (15-ounce) cans cannellini beans, rinsed and drained
- ¼ cup red wine vinegar
- 2 shallots, sliced thin (¾ cup)
- 3 ounces (3 cups) baby arugula

1 FOR THE FRICO Combine Manchego and Parmesan in bowl. Sprinkle half of cheese mixture evenly over bottom of cold 10-inch nonstick skillet. Cook over medium heat until edges are lacy and light golden, 2 to 3 minutes. Remove skillet from heat and let sit for 1 minute. Using 2 spatulas, carefully flip frico. Return to medium heat and cook until second side is deep golden brown, about 1 minute. Carefully slide frico onto plate. Wipe skillet clean with paper towels and repeat with remaining cheese. Let frico cool completely, then crumble into bite-size pieces. (Frico can be stored in airtight container at room temperature for up to 5 days.)

2 FOR THE SALAD Heat 1 tablespoon oil, garlic, and sage sprig in medium saucepan over medium-high heat until garlic is just beginning to brown, 2 to 3 minutes. Add 2 cups water and 1 teaspoon salt and bring to simmer. Off heat, add beans, cover, and let sit for 20 minutes. Combine vinegar and shallots in large bowl and let sit for 20 minutes.

3 Drain beans and discard garlic and sage sprig. Add beans to shallot mixture and toss until thoroughly combined. Season with salt and pepper to taste. Let sit for at least 20 minutes or up to 6 hours.

4 Add arugula, minced sage, and remaining ¼ cup oil to beans and toss to combine. Transfer to serving platter and top with frico. Serve.

KEITH'S TIPS

› I like to make the frico using equal parts tangy Manchego and nutty Parmesan, but feel free to use just one or the other. Or try an aged Asiago or Gouda.

› This salad works best with large, meaty white beans, such as cannellini, Great Northern, or butter beans, but small white beans work too.

SWEET POTATO AND LENTIL SALAD WITH FRIED SHALLOTS

Serves 6 to 8

Total Time: 1¼ hours, plus 1 hour soaking

WHY I LOVE THIS RECIPE Small black lentils have a slightly spicy earthiness that pairs well with fall flavors. A quick brine in warm salt water helps to season them and soften their skins, leading to very few blowouts when cooking. Creamy chunks of roasted sweet potatoes and substantial bites of Tuscan kale complement the lentils. Fried shallots do double duty: The crispy pieces are the perfect topping, while the oil used to fry the shallots is incorporated into the dressing, adding a subtle sweetness to the entire salad.

	Table salt for soaking lentils
1½	cups black lentils, picked over and rinsed
1½	pounds sweet potatoes, peeled and cut into ½-inch pieces (5 cups)
½	cup plus 2 tablespoons vegetable oil, divided
¾	teaspoon table salt, divided
¼	teaspoon pepper
3	shallots, sliced thin
2	tablespoons sherry vinegar
1	teaspoon mayonnaise
1	teaspoon Dijon mustard
8	ounces Tuscan kale, stemmed and sliced into ¼-inch strips (4½ cups)
4	ounces goat cheese, crumbled

1 Dissolve 1½ teaspoons salt in 4 cups warm water in bowl. Add lentils; soak at room temperature for 1 hour. Drain well.

2 Meanwhile, adjust oven rack to lower-middle position and heat oven to 400 degrees. Toss sweet potatoes with 2 tablespoons oil, ½ teaspoon salt, and pepper. Spread sweet potatoes on rimmed baking sheet and roast until well browned and tender, 20 to 25 minutes, stirring halfway through roasting. Let cool slightly, about 5 minutes. (Sweet potatoes can be roasted up to 1 day ahead. Bring to room temperature before using.)

3 Combine shallots and remaining ½ cup oil in medium bowl. Microwave for 5 minutes. Stir and continue to microwave 2 minutes longer. Repeat stirring and microwaving in 2-minute increments until beginning to brown (4 to 6 minutes). Repeat stirring and microwaving in 30-second increments until deep golden brown (30 seconds to 2 minutes). Using slotted spoon, transfer shallots to paper towel–lined plate; season with salt to taste. Let drain and crisp, about 5 minutes. Set oil aside to cool completely for dressing. (Shallots and shallot oil can be stored separately in airtight containers at room temperature for up to 3 days.)

4 Drain lentils well. Bring lentils and 6 cups water to boil in medium saucepan over high heat. Reduce heat and simmer gently until lentils are just tender, 20 to 25 minutes. Drain.

5 Combine vinegar, mayonnaise, mustard, and remaining ¼ teaspoon salt in large bowl and season with pepper to taste. Whisk until mixture is milky in appearance and no lumps of mayonnaise remain. Whisking constantly, very slowly drizzle reserved shallot oil into vinegar mixture until glossy and lightly thickened, with no pools of oil visible. (Dressing can be refrigerated for up to 3 days; whisk to recombine before serving.)

6 Add kale, sweet potatoes, and lentils to dressing and toss to combine. Season with salt and pepper to taste. Transfer to serving platter and sprinkle with goat cheese and fried shallots. Serve.

KEITH'S TIP

› Salt-soaking helps keep the lentils intact, but if you don't have time, they'll still taste great.

SPICED PANNA COTTA WITH CANDIED MAPLE PECANS

Serves 8

Total Time: 1¼ hours, plus 6 hours chilling

WHY I LOVE THIS RECIPE Panna cotta is a go-to entertaining dessert for me. It can be made well in advance, and it's easy to customize the flavor to go with the rest of the menu. For this version, I use sweet, warm spices—cinnamon, cloves, and ginger—to complement the tangy buttermilk base. To add some contrasting texture and reinforce the fall vibes, I sprinkle the panna cotta with some easy maple-glazed pecans.

PANNA COTTA

½	cup (3½ ounces) sugar
2	teaspoons unflavored gelatin
	Pinch table salt
2	cups heavy cream
2	cloves
1	cinnamon stick
¼	teaspoon ground ginger
2	cups buttermilk

CANDIED MAPLE PECANS

¾	cup pecan halves
2	tablespoons pure maple syrup, plus extra for serving
1	teaspoon vegetable oil
⅛	teaspoon table salt

KEITH'S TIPS

> Make sure to unmold the panna cotta onto chilled plates. And if you'd rather not fuss with unmolding, use 5- to 6-ounce glasses instead of the ramekins and serve in the glasses.

> Because this contains gelatin, the panna cotta is not vegetarian. There are vegetarian substitutes for gelatin, but they require different treatment than gelatin, and the effectiveness of different brands varies. If using a vegetarian gelatin, I suggest making a test batch of the panna cotta in advance of your party.

1 **FOR THE PANNA COTTA** Whisk sugar, gelatin, and salt in small saucepan until very well combined. Whisk in cream and let sit for 5 minutes. Add cloves, cinnamon, and ginger and cook over medium heat, stirring occasionally, until mixture registers 150 to 160 degrees, about 5 minutes. Remove from heat and let mixture cool to 105 to 110 degrees, about 15 minutes. Strain cream mixture through fine-mesh strainer into medium bowl. Gently whisk in buttermilk.

2 Set eight 5-ounce ramekins on rimmed baking sheet. Divide buttermilk mixture evenly among ramekins. Invert second rimmed baking sheet on top of ramekins and carefully transfer to refrigerator. Chill for at least 6 hours or up to 3 days. (If chilling for more than 6 hours, cover each ramekin with plastic wrap instead of a baking sheet.)

3 **FOR THE PECANS** Adjust oven rack to middle position and heat oven to 350 degrees. Spread pecans in single layer on rimmed baking sheet and toast until fragrant and slightly darkened, 8 to 12 minutes, shaking sheet halfway through toasting. While nuts toast, combine maple syrup, oil, and salt in medium bowl. Transfer nuts to bowl with maple syrup mixture and toss to combine. Do not wash sheet.

4 Line now-empty sheet with parchment paper. Spread nuts on prepared sheet in single layer and bake until nuts are crisp and dry, 9 to 11 minutes, stirring every 3 minutes. Transfer sheet to wire rack and let nuts cool completely, about 20 minutes. Transfer nuts to cutting board and coarsely chop. (Nuts can be stored in airtight container at room temperature for up to 5 days.)

5 Working with 1 panna cotta at a time, insert paring knife between panna cotta and side of ramekin. Gently run knife around edge of ramekin to loosen panna cotta. Cover ramekin with chilled serving plate and invert panna cotta onto plate. (You may need to gently jiggle ramekin.) Drizzle each panna cotta with extra maple syrup, sprinkle with pecans, and serve.

Erin McMurrer's

VEGETARIAN LUNCHEON

SERVES 4 TO 6

» PEAR-MINT SPARKLING ICED GREEN TEA

» RED LEAF AND WATERCRESS SALAD WITH FENNEL, APPLE, PARMESAN, AND HAZELNUTS

» CELERY ROOT GALETTE WITH BLUE CHEESE AND WALNUTS

» GINGERED PEAR AND CRANBERRY COBBLER

Erin McMurrer

I designed this gathering to showcase my love for fall and winter produce, along with nuts and cheeses, in dishes that let each ingredient really shine. These combinations represent similar dishes and techniques I learned early in my career when I trained at Hamersley's Bistro in Boston. I was fortunate to have worked under chef Gordon Hamersley and to have learned from him the importance of treating each ingredient with respect, preparing in-season ingredients at their peak, pairing ingredients and dishes that balance and complement each other, and keeping things simple so flavors and nuances come through clearly. These lessons also come into play here at ATK when we develop new recipes. While I love to serve this menu for a luncheon gathering, it's also hearty enough to make a wonderful dinner. It truly reflects how I like to eat to this day.

MY GAME PLAN

UP TO 3 DAYS AHEAD
〉 Prepare the green tea infusion for the Pear-Mint Sparking Iced Green Tea.

UP TO 2 DAYS AHEAD
〉 Make the dough for the Celery Root Galette with Blue Cheese and Walnuts. (Alternatively, you can make it up to 1 month ahead and freeze it; transfer it to the refrigerator 2 days before using.)
〉 Roast the celery root for the galette.

UP TO 1 DAY AHEAD
〉 Make the vinaigrette for the Red Leaf and Watercress Salad with Fennel, Apple, Parmesan, and Hazelnuts.
〉 Prep the greens, fennel, and nuts for the salad.
〉 Combine the dry topping ingredients for the Gingered Pear and Cranberry Cobbler.
〉 If using frozen cranberries for the cobbler, transfer them to the refrigerator to thaw.

UP TO A COUPLE OF HOURS AHEAD
〉 Bake the galette ahead and serve it at room temperature, if you like.
〉 Prepare the filling for the cobbler.

PEAR-MINT SPARKLING ICED GREEN TEA

Makes 6 drinks

Total Time: 15 minutes, plus 1 hour steeping and
1 hour chilling

WHY I LOVE THIS RECIPE Iced tea is one of my favorite summer beverages, but it can be inconsistent at best depending on who prepares it, the quality of the tea, and the brewing method used. Since my colleague Lan Lam took a deep dive and created a road map for how to make the best iced tea, I have been hooked. Lan's recipe uses loose-leaf tea and a hybrid hot-cold brewing method. Following both of these key steps guarantees complex flavor and distinctive aromas. Here's my spin, with the bonus addition of effervescence. I steep the tea, pear, and mint and strain the mixture, then add sparkling water just before serving.

GREEN TEA INFUSION

- 2 ripe but firm Bosc or Bartlett pears, halved, cored, peeled
- 2 tablespoons loose-leaf green tea
- 2 cups hot water (175 degrees)
- 1 cup ice water
- 3 tablespoons chopped fresh mint, plus mint sprigs for serving
- 1–2 tablespoons sugar
- 1 tablespoon lemon juice

TO SERVE

- 1 cup sparkling water, chilled

1 FOR THE INFUSION Shred pears on large holes of box grater to yield 1 cup pulp; set aside. Place tea in medium bowl. Add hot water and steep for 4 minutes. Stir in grated pear, ice water, chopped mint, sugar, and lemon juice until sugar has dissolved. Let steep for 1 hour. Strain infusion through fine-mesh strainer into pitcher (or strain into second bowl and transfer to pitcher). Refrigerate for at least 1 hour or up to 3 days.

2 To serve, add sparkling water to green tea infusion. Pour into ice-filled glasses and garnish with mint sprigs.

ERIN'S TIPS

> Buy the pears a week in advance to be sure they ripen fully; if they are ripe before you make the concentrate, just pop them into the refrigerator for up to 5 days.

> Chinese green tea will produce a grassy, floral tea, whereas Japanese green tea is more savory. Whatever you choose, use loose-leaf tea, not tea bags.

> To ensure that your water is at the proper temperature, start with 1½ cups boiling water; add cold water, a little at a time, and stir with an instant-read thermometer until the water registers 175 degrees; then measure out 2 cups.

> Your ice water should be half ice and half water.

> If you like, you can leave out the pear and mint for a simpler sparkling iced green tea.

RED LEAF AND WATERCRESS SALAD WITH FENNEL, APPLE, PARMESAN, AND HAZELNUTS

Serves 4 to 6

Total Time: 25 minutes

WHY I LOVE THIS RECIPE A dish that appears to be the easiest to make—like a salad—often is the most likely to go wrong unless you take time to understand how best to approach it. This was one of the first lessons I learned at Hamersley's Bistro. Gordon took great pride in the salads we served, putting much thought and care into the flavors and textures. He kept a sharp eye on each salad that left the kitchen and didn't hesitate to have us start over. Once you understand the fundamentals, the sky's the limit with the number of winning combinations you can put together. I love how balanced this salad is with its vegetal, fruity, and nutty flavors and crisp, crunchy, soft textures.

VINAIGRETTE

- 1 tablespoon champagne or white wine vinegar
- 1½ teaspoons minced shallot
- ½ teaspoon mayonnaise
- ½ teaspoon Dijon mustard
- ⅛ teaspoon table salt
- 3 tablespoons extra-virgin olive oil

SALAD

- 1 small head red leaf lettuce (8 ounces), torn into bite-sized pieces
- 3 ounces (3 cups) watercress, torn into bite-size pieces
- 1 Honeycrisp apple, cored, halved, and sliced very thin
- 1 small fennel bulb, ¼ cup fronds chopped coarse, stalks discarded, bulb halved, cored, and sliced very thin
- ½ cup fresh parsley leaves
- 1½ ounces Parmesan cheese, shaved, divided
- ¼ cup coarsely chopped toasted and skinned hazelnuts, divided

1 **FOR THE VINAIGRETTE** Whisk vinegar, shallot, mayonnaise, mustard, and salt in medium bowl until mixture is milky in appearance and no lumps of mayonnaise remain. Whisking constantly, very slowly drizzle oil into vinegar mixture until glossy and lightly thickened, with no pools of oil visible. If pools of oil are visible on surface as you whisk, stop addition of oil and whisk until mixture is well combined, then resume whisking in oil in slow stream. Vinaigrette should be glossy and lightly thickened, with no pools of oil on surface. Season with pepper to taste. (Vinaigrette can be refrigerated for up to 1 day; bring to room temperature and whisk to recombine before serving.)

2 **FOR THE SALAD** Place lettuce, watercress, apple, fennel fronds, sliced fennel, parsley, half of Parmesan, and 2 tablespoons hazelnuts in large bowl and toss to combine. Drizzle with vinaigrette and toss until greens are evenly coated. Season with salt and pepper to taste. Sprinkle with remaining Parmesan and remaining 2 tablespoons hazelnuts. Serve immediately.

ERIN'S TIPS

> Using a head lettuce (which provides bulk and has a relatively mild flavor) plus an accent lettuce (spicy, bitter, crunchy, or frilly) makes the salad pop.

> I'm usually more heavy handed with neutral herbs such as parsley and then add more modest amounts of stronger herbs (chives, tarragon, mint, etc.).

> Including a variety of fruits (fresh or dried) and vegetables (raw or cooked), cheeses, and nuts is a quick and creative way to add interest and a wide range of flavors and textures. Be sure to thinly slice fruits and vegetables so that they mix evenly with the greens (a mandoline is great for this).

> I'm a strong believer in properly emulsified vinaigrettes because it ensures that the dressing will cling to the salad and that you will have balanced flavor in every bite.

CELERY ROOT GALETTE WITH BLUE CHEESE AND WALNUTS

Serves 4 to 6

Total Time: 2 hours, plus 1½ hours chilling

WHY I LOVE THIS RECIPE My former colleague Andrew Janjigian developed a masterpiece of a whole-wheat galette crust years ago, and it is my perennial favorite. Its rustic nature brings me back to my Hamersley's Bistro days, when we created savory, seasonal galettes. For an earthy twist, I include ground nuts. A tangy glaze and a citrusy gremolata add a bright flourish to this galette.

DOUGH

1	cup (5 ounces) all-purpose flour
½	cup (2¾ ounces) whole-wheat or rye flour
½	cup chopped walnuts
1	tablespoon sugar
¾	teaspoon table salt
10	tablespoons unsalted butter, cut into ½-inch pieces and chilled
7	tablespoons ice water
1	teaspoon distilled white vinegar

FILLING

3	tablespoons plus 1 teaspoon extra-virgin olive oil, divided
1½	pounds celery root, peeled and cut into ¾-inch pieces
1	teaspoon kosher salt, divided
⅛	teaspoon pepper
6	ounces (6 cups) baby spinach
1½	pounds leeks, white and light green parts only, sliced ½ inch thick and washed thoroughly (4½ cups)
3	sprigs fresh thyme, plus ½ teaspoon minced
2	tablespoons crème fraîche
1	tablespoon Dijon mustard
3	tablespoons orange juice
2	tablespoons honey
2	teaspoons distilled white vinegar
3	ounces blue cheese, crumbled (¾ cup), divided
1	large egg, lightly beaten

GREMOLATA

2	tablespoons minced fresh parsley
1	teaspoon grated orange zest
1	garlic clove, minced

1 FOR THE DOUGH Pulse all-purpose flour, whole-wheat flour, walnuts, sugar, and salt in food processor until walnuts are finely ground, 8 to 10 pulses. Add butter and pulse until butter is cut into pea-size pieces, about 10 pulses. Transfer mixture to medium bowl and sprinkle with water and vinegar. Using rubber spatula, fold mixture until loose, shaggy mass forms with some dry flour remaining (do not overwork). Transfer mixture to center of large sheet of plastic wrap, press gently into rough 4-inch square, and wrap tightly. Refrigerate for 45 minutes.

2 Transfer dough to lightly floured counter. Roll into 11 by 8-inch rectangle with short side parallel to counter edge. Starting at bottom of dough, fold into thirds like business letter into 8 by 4-inch rectangle. Turn dough 90 degrees counterclockwise. Roll out lengthwise again into 11 by 8-inch rectangle and fold into thirds. Turn dough 90 degrees counterclockwise and repeat rolling and folding dough into thirds, then fold dough in half to create 4-inch square. Press top of dough gently to seal. Wrap tightly in plastic wrap and refrigerate for at least 45 minutes or up to 2 days (or freeze for up to 1 month).

3 FOR THE FILLING Adjust oven rack to lower-middle position, place baking stone on rack, and heat oven to 425 degrees. Heat 1 tablespoon oil in 12-inch skillet over medium heat until shimmering. Add celery root, ½ teaspoon salt, and pepper and cook, stirring occasionally, until softened and lightly browned, 5 to 7 minutes. Place skillet on baking stone and roast until deep golden brown and tender, 8 to 16 minutes, stirring halfway through roasting. Being careful of hot skillet handle, transfer celery root to plate; set aside. (Celery root can be refrigerated for up to 2 days.) Wipe skillet clean with paper towels.

4 Meanwhile, place spinach and ¼ cup water in large microwave-safe bowl. Cover bowl with large dinner plate (plate should completely cover bowl and not rest on spinach). Microwave on high until spinach is wilted and decreased in volume by half, 3 to 4 minutes. Using potholders, remove bowl from microwave and keep covered for 1 minute. Carefully remove plate and transfer spinach to colander set in sink. Using back of rubber spatula, gently press spinach against colander to release excess liquid. Transfer spinach to cutting board and chop. Return spinach to colander and press again with rubber spatula.

5   Heat 1 tablespoon oil in now-empty skillet over medium heat until shimmering. Add leeks and minced thyme; cover; and cook, stirring occasionally, until leeks are tender and beginning to brown, 5 to 7 minutes. Transfer leek mixture to medium bowl, add spinach, crème fraîche, and mustard and gently stir to combine. Season with salt and pepper to taste; set aside. Wipe skillet clean with paper towels.

6   Bring 3 tablespoons water, orange juice, honey, vinegar, and thyme sprigs to simmer in again-empty skillet over medium-high heat. Cook, stirring constantly, until reduced to syrup consistency, about 2 minutes. Off heat, discard thyme springs. Add celery root to skillet and toss gently to coat with glaze.

7   Remove dough from refrigerator and let sit at room temperature for 15 minutes. Roll dough into 14-inch circle on generously floured counter. Trim edges as needed to form uniform circle. Transfer dough to parchment paper–lined rimmed baking sheet (dough will hang over edges of sheet). With plastic drinking straw or tip of paring knife, cut five ¼-inch circles in dough (one at center, and four evenly spaced midway from center to edge of dough). Brush top of dough with 2 teaspoons oil.

8   Spread half of leek and spinach filling evenly over dough, leaving 2-inch border around edge. Sprinkle with 6 tablespoons blue cheese and top with remaining leek and spinach filling. Evenly distribute celery root over filling. Sprinkle with remaining 6 tablespoons blue cheese and drizzle with remaining 2 teaspoons oil. Carefully grasp one edge of dough and fold up outer 2 inches over filling. Repeat around circumference of tart, overlapping dough every 2 to 3 inches; gently pinch pleated dough to secure, but do not press dough into filling. Brush dough with egg and sprinkle with remaining ½ teaspoon salt.

9   Reduce oven temperature to 375 degrees. Place sheet on baking stone and bake galette until crust is deep golden brown and filling is beginning to brown, 35 to 45 minutes. Transfer galette, still on sheet, to wire rack and let cool for 10 minutes.

10   **FOR THE GREMOLATA** Combine all ingredients in bowl. Using wide metal spatula, loosen galette from parchment and carefully slide it off parchment onto cutting board. Sprinkle with gremolata, cut into wedges, and serve.

ERIN'S TIPS

› I like to serve the tart warm, but it's also wonderful at room temperature.

› If you only have plastic wrap that is 12 inches wide, it can be cumbersome to gather the voluminous shaggy dough mass. I crisscross two sheets of plastic over a medium bowl, then push down to line the bowl, making sure that both pieces lay flat. I then transfer the contents from the mixing bowl and gather the ends of the plastic while pressing down and compacting the mixture. I twist tightly, remove the bundle, and press the dough into a 4-inch square.

› It can be easy to lose track of how many times you roll and fold the dough in step 2. I create a small strip of flour at the top of my cutting board and each time I complete a roll and fold, I make a swipe through the flour.

GINGERED PEAR AND CRANBERRY COBBLER

Serves 8

Total Time: 1¼ hours

WHY I LOVE THIS RECIPE One of the first recipes that
I developed when I started at ATK 20 years ago was a
blueberry cobbler. It remains a favorite of mine because
it is a humble dessert where the blueberries play the starring
role along with the tender, rustic, lightly crisped drop biscuit
topping. Building from that foundation, I created this version
starring the classic fall combination of pears and cranberries, jazzed up with ginger, lime, and baking spices. Sliced
almonds make the biscuit crust even crisper and more
flavorful. I love serving this warm with a scoop of vanilla or
ginger ice cream on top. The temperature contrast brings
the dessert over the top.

FILLING

- 6 ounces (1½ cups) fresh or thawed frozen cranberries
- 6 tablespoons sugar
- 1 teaspoon grated fresh ginger
- 1 teaspoon cornstarch
- ¼ teaspoon ground cardamom
- ¼ teaspoon ground cinnamon
- ½ teaspoon grated lime zest plus 2 teaspoons juice
  Pinch table salt
- 1½ pounds ripe but firm Bartlett pears, peeled, halved, and cored
- 1½ pounds ripe but firm Bosc pears, peeled, halved, and cored

BISCUIT TOPPING

- 1 cup (5 ounces) all-purpose flour
- 2 tablespoons stone-ground cornmeal
- ¼ cup (1¾ ounces) plus 2 teaspoons sugar, divided
- 2 teaspoons baking powder
- ¼ teaspoon baking soda
- ¼ teaspoon table salt
- ⅓ cup buttermilk
- 4 tablespoons unsalted butter, melted
- ½ teaspoon vanilla extract
- 2 tablespoons sliced almonds

1 **FOR THE FILLING** Adjust oven rack to lower-middle position and heat oven to 375 degrees. Pulse cranberries, sugar, ginger, cornstarch, cardamom, cinnamon, lime zest and juice, and salt in food processor until cranberries are coarsely chopped, about 5 pulses; transfer to large bowl. Cut each pear half into 4 wedges, then cut each wedge in half crosswise (pieces should be about 1½ inches). Transfer to bowl with cranberry mixture and toss gently to combine. Transfer mixture to 9-inch square baking dish and bake until filling is hot and starting to bubble around edges, 15 to 25 minutes.

2 **FOR THE TOPPING** Meanwhile, whisk flour, cornmeal, ¼ cup sugar, baking powder, baking soda, and salt together in large bowl. Whisk buttermilk, melted butter, and vanilla together in small bowl. Just before filling is cooked, add buttermilk mixture to flour mixture and stir with rubber spatula until just combined and no dry pockets remain.

3 Remove filling from oven and increase oven temperature to 425 degrees. Pat topping mixture into circle and score into 8 pie wedges. Shape each wedge into a rough round and place on top of filling, spacing them at least ½ inch apart. Sprinkle each piece with almonds and remaining 2 teaspoons sugar. Return dish to oven and bake until filling is bubbling and biscuits are golden brown on top and toothpick inserted into center comes out clean, 15 to 18 minutes. Let cobbler cool on wire rack for 20 minutes before serving.

ERIN'S TIPS

> Instead of the 9-inch square baking dish, you can use an 8-inch square baking dish or a 9-inch pie pan.

> The filling can be prepared and transferred to the baking dish a couple of hours before baking, but the biscuit topping should be mixed just prior to baking to ensure that it rises properly.

> Since heat causes the pectin in pears to break down, it's important to cook with pears that are firm but not rock-hard. When you press the neck, it should give only slightly and feel a bit softer than a russet potato—the meaning of "firm but ripe."

> Using a combination of Bartlett and Bosc pears adds more complexity in both flavor and texture.

> You will have leftovers—which is a good thing. You can reheat the cobbler in a 350 degree oven for 10 to 15 minutes.

Steve Dunn's

DOUBLE-DATE NIGHT

SERVES 4

» **BIJOU COCKTAILS**

» **SMOKED SALMON CRISPS**

» **SAUTÉED CHILEAN SEA BASS WITH CREAMY COCONUT RICE AND BABY BOK CHOY**

» **RASPBERRY NAPOLEONS WITH BITTERSWEET CHOCOLATE SAUCE**

Steve Dunn

If I'm cooking a date night–worthy meal, I want it to feel special—hence the sophisticated cocktail, beautiful hors d'oeuvre, restaurant-esque entrée, and a dessert that would look right at home in a pastry shop window. Entertaining for me is all about the quality of the food, drink, and time I get to share with others, so I spend most of my time crafting a menu that not only tastes great, but that also doesn't require my constant attention after my guests arrive. I like to keep things elegant yet simple, so that everyone relaxes and feels comfortable right away. I love having folks join me in the kitchen, the heart of my home, so as I have done here, I usually design menus that allow an opportunity for guests to roll up their sleeves and help when it comes time to serve cocktails and get the meal on the table.

MY GAME PLAN

UP TO 1 WEEK AHEAD
> Make the Bijou Cocktails.

UP TO 2 DAYS AHEAD
> Make the mousse, the pastry, and the chocolate sauce for the Raspberry Napoleons with Bittersweet Chocolate Sauce. If you plan on using a pastry bag for the mousse, you can refrigerate it right in the bag. (And don't forget to allow time for thawing the phyllo dough before baking it!)

UP TO 1 DAY AHEAD
> Cut the salmon into pieces for the Smoked Salmon Crisps. (Save assembly for within an hour of guests' arrival so that the chips stay crisp.)

UP TO SEVERAL HOURS AHEAD
> Make the broth for the Sautéed Chilean Sea Bass with Creamy Coconut Rice and Baby Bok Choy.

BIJOU COCKTAILS

Makes 4 cocktails

Total Time: 5 minutes, plus 2 hours chilling

WHY I LOVE THIS RECIPE   This drink has everything I want in a cocktail and feels like a special occasion in a glass. It's simple to make yet has a complex flavor profile, it's boozy without feeling heavy, and it's beautiful when served up in a chilled coupe or Nick and Nora glass. For a romantic couples date night, I want something that feels thoughtful and special, and the inclusion of Chartreuse is a fun conversation starter. This liqueur has a rich and interesting backstory, having been produced since the 18th century by Carthusian monks in the French valley of Chartreuse from a closely guarded recipe.

4	ounces London dry gin
4	ounces green Chartreuse
4	ounces sweet vermouth
4	ounces water
¼	teaspoon orange bitters

1   Combine gin, Chartreuse, vermouth, water, and bitters in serving pitcher or large container. Cover and refrigerate until well chilled, at least 2 hours. (Bijou can be refrigerated in an airtight container for up to 1 week.)

2   Stir cocktail to recombine, then serve in chilled cocktail glasses.

STEVE'S TIPS

› Don't substitute yellow Chartreuse, which is sweeter and has a different flavor.

› This is also a great cocktail to make ahead in a bigger batch, both because it's so simple and it's made up of spirits; there is no citrus juice to develop off flavors or bitterness by sitting in the refrigerator for an extended period of time. What's more, the measured added water means that you don't even need to add ice cubes before serving. The water ensures the perfect amount of dilution so that you can serve this cocktail straight up to your guests from the fridge.

SMOKED SALMON CRISPS

Makes 16 crisps

Total Time: 10 minutes

WHY I LOVE THIS RECIPE   I love finding ways to simplify and modernize classic dishes. This one is a riff on blinis with caviar; I substitute potato chips for the tiny pancakes and readily available (and much more affordable) smoked salmon for the caviar. A dollop of crème fraîche (or sour cream), the briny pop of a caper, and a garnish of tender chives (dill or tarragon also work) elevate this simple nosh into something quite special.

16	large potato chips
4	ounces smoked salmon, cut into 16 pieces
2	tablespoons crème fraîche
16	capers, patted dry
1	tablespoon minced fresh chives

Top each chip with piece of salmon, then dollop with crème fraîche and top with a caper and light sprinkle of chives. Arrange crisps attractively on platter. Serve immediately.

STEVE'S TIPS

› My preference is for kettle-style potato chips, which tend to be sturdier, but you can use your favorite chip.

› For a fancier presentation, slice the chives on the bias into 1-inch lengths.

SAUTÉED CHILEAN SEA BASS WITH CREAMY COCONUT RICE AND BABY BOK CHOY

Serves 4

Total Time: 1 hour

WHY I LOVE THIS RECIPE I made an iteration of this dish the first time I cooked for my wife, and it's one I continue to cook for special occasions. It's elegant and a bit restauranty, but approachable and easy to pull off with a bit of planning. The dish hits all the right notes with buttery-flaky fish, lush-creamy rice, and a light but deeply flavorful broth dotted with tender greens. I like to invite a guest into the kitchen, asking them to spoon rice onto each plate. I add the fish, they ladle the broth, and then I garnish and serve.

3	cups chicken broth
1	(1-inch) piece ginger, peeled and sliced ¼ inch thick
1	lemongrass stalk, trimmed to bottom 4 inches, halved lengthwise
½	star anise pod
2¾	cups water, divided
1¼	teaspoons table salt, divided
⅛	teaspoon plus ¼ teaspoon pepper
1	cup jasmine rice
¾	cup coconut milk
¼	cup minced cilantro, divided
1	tablespoon grated lemon zest
4	(6- to 8-ounce) skinless Chilean sea bass fillets
2	tablespoons vegetable oil
4	heads baby bok choy (4 ounces each), stalks sliced ¼ inch thick and greens chopped coarse

1 Bring broth, ginger, lemongrass, and star anise to simmer in small saucepan and cook for 20 minutes. Season with salt and pepper to taste. Strain broth, discarding solids, and return to now-empty saucepan. Set aside.

2 Meanwhile, bring 2½ cups water, ¾ teaspoon salt, and ⅛ teaspoon pepper to boil in medium saucepan over high heat. Stir in rice, return to simmer, and cook until al dente, 6 to 8 minutes; drain rice in colander.

3 Bring coconut milk and remaining ¼ cup water to simmer in now-empty saucepan over medium-high heat. Stir in rice, 3 tablespoons cilantro, and lemon zest. Off heat, cover and let rice sit until tender, about 15 minutes.

4 Meanwhile, pat fish dry with paper towels and sprinkle with remaining ½ teaspoon salt and ¼ teaspoon pepper. Heat oil in 12-inch nonstick skillet over medium-high heat until shimmering. Place fillets in skillet and cook until well browned on first side, about 4 minutes. Using 2 spatulas, flip fillets and continue to cook until fish registers 135 degrees, 2 to 4 minutes.

5 While fish cooks, bring broth to simmer over medium-high heat. Add bok choy and simmer until tender, about 5 minutes; remove from heat and cover to keep warm. Divide rice among 4 warm shallow bowls and top with fish. Spoon broth and bok choy around bass and sprinkle with remaining 1 tablespoon cilantro. Serve immediately.

RASPBERRY NAPOLEONS WITH BITTERSWEET CHOCOLATE SAUCE

Serves 4

Total Time: 1¾ hours, plus 1 hour cooling and 2 hours chilling

WHY I LOVE THIS RECIPE This is a fun, delicious, cheffy-looking dessert that will impress all at your table. All the components can be made in advance and then quickly plated just before serving. When it comes time to assemble the components, that's another nice opportunity to invite someone into the kitchen to help. The combination of creamy fruit mousse and crisp, buttery pastry is a match made in heaven. The ganache sauce is the perfect complement to the raspberry mousse and makes for a smashing presentation. A smattering of fresh raspberries or a pillow of whipped cream would also be lovely on the plate.

RASPBERRY MOUSSE

- ½ teaspoon unflavored gelatin
- 1 tablespoon water
- 8 ounces (1½ cups) fresh or thawed frozen raspberries
- ⅓ cup sugar
- 1 tablespoon unsalted butter
  Pinch table salt
- 2 large egg yolks
- 1¼ teaspoons cornstarch
- ¾ cup heavy cream

PASTRY LAYERS

- 3 tablespoons plus 1 teaspoon sugar
  Pinch table salt
- 5 (14 by 9-inch) phyllo sheets, thawed
- 4 tablespoons unsalted butter, melted

CHOCOLATE SAUCE

- 2 ounces bittersweet chocolate, chopped fine
- ¼ cup heavy cream

1 **FOR THE MOUSSE** Sprinkle gelatin over water in large bowl and let sit until gelatin softens, about 5 minutes. Combine raspberries, sugar, butter, and salt in medium saucepan. Mash lightly with whisk and stir until no dry sugar remains. Cook over medium heat, whisking frequently, until mixture is simmering and raspberries are almost completely broken down, 4 to 6 minutes; remove from heat.

2 Whisk egg yolks and cornstarch together in medium bowl until combined. Whisking constantly, slowly add ½ cup raspberry mixture to yolk mixture to temper, then whisk tempered yolk mixture into remaining raspberry mixture. Return saucepan to medium heat and cook, whisking constantly, until mixture thickens and bubbles, about 1 minute. Pour through fine-mesh strainer set over gelatin mixture, pressing on solids to extract as much liquid as possible; discard solids. Stir raspberry mixture until gelatin has dissolved. Let curd sit, stirring occasionally, until thickened slightly and cooled to room temperature, about 1 hour.

3 Using stand mixer fitted with whisk, whip cream on medium-low speed until foamy, about 1 minute. Increase speed to high and whip until soft peaks form, 1 to 2 minutes. Transfer one-third of whipped cream to curd; whisk gently until mixture is lightened. Using rubber spatula, gently fold in remaining cream until mixture is fully combined and no white streaks remain. Cover and refrigerate until mousse is fully set, at least 2 hours or up to 2 days.

4 **FOR THE PASTRY LAYERS** Adjust oven rack to middle position and heat to 400 degrees. Line a rimmed baking sheet with parchment paper. Combine sugar and salt in small bowl. Lay 1 sheet of phyllo dough on cutting board. Keep remaining sheets covered with a damp towel to keep from drying out. Brush phyllo with melted butter and sprinkle with 2 teaspoons sugar mixture, then top with second phyllo sheet. Repeat layering with remaining butter, sugar mixture, and phyllo sheets, finishing top layer of phyllo with butter and sugar mixture. Cut phyllo lengthwise into thirds, then cut crosswise into quarters to create twelve 3½ by 3-inch pieces. Transfer pieces to prepared sheet, cover with second piece of parchment, place second rimmed baking sheet over parchment, and press down firmly.

5   Bake phyllo until golden brown (remove top sheet to check), 12 to 22 minutes. Remove phyllo from oven, remove top baking sheet and parchment sheet, and allow pastry to cool to room temperature, about 30 minutes. (Cooled phyllo pieces can be stored in airtight container for up to 2 days.)

6   **FOR THE SAUCE** Microwave chocolate and cream in bowl at 50 percent power, stirring occasionally, until melted and smooth, 2 to 4 minutes. Use immediately, or cover and refrigerate for up to 2 days.

7   **TO ASSEMBLE** Transfer mousse to piping bag fitted with star tip. Pipe small dot of mousse onto center of 4 chilled plates to anchor pastry. Top each dot with pastry piece, then pipe half of mousse evenly over phyllo. Top with phyllo pieces, followed by remaining mousse. Top with remaining phyllo pieces, then drizzle with chocolate sauce. Serve immediately.

STEVE'S TIPS

›   Phyllo dough is also available in larger, 18 by 14-inch sheets; if using, cut them in half to make 14 by 9-inch sheets.

›   Don't thaw the phyllo in the microwave; let it sit in the refrigerator overnight or on the counter for 4 to 5 hours.

›   If you don't have a pastry bag, you can simply dollop the mousse onto the plate and phyllo layers with a small spoon.

›   If you make the chocolate sauce ahead, reheat it gently in the microwave in 10-second bursts until it reaches drizzling consistency.

Camila Chaparro's

MEXICAN BRUNCH

SERVES 6

» **HIBISCUS MARGARITAS**

» **CHILAQUILES VERDES WITH SHEET-PAN FRIED EGGS**

» **FRUIT STAND SALAD WITH CHILE AND LIME**

» **MEXICAN CHOCOLATE CONCHAS**

Camila Chaparro

Food is one of the best ways to be virtually transported to a different time or place, and this menu brings me back to a few spectacular years when I lived in Mexico City, one of the most energetic, vibrant, and culturally rich cities I've experienced. During the time I lived there, I would occasionally treat myself (or bring visiting friends and family) to a Saturday brunch served in a beautiful open-air courtyard with a fountain in the middle, always artfully decorated with fruit and flowers. There they served an array of traditional Mexican breakfast dishes, from made-to-order squash blossom quesadillas with stringy queso Oaxaca to sweet and savory tamales, chilaquiles, and pan dulce, all washed down with fresh juices, thick chocolate champurrado, or sweet, warmly spiced café de olla. While I couldn't possibly do justice to re-creating that brunch at home, this menu captures a few of my favorites. All that's left to add is some freshly brewed coffee and fresh fruit juices to round out a satisfying meal with family or friends. ¡Provecho!

MY GAME PLAN

UP TO 1 MONTH AHEAD
> Make the hibiscus syrup and the rim sugar for the Hibiscus Margaritas.

UP TO 3 DAYS AHEAD
> Make the tomatillo sauce for the Chilaquiles Verdes with Sheet-Pan Fried Eggs.

UP TO 1 DAY AHEAD
> Mix the ingredients for the margaritas.
> Prep garnishes (onion, cilantro, cheese, radishes) for the chilaquiles.
> Cut up the fruits and vegetables that will not oxidize for the Fruit Stand Salad with Chile and Lime: Pineapple, melon, cucumber, and jicama are all OK to do ahead. (I don't recommend cutting mango in advance.) Store each element separately.
> Make the dough and the crust for the Mexican Chocolate Conchas. (Note that you can make the dough the morning of your brunch, but it needs to rise at room temperature for 1 hour before being shaped and then an additional hour after shaping. I usually make the dough a day ahead and place it in the refrigerator for the first rise, between 8 and 24 hours.)

UP TO A FEW HOURS AHEAD
> Rim the glasses for the margaritas.
> Assemble the platter for the fruit stand salad.
> Bake the conchas.

HIBISCUS MARGARITAS

Makes 6 cocktails

Total Time: 35 minutes, plus 1 hour chilling

WHY I LOVE THIS RECIPE There are few cocktails more closely associated with Mexico than the margarita. Thought to be developed in the early 20th century in Tijuana and classically made with tequila, orange liqueur, and lime juice, it has been one of my favorite drinks since my first sip many years ago. This version, with dried hibiscus flowers, has a gorgeous, deep pink color and tart-sweet cranberry-like flavor. The water added to the cocktail mixture before refrigerating it accounts for the dilution that would normally occur from shaking the drink; adding the water means that you can serve this straight from the fridge. The hibiscus syrup makes enough for 12 cocktails; you can double the rest of the recipe, if you like, or refrigerate the remaining syrup for another batch of margaritas later.

HIBISCUS SYRUP

12	ounces water
1	ounce (¾ cup) dried hibiscus flowers
1½	cups sugar

HIBISCUS RIM SUGAR

¼	cup dried hibiscus flowers
¼	cup sugar
¼	teaspoon table salt

MARGARITAS

7½	ounces blanco tequila
6	ounces lime juice, plus lime wedges for rimming glasses
4½	ounces water
1½	ounces orange liqueur

1 **FOR THE SYRUP** Bring water and hibiscus to boil in small saucepan. Off heat, cover and let steep for 15 minutes. Strain mixture through fine-mesh strainer into bowl, pressing on solids to extract as much liquid as possible; discard solids. Whisk in sugar until dissolved. (You should have about 15 ounces syrup. Syrup can be refrigerated for up to 1 month.)

2 **FOR THE RIM SUGAR** Grind hibiscus in spice grinder until finely ground, 30 to 60 seconds. Combine hibiscus powder, sugar, and salt in small bowl. (Sugar can be stored in airtight container for up to 1 month.)

3 **FOR THE MARGARITAS** Combine 7½ ounces hibiscus syrup, tequila, lime juice, water, and orange liqueur in storage container. Refrigerate until flavors meld and mixture is well chilled, at least 1 hour or up to 1 day. Stir before serving.

4 Spread hibiscus rim sugar into even layer in shallow bowl. Moisten about ½ inch of chilled margarita or old-fashioned glass rims by running lime wedge around outer edge; dry any excess juice with paper towel. Roll moistened rims in sugar to coat. Remove any excess sugar that falls into glass. Serve margaritas in prepared glasses filled with ice.

CAMILA'S TIPS

› You can find dried hibiscus flowers (called "flor de jamaica" in Spanish) in Latin grocery stores or online.

› The hibiscus rim sugar looks pretty and adds a sweet-tart start to your sipping, but these margaritas are also delicious without it.

CHILAQUILES VERDES WITH SHEET-PAN FRIED EGGS

Serves 6

Total Time: 1 hour

WHY I LOVE THIS RECIPE Upon first experiencing the delight that are chilaquiles, I was disappointed to learn that they are traditionally a breakfast dish—because I could eat them at any meal! Created as a way to use up leftover tortillas, chilaquiles involve frying tortilla pieces until crisp and then coating them in a sauce, in this case a tangy, cilantro-forward green sauce with a base of tomatillos and green chiles (I've used both a sweeter poblano and a spicier, grassier serrano). As a shortcut, I start with tortilla chips; once they have softened to a crispy-tender-chewy texture, they're a vehicle for a variety of toppings, which could include shredded chicken, chorizo, or fried eggs, along with crumbled cheese, cilantro, onions, and a drizzle of Mexican crema. To make this easier to pull off as part of a menu, in addition to the tortilla chip shortcut, I use canned tomatillos, as well as "fry" the eggs on a sheet pan to make cooking them all at once more hands-off.

1	(26-ounce) can whole tomatillos, drained
1	small white onion (half peeled and quartered, half sliced thin)
1	poblano chile, halved, stemmed, seeded, and pressed flat
1	serrano chile, stemmed and seeded
3	garlic cloves, peeled
2	teaspoons plus ¼ cup vegetable oil, divided
1	cup coarsely chopped fresh cilantro leaves and tender stems, plus ½ cup coarsely chopped fresh cilantro
1½	cups chicken or vegetable broth
¾	teaspoon table salt, divided
6	large eggs
½	teaspoon pepper
10	ounces tortilla chips
1	avocado, peeled, pitted, and cut into ½-inch pieces
4	ounces queso fresco, crumbled (1 cup)
2	radishes, trimmed and sliced thin
2	tablespoons Mexican crema

1 Adjust oven rack to upper-middle position and heat broiler. Line rimmed baking sheet with aluminum foil. Gently toss tomatillos, quartered onion half, poblano, serrano, and garlic with 2 teaspoons oil on prepared sheet. Arrange vegetables in even layer, placing chiles skin side up. Broil until tomatillos and chiles are spotty brown and tomatillo skins begin to burst, 7 to 10 minutes. Let cool 10 minutes, then remove charred skins from poblanos (leave skins on tomatillos and serrano intact). Transfer vegetables and any accumulated juices to blender. Add chopped cilantro leaves and stems to blender and process until smooth, about 30 seconds, scraping down sides of blender jar as needed.

2 Discard aluminum foil from baking sheet and wipe sheet clean with paper towels; set aside. Adjust oven temperature to 425 degrees. Heat 2 tablespoons oil in Dutch oven over medium-high heat until shimmering. Carefully add tomatillo sauce (sauce will spatter), broth, and ¼ teaspoon salt. Bring to simmer and cook, stirring occasionally, until sauce thickens slightly and darkens in color, about 5 minutes. Off heat, season with salt to taste. (Sauce can be refrigerated up to 3 days.)

3 Place now-empty sheet in oven and heat for 15 minutes. Meanwhile, crack eggs into large measuring cup or pitcher. Carefully remove hot sheet from oven and drizzle with remaining 2 tablespoons oil, tilting sheet to coat evenly. Quickly pour eggs onto hot sheet and sprinkle with pepper and remaining ½ teaspoon salt. Transfer sheet to oven (eggs will slide around a bit) and bake 3 to 4 minutes (for set whites and runny yolks) or 5 to 6 minutes (for set whites and jammy yolks).

4 While eggs finish cooking, return sauce to brief simmer over medium-high heat. Off heat, stir in chips and toss gently to coat, taking care not to break up chips. Transfer chilaquiles to large serving platter, continuing to toss chips gently in sauce as needed to coat remaining chips. Working quickly, slide eggs on top, then sprinkle with avocado, queso fresco, radishes, remaining sliced onion, and chopped cilantro. Drizzle with crema and serve immediately.

CAMILA'S TIPS

> If you find only 28-ounce cans of tomatillos, go ahead and just add those extra 2 ounces.

> Proper timing is crucial so that the sauced chips don't sit for too long and get too soft: Have all the needed garnishes ready to go, coat the chips in the sauce just as the eggs finish cooking, and serve immediately.

> Use tortilla chips that are on the thicker side. I like Mi Niña Tortilla Chips and On the Border Café Style Tortilla Chips. I don't recommend Tostitos chips here, as they are too thin and too salty.

> If you can't find Mexican crema, substitute sour cream, thinned with milk to a drizzling consistency.

FRUIT STAND SALAD WITH CHILE AND LIME

Serves 6

Total Time: 30 minutes

WHY I LOVE THIS RECIPE Go to any plaza or busy street corner throughout Mexico and you're bound to find a vendor selling juicy, colorful spears and chunks of tropical fruit and vegetables artfully arranged in plastic cups. After you choose your combination, you top your selection with a squeeze of fresh lime juice and a drizzle of bottled hot sauce and/or a sprinkle of chile-lime salt (such as Tajín brand). For the uninitiated, the combination may sound odd, but oh, how it works (and soon you'll be sprinkling Tajín on everything)! To serve, I like to arrange the fruit and vegetables attractively on a large platter and offer plenty of lime wedges and seasoning on the side for sprinkling, along with cups or mason jars for my guests to create their own selection.

- 1 pineapple, peeled, cored, and cut lengthwise into 1-inch-thick wedges
- 2 mangos, peeled, pitted, and cut lengthwise into 1-inch-thick wedges
- 1 cantaloupe or honeydew, peeled, halved, seeded, and cut into 1-inch-thick wedges
- 1 jicama (12 ounces), peeled, quartered, and sliced ½ inch thick
- 1 English cucumber, peeled, quartered lengthwise, and cut into 3-inch lengths on bias

  Chile-lime seasoning

  Lime wedges

Arrange fruit attractively on platter and serve with chile-lime seasoning and lime wedges.

CAMILA'S TIPS

› You can substitute watermelon for the cantaloupe or honeydew.

› I've suggested cutting the fruit and vegetables into spears or wedge shapes, which facilitates picking up the pieces with your fingers. But you can cut everything into 1-inch chunks, if you prefer.

MEXICAN CHOCOLATE CONCHAS

Makes 6 conchas

Total Time: 1¾ hours, plus 2 hours rising

WHY I LOVE THIS RECIPE Conchas are Mexico's best-known, and arguably most-loved, pan dulce (sweet bread). These lightly sweet, fluffy, tender buns are traditionally topped with a vanilla or chocolate cookie-like crust that's scored to look like a shell (concha means "seashell" in Spanish). In this version, I've added the flavors of Mexican hot chocolate—a favorite drink of mine and a common concha accompaniment—to the crust to combine two favorites in one bite.

ROLLS

2	cups (11 ounces) bread flour
1½	teaspoons instant or rapid-rise yeast
½	cup plus 2 tablespoons (5 ounces) water, room temperature
1	large egg, room temperature
2	tablespoons granulated sugar
1	teaspoon table salt
6	tablespoons unsalted butter, cut into 6 pieces and softened

CRUST

½	cup (2 ounces) confectioner's sugar
⅓	cup (1¾ ounces) bread flour, plus extra flour for rolling
5	tablespoons (2 ounces) vegetable shortening
1½	tablespoons cocoa powder
1½	teaspoons Ceylon cinnamon
1	teaspoon vanilla extract
½	teaspoon instant espresso powder
	Pinch table salt

1 FOR THE ROLLS Whisk flour and yeast together in bowl of stand mixer. Whisk water and egg together in 2-cup liquid measuring cup until combined. Using dough hook on low speed, add water mixture to flour mixture and mix until cohesive dough starts to form and no dry flour remains, about 2 minutes, scraping down bowl as needed. Let rest for 15 minutes.

2 Add granulated sugar and salt to dough and knead on medium-low speed until incorporated, about 30 seconds. Increase speed to medium and, with mixer running, add butter 1 piece at a time, allowing each piece to incorporate before adding next, about 5 minutes total, scraping down bowl and dough hook as needed. Continue to knead until dough is elastic and pulls away cleanly from sides of bowl, about 10 minutes longer. Transfer dough to greased large bowl. Cover with plastic and let rise at room temperature until doubled in volume, about 1 hour. (Dough also can be placed in refrigerator to rise for at least 8 hours or up to 24 hours.)

3 FOR THE CRUST While dough rises, in clean, dry, mixer bowl, combine confectioner's sugar, flour, shortening, cocoa powder, cinnamon, vanilla, espresso powder, and salt. Fit mixer with paddle attachment and mix on low speed, scraping down bowl as needed, until mixture is homogeneous and has the texture of Play-Doh, about 2 minutes. Transfer mixture to counter and divide into 6 equal pieces. Roll into balls, place on plate, and cover with plastic. Refrigerate for at least 30 minutes or up to 24 hours.

4 Draw or trace 4-inch circle in center of 1 side of zipper-lock bag. Cut open seams along both sides of bag, leaving bottom seam intact so bag opens completely. Line rimmed baking sheet with parchment paper. Turn out concha dough onto clean counter and divide into 6 equal portions. Working with 1 piece of dough at a time (keep remaining pieces covered), form into rough ball by bringing edges of dough together and pinching edges to seal so that top is smooth. Place ball seam side down on clean counter and, using your cupped hand, drag in small circles until dough feels taut and round. Repeat with remaining dough pieces, scraping counter clean with bench scraper as needed. Evenly space 6 dough balls on prepared sheet and poke any air bubbles in dough balls with tip of paring knife.

5 Place reserved cut bag, marked side down, on counter. Place ¼ cup flour in small bowl. Working with 1 ball of crust at a time, toss gently in flour to coat, then open bag and place ball in center of circle. Fold other side of bag over ball and, using glass pie plate or baking dish, gently press crust to 4-inch diameter, using circle drawn on bag as guide. Carefully turn out disk into your palm, then gently place on top of 1 ball of concha dough, pressing very gently to mold crust to dough. Repeat with remaining balls of crust and remaining concha dough balls, wiping bag clean with paper towels as needed.

6 Using butter knife, score crust of each roll with series of concentric curved lines emanating from a single point to create a seashell pattern. Do not cut through topping completely or cut into concha dough. Cover rolls loosely with greased plastic and let rise at room temperature until doubled in size, 1 to 1½ hours.

7 Adjust oven rack to middle position and heat oven to 350 degrees. Bake until buns are golden brown and register at least 205 degrees in center, about 25 minutes, rotating sheet halfway through baking. Transfer sheet to wire rack and let cool for 15 minutes. Serve.

VARIATION

ORANGE BLOSSOM–CHOCOLATE CONCHAS
In the concha dough, reduce water to ¼ cup and add 5 teaspoons orange blossom water, 2 teaspoons grated orange zest, and ¼ cup orange juice to egg; whisk to combine. Omit Ceylon cinnamon from the crust.

CAMILA'S TIP
> Ceylon cinnamon, the type of cinnamon used in Mexico, is more floral and citrusy, less intense, and not as spicy as cassia cinnamon, the type most commonly used in the U.S. Ceylon cinnamon is readily available in large grocery stores and online. Don't substitute cassia cinnamon in this recipe.

Matthew Fairman's

GUMBO WEATHER GET-TOGETHER

SERVES 8

» **BIG-BATCH SAZERACS**

» **FRIED OYSTER PO' BOY SLIDERS**

» **SMOKY CHICKEN AND ANDOUILLE GUMBO**

» **BANANAS FOSTER BREAD PUDDING**

Matthew
Fairman

When the wind brings a chill down into Louisiana from the north, and the humidity seems to drive the cold right through your jacket and straight into your bones, there's no better way to keep cozy and buoy your spirits than to put on a pot of gumbo. In fact, down here a cold patch is often simply called "gumbo weather," and it's the most encouraging name I can imagine for a stretch of dreary days and wet cold. All the more reason to gather with friends and family and share a spread of some of the all-time most soothing New Orleans–themed comfort foods: crispy fried oysters; a chicken and sausage gumbo redolent of smoked pork and roasty notes from a dark roux; a rich, warm banana bread pudding nestled next to some melting ice cream; and a strong rye whiskey cocktail. Whether you're planning a spread for a winter game day or just looking for an excuse to invite people over and indulge in some classic Louisiana cooking, hearts are sure to be warmed and taste buds are guaranteed to be satisfied.

MY GAME PLAN

UP TO 1 MONTH AHEAD
› Make the Big-Batch Sazeracs.

UP TO 2 OR 3 DAYS AHEAD
› Make the stock and shred the meat for the Smoky Chicken and Andouille Gumbo up to 2 days ahead of making the gumbo. (Both of these elements freeze really well too.)
› Alternatively, you can make the gumbo itself up to 2 days ahead (the finished gumbo also freezes well).

UP TO SEVERAL HOURS AHEAD
› Bake the Bananas Foster Bread Pudding. (When ready to serve, you can reheat it in a 325-degree oven for 15 to 20 minutes.)
› Shuck the oysters, if you purchased in-shell oysters.

BIG-BATCH SAZERACS

Makes 8 cocktails

Total Time: 10 minutes, plus 2 hours chilling

WHY I LOVE THIS RECIPE Aromatic and complex in flavor, the Sazerac is one of America's oldest cocktails and a signature drink of New Orleans. The fact that it remains hugely popular around the Crescent City—a place known for storied bars and famous drinks and that still boasts a booming, growing cocktail scene—is a testament to its excellence. This classic is easy to make ahead in large batches, ready to pour for a group at a moment's notice. The measured added water means that you don't need to add ice cubes and shake before serving and ensures the perfect amount of dilution so that you can serve the cocktail straight up to your guests, right from the fridge.

16	ounces rye whiskey
8	ounces water
8	teaspoons sugar
1	teaspoon Peychaud's bitters
1	tablespoon absinthe or Herbsaint
8	(3-inch) strips lemon peel

1 Stir rye, water, sugar, and bitters in serving pitcher or large container until sugar has dissolved. Cover and refrigerate until well chilled, at least 2 hours or up to 1 month.

2 Pour absinthe into 1 chilled old-fashioned glass, then tilt and rotate glass to coat interior wall. Pour excess absinthe into second chilled old-fashioned glass and tilt and rotate glass to coat interior. Repeat pouring off excess absinthe and coating interiors of 6 more old-fashioned glasses; discard excess absinthe.

3 Stir cocktail to recombine, then pour into prepared glasses. Pinch lemon peel over each drink, rub outer edge of glass with peel, then garnish with lemon peel and serve.

MATTHEW'S TIPS

› If serving only 1 or 2 cocktails at a time, pour ½ teaspoon absinthe into first glass in step 2.

› My preferred tool for making strips of citrus peel is a Y-shaped peeler.

FRIED OYSTER PO' BOY SLIDERS

Serves 8

Total Time: 55 minutes

WHY I LOVE THIS RECIPE Fried oysters are so delicious, simple, and fast (especially if you can source shucked oysters) that they're one of the few dishes I'll happily fry at home. These briny oysters are flash fried with a light, crispy coating that's flavored with Creole seasoning and bright, fiery Tabasco. "Dressed" in the style of a po' boy (with iceberg lettuce, mayonnaise, tomato, and dill pickle) and nestled into a toasted slider bun, they'll fly off the platter.

- 1 pound shucked oysters in their liquor, picked over for shells
- ½ cup buttermilk
- 2 tablespoons Tabasco sauce, plus extra for drizzling
- ¾ cup all-purpose flour
- ¾ cup cornmeal
- 1 tablespoon Tony Chachere's Original Creole Seasoning
- 2 quarts peanut or vegetable oil for frying
- 8 slider buns or soft dinner rolls, split crosswise and lightly toasted
- ⅓ cup mayonnaise
- 1 cup shredded iceberg lettuce
- 8 thin tomato slices
- 8 dill pickle slices

1 Adjust oven rack to middle position and heat oven to 200 degrees. Combine oysters, buttermilk, and Tabasco in bowl. Whisk flour, cornmeal, and Creole seasoning together in shallow dish.

2 Set wire rack over rimmed baking sheet and line one half of rack with triple layer of paper towels. Add oil to large Dutch oven until it measures about 1½ inches deep and heat over medium-high heat to 400 degrees.

3 Using slotted spoon or fork, remove half of oysters from buttermilk mixture, letting excess drain off, and transfer to flour mixture. Gently toss oysters to coat with flour mixture. Working with 1 or 2 oysters at a time, shake off excess flour mixture and add to hot oil. Fry, stirring occasionally, until oysters are golden brown and bubbling has subsided, about 2 minutes. Adjust burner, if necessary, to maintain oil temperature between 375 and 400 degrees. Using wire skimmer or slotted spoon, transfer oysters to prepared paper towels and let drain for 30 seconds, turning once while draining. Move oysters to open side of rack and keep warm in oven. Return oil to 400 degrees and repeat with remaining oysters; keep warm in oven.

4 Arrange bun tops and bottoms on serving platter. Spread mayonnaise over bun tops and arrange lettuce on bun bottoms. Arrange oysters evenly over lettuce and drizzle with extra Tabasco. Top with tomato slices, pickle slices, and bun tops. Serve immediately.

MATTHEW'S TIPS

> I think the unique flavor of Tabasco pairs exceptionally well with oysters, but you can substitute another Louisiana-style hot sauce if you prefer.

> Use a Dutch oven that holds 6 quarts or more.

> These fried oysters make an excellent snack on their own, without the buns. I often serve them with a sauce made by simply stirring together mayonnaise with a generous amount of chopped fresh dill, lemon juice and zest, a minced garlic clove, and extra-virgin olive oil.

> Look for fresh shucked oysters sold by the pint at your local seafood counter. The number of oysters in a pint can vary from as few as 16 to more than 30. If your oysters are on the large side, 1 will be enough to fill a bun, but if they're much smaller, you may need as many as 3.

> If you can't find fresh oysters locally, I suggest buying oysters in their shells from one of these online purveyors: Murder Point Oysters, Bon Secour Fisheries, Real Oyster Cult, and Taylor Shellfish Farms.

SMOKY CHICKEN AND ANDOUILLE GUMBO

Serves 8

Total Time: 4¾ hours

WHY I LOVE THIS RECIPE An excellent from-scratch gumbo is a quintessential pleasure of life in Louisiana and a proud addition to the culinary repertoire of any American home cook. Perhaps more persuasively, it's undeniably and irresistibly delicious. An intensely savory pork and chicken stock lays the foundation. Toasting flour in oil until it's the color of cinnamon not only gives this gumbo its signature, deep roasted flavor and alluringly dark color but also quickens the process of making the roux. It all adds up to an extraordinarily compelling gumbo. To stick with tradition, put on a pot of rice (see page 24) too.

ENRICHED CHICKEN STOCK
- ¼ cup vegetable oil
- 1 (4-pound) whole chicken, giblets discarded
- 12 cups chicken broth
- 2 (12-ounce) smoked ham hocks
- 1 onion, halved
- 6 garlic cloves, smashed
- 5 sprigs fresh thyme
- 1 tablespoon black peppercorns
- 2 bay leaves

GUMBO
- 1 cup vegetable oil
- 1 cup all-purpose flour
- 2 onions, chopped
- 2 green bell peppers, stemmed, seeded, and chopped
- 3 celery ribs, chopped
- 1 tablespoon sugar
- 1 teaspoon table salt
- 10 garlic cloves, minced
- 2 tablespoons minced fresh thyme
- 2 teaspoons black pepper
- 1 teaspoon smoked paprika
- 1 teaspoon white pepper
- ½ teaspoon cayenne pepper
- 1½ pounds andouille sausage, halved lengthwise and sliced ½ inch thick
- 3 bay leaves
- 1 pound fresh okra, caps trimmed, cut into ½-inch pieces (optional)
- 8 scallions, sliced thin
  Crystal Hot Sauce

1 FOR THE STOCK Heat oil in large Dutch oven over medium-high heat until shimmering. Add chicken and cook, turning as needed, until well browned on all sides, 10 to 12 minutes. Add broth, ham hocks, onion, garlic,

thyme sprigs, peppercorns, and bay leaves and bring to simmer over high heat. Reduce heat to low, cover, and simmer until chicken breast registers at least 160 degrees and thighs register at least 175 degrees, about 45 minutes.

2   Transfer chicken to cutting board and let rest until cool enough to handle, about 30 minutes. Meanwhile, cover pot and continue to simmer stock until ham hocks are tender, about 1 hour. Pull meat from chicken; add skin and bones to stock while it simmers. Using 2 forks, shred chicken into bite-size pieces. Transfer chicken to bowl, cover, and refrigerate while finishing stock.

3   Transfer ham hocks to cutting board, let cool slightly, then shred into bite-size pieces with 2 forks; discard skin and bones. Add ham to bowl with chicken. Strain stock through fine-mesh strainer set over large bowl or container and let settle for 15 minutes. Skim excess fat from surface using wide shallow spoon or ladle. (Cooled stock and shred-ded chicken and ham can be refrigerated separately for up to 3 days or frozen for up to 1 month. Bring stock to room temperature before adding to gumbo.)

4   **FOR THE GUMBO** Heat oil in now-empty Dutch oven over medium-high heat until just smoking. Add flour and cook, whisking constantly, until roux is the color of cinnamon, 6 to 10 minutes. (Roux will begin to smoke during final few minutes of cooking.)

5   Reduce heat to medium and add onions, bell peppers, celery, sugar, and salt. Cook, stirring and scraping bottom of pot often, until vegetables are softened and beginning to break down, about 15 minutes.

6   Stir in garlic, thyme, black pepper, paprika, white pepper, and cayenne and cook until fragrant, about 2 minutes. Stir in stock, sausage, and bay leaves and bring to simmer. Cover, reduce heat to low, and simmer until flavors have melded and sausage is tender, about 1 hour. Season to taste with salt.

7   Discard bay leaves. Skim excess fat from surface of gumbo. Add okra, if using, and shredded chicken and ham, and cook, covered, until okra is tender, 15 to 20 minutes. Season again with salt to taste. Sprinkle individual portions with scallions and serve with hot sauce.

MATTHEW'S TIPS

› Making the roux this quickly requires close attention and quick, constant whisking, as the flour will burn if left unattended for even a few moments. If the flour seems to be darkening too fast, reduce the heat and continue to whisk constantly until your roux has reached the cinnamon color.

› Good-quality andouille can be hard to find outside of communities with Cajun roots. You can order Louisiana andouille online from places like Jacob's World Famous Andouille in Laplace and Bourgeois Meat Market in Thibodaux. I don't recommend buying andouille that's widely available nationwide but not made in Louisiana (such as Aidells and Johnsonville). The best locally made smoked sausage you can find around you will be a better choice.

› If fresh okra is unavailable, you can substitute frozen cut okra; don't thaw it.

› We Louisianans are particular about our hot sauces. I like the relatively mild heat of Crystal with this gumbo, but you can substitute another Louisiana-style hot sauce.

› Though you can serve it right away, this gumbo gets even better with time. I always make it ahead and let it rest at least overnight.

BANANAS FOSTER
BREAD PUDDING

Serves 8 to 10

Total Time: 1¾ hours, plus 45 minutes cooling

WHY I LOVE THIS RECIPE When it comes to sweets, I'm a lover of all things banana. This recipe, which is essentially two classic New Orleans desserts in one, doesn't disappoint, demonstrating how dynamic bananas can be. Mashed ripe bananas, brown sugar, and warm spices flavor the custardy bread pudding, which is stiff enough to stand proud on the plate but remains light and tender. A traditional bananas foster—with its lightly caramelized bananas bathed in rum and banana liqueur—is a winning choice for the topping. Flambéing the rum (use a long-handled lighter to stay comfortably distant from the flames) makes for an exciting final flourish to an excellent dinner. Take this even more over the top by serving it with vanilla ice cream.

BANANA BREAD PUDDING

- 3 ripe but firm bananas, peeled and mashed (1½ cups)
- 1 cup (7 ounces) packed brown sugar
- 9 large egg yolks
- ¼ cup banana liqueur
- 1 tablespoon vanilla extract
- 1 teaspoon table salt
- ¾ teaspoon ground cinnamon
- ½ teaspoon ground nutmeg
- 2 cups whole milk
- 2 cups heavy cream
- 14 ounces hearty white sandwich bread, cut into ¾-inch cubes (10 cups), staled overnight
- 3 tablespoons turbinado sugar

BANANAS FOSTER TOPPING

- 4 tablespoons unsalted butter
- ½ cup packed brown sugar
- ½ teaspoon ground cinnamon
- ¼ teaspoon table salt
- ⅛ teaspoon ground nutmeg
- 4 ripe but firm bananas, peeled, halved lengthwise, and halved crosswise
- ¼ cup aged rum
- 2 tablespoons banana liqueur
- 1 teaspoon lemon juice
- ½ cup pecans, toasted and chopped

1 FOR THE BREAD PUDDING Adjust oven rack to middle position and heat oven to 325 degrees. Whisk bananas, brown sugar, egg yolks, liqueur, vanilla, salt, cinnamon, and nutmeg in large bowl until sugar has dissolved. Whisk in milk and cream until combined. Add bread cubes and toss to coat. Let bread soak for 30 minutes, stirring occasionally.

2 Transfer bread mixture to greased 13 by 9-inch baking dish and spread into even layer. Sprinkle with turbinado sugar and bake until pudding has just set, center registers 170 degrees, and pressing center of pudding with finger reveals no runny liquid, 45 to 60 minutes. Transfer to wire rack and let cool until pudding is set, about 45 minutes.

3 FOR THE TOPPING Melt butter in 12-inch skillet over medium heat. Stir in brown sugar, cinnamon, salt, and nutmeg and cook, stirring frequently until sugar has dissolved, about 2 minutes.

4 Arrange bananas cut side down in skillet and cook until glossy and golden on bottom, 1 to 1½ minutes. (Skillet will be very full at first, but bananas will shrink as they cook.) Flip bananas and continue to cook until tender but not mushy, 1 to 1½ minutes.

5 Off heat, add rum and banana liqueur and let warm slightly, about 5 seconds. Wave long-handled lighter or lit match over the pan until alcohol ignites, then shake pan to distribute flame over entire pan. When flames subside, stir in lemon juice. Serve bread pudding topped with bananas and sauce and sprinkled with toasted pecans.

> **MATTHEW'S TIPS**
> › You can quickly "stale" fresh bread pieces by baking them on rimmed baking sheets in a 325-degree oven for about 15 minutes, stirring occasionally.
>
> › For a banana liqueur, I like Tempus Fugit Spirits Creme de Banane.
>
> › For a taller bread pudding, use a deeper, smaller rectangular casserole (about 8 by 11 inches) with at least a 2½-quart capacity.
>
> › Local French bread, the kind traditionally used for po' boys, creates an especially light texture. If you have access to this type of bread, substitute an equal amount by volume (10 cups); it will weigh less than hearty white sandwich bread.

Elle Simone Scott's

MIDWESTERN FAMILY CLASSICS

SERVES 6

» **PORK CHOP POTATO BAKE CASSEROLE**

» **SOUTHERN PUNCH BOWL SEVEN-LAYER SALAD**

» **VINTAGE TRIPLE-LAYER "CHRISTMAS" JELL-O**

Elle
Simone
Scott

I've been a professional chef for many years and have learned tons of new techniques and methods of cooking along the way, but I've also realized that when it comes to cooking for my family, they like the classic family recipes. So my go-to in the kitchen is always quintessential Midwestern comfort food. Visiting farms in the Upper Peninsula of Michigan has inspired the way I cook, just as much as my family's inclination to fuse Southern cuisine with European cuisine, which is common in the Midwest. My grandmother was often inspired by recipes that she found on product labels and in the food section of the *Detroit Free Press*. She delighted in adapting them, using her own techniques and methods to give them a homier feel. My grandmother was a hardworking medical professional whose favorite pastime was traveling on cruises with friends, but she loved nothing more than to cook for her family and make our favorite dishes. She handed these recipes down to me; they were her personal favorites, and of course, they include her extra cooking magic. They are also my favorites and remind me of home.

MY GAME PLAN

UP TO 2 DAYS AHEAD
› Make the first layer of the Vintage Triple-Layer "Christmas" Jell-O.

UP TO 1 DAY AHEAD
› Assemble the Pork Chop Potato Bake Casserole. Take out of the fridge about 1 hour before baking.
› Make the Southern Punch Bowl Seven-Layer Salad.
› Finish making the "Christmas" Jell-O.

PORK CHOP POTATO BAKE CASSEROLE

Serves 6

Total Time: 1 hour

WHY I LOVE THIS RECIPE This recipe was beloved in our home because it's so versatile, and also because all the ingredients were usually already in the pantry. It's what I like to call a "one-pot-shot," and it makes the most of shortcuts like frozen hash browns and condensed soup. You can also double the recipe for a crowd.

6	(4- to 6-ounce) boneless pork chops, ½ to ¾ inch thick, trimmed
4	teaspoons vegetable oil, divided
2½	teaspoons table salt, divided
2	teaspoons pepper, divided
1	(10.5-ounce) can condensed cream of celery or mushroom soup
½	cup whole or 2% milk
½	cup sour cream
6	cups frozen shredded O'Brien-style hash brown potatoes, thawed
3	cups canned French-fried onions (about 6 ounces), divided
4	ounces Colby Jack cheese, shredded (1 cup), divided

1 Adjust oven rack to middle position and heat oven to 350 degrees. Pat pork dry with paper towels, rub with 1 tablespoon oil, and sprinkle with 1¼ teaspoons salt and 1 teaspoon pepper. Heat remaining 1 teaspoon oil in 12-inch nonstick skillet over medium-high heat until just smoking. Brown pork, about 3 minutes per side; transfer to plate.

2 Whisk soup, milk, sour cream, remaining 1¼ teaspoons salt, and remaining 1 teaspoon pepper together in large bowl. Stir in potatoes, ¾ cup onions, and ½ cup cheese. Transfer potato mixture to greased 13 by 9-inch baking dish and spread into even layer. Arrange pork on top of potato mixture and cover loosely with aluminum foil. (Casserole can be refrigerated for up to 1 day.) Place dish on rimmed baking sheet, transfer sheet to oven, and bake until bubbling around edges, 30 to 40 minutes.

3 Combine remaining 2¼ cups onions and remaining ½ cup cheese in small bowl. Remove foil and sprinkle onion mixture on top. Bake until cheese is melted and topping is lightly browned, about 5 minutes. Let cool slightly before serving.

ELLE'S TIPS

> Other types of boneless cutlets can be used in place of the pork. One of my favorite alternatives is lamb, and I've also had good success with chicken.

> Be sure to purchase shredded hash brown potatoes rather than the cubed variety. I'm partial to O'Brien-style hash browns, since they contain diced onion and bell pepper.

SOUTHERN PUNCH BOWL SEVEN-LAYER SALAD

Serves 6

Total Time: 30 minutes

WHY I LOVE THIS RECIPE Seven-layer salad is one of those crowd-pleasing recipes that always appears on our table during holidays and family celebrations. You literally just dig in! My favorite part of this salad is the punch bowl visuals. There are seven traditional layered toppings for the lettuce, but you can really create whatever flavor and visual profile you like. You can also add herbs and spices to the mayonnaise if you want: Try curry powder, tarragon, or thyme.

1	pound bacon, chopped
1	cup mayonnaise
2	tablespoons sugar
1	head iceberg lettuce (2 pounds), cored and chopped coarse
8	hard-cooked large eggs, 4 cut into quarters and 4 chopped coarse
1	large tomato, cored and cut into ½-inch pieces
1	large red onion, chopped fine
1¾	cups frozen peas, thawed
4	ounces sharp cheddar cheese, shredded (1 cup)
4	scallions, sliced thin (optional)

1 Cook bacon in 12-inch skillet over medium heat until rendered and crispy, 5 to 7 minutes. Using slotted spoon, transfer bacon to paper towel–lined plate.

2 Whisk mayonnaise and sugar together in bowl. Arrange half of lettuce in even layer in bottom of large serving bowl. Arrange quartered eggs upright around bottom of bowl, wedged between lettuce and wall of dish. Layer remaining lettuce, tomato, onion, and peas in bowl (in that order). Spread chopped eggs over top, then spread mayonnaise mixture evenly over salad. Sprinkle with bacon; cheese; and scallions, if using. Serve.

ELLE'S TIPS

> The assembled salad can be served immediately, but I think it tastes better after sitting in the refrigerator overnight, which lets everything meld.

> You will need a large (at least 4½-quart) serving bowl. A glass trifle bowl with straight sides is best for highlighting the layers of ingredients.

VINTAGE TRIPLE-LAYER "CHRISTMAS" JELLO

Serves 10 to 12

Total Time: 30 minutes, plus 10 hours cooling and chilling

WHY I LOVE THIS RECIPE Festive in both looks and flavor, this 50-plus-year-old recipe is a Christmas classic, but trust me, it tastes just as delicious at other times of year! It always reminds me of my cousins sneaking into the fridge in the middle of the night for leftovers. As a child, I did not enjoy this dessert, since it was traditionally made with cottage cheese. (I'm still not a huge fan of cottage cheese.) I've since learned some ways to rework the recipe, so nowadays I use ricotta and mascarpone (both of which I love) instead.

4 cups boiling water plus 4 cups cold water, divided

2 (3-ounce) boxes lime-flavored Jell-O

2 tablespoons unflavored gelatin, divided

8 ounces (1 cup) whole-milk ricotta cheese

½ cup marshmallow crème

½ cup canned crushed pineapple, drained

2 ounces (¼ cup) mascarpone cheese, room temperature

2 tablespoons confectioners' sugar

1 teaspoon vanilla extract

2 (3-ounce) boxes cherry-flavored Jell-O

1 Whisk 2 cups boiling water, lime Jell-O, and 2 teaspoons gelatin in large bowl until gelatin has fully dissolved. Stir in 2 cups cold water, then transfer to 13 by 9-inch baking dish. Cover and refrigerate until fully set, about 4 hours.

2 Stir ricotta, marshmallow crème, pineapple, mascarpone, sugar, and vanilla in bowl until well combined. Working quickly, sprinkle 2 teaspoons gelatin over mixture and whisk to combine thoroughly. Using rubber spatula, dollop small piles of ricotta mixture around edge of dish with Jell-O. Dollop more ricotta mixture into center of dish, then spread until even layer covers all of Jell-O layer. Cover and refrigerate until ricotta mixture is set, about 1 hour.

3 Meanwhile, whisk cherry Jell-O, remaining 2 cups boiling water, and remaining 2 teaspoons gelatin in clean large bowl until gelatin has fully dissolved. Stir in remaining 2 cups cold water and let mixture cool to room temperature, about 1 hour. Gently spoon gelatin mixture over ricotta mixture, cover, and refrigerate until fully set, at least 4 hours or up to 24 hours. Cut into squares and serve.

ELLE'S TIPS

› For an accurate measurement of boiling water, bring a kettle of water to a boil and then measure out the desired amount.

› It's important to wait for each layer to fully set before adding the next.

› Don't substitute fresh pineapple. It contains an enzyme that prevents the gelatin from setting (this enzyme is inactivated by the canning process).

› My family uses Marshmallow Fluff and traditionally serves this dessert with Cool Whip for dolloping on top.

Erica Turner's

TRADITIONAL ANATOLIAN DINNER

SERVES 4

» SIGARA BÖREĞI

» CACIK

» EZME SALAD

» ADANA KEBAB WITH SUMAC ONIONS

» KATMER

Erica
Turner

When I lived in Turkey, I fell in love with the culture, the people, the land, and of course, the cuisine. Since moving back to the United States, I often find myself homesick for so many of the foods and traditions I embraced when I lived there. This dinner is special to me because it reminds me of weekend evenings spent with friends on my rooftop balcony or under the canopies at my favorite restaurant in the old part of Gaziantep (the city is known as the gastronomy capital of Turkey). There's a saying popularized by Turkish comedian Cem Yılmaz that goes, "Little, little into the middle." It refers to the art of meze, a lot of little plates filling the middle of the table and made for sharing with everyone. While this meal is not meze centered, it still incorporates those values of communal or family-style dining. And it conjures up wonderful memories of hot summer nights under the stars in Antep with dear friends and neighbors. I hope that in making it, you'll create some new memories or traditions of your own.

MY GAME PLAN

UP TO 2 DAYS AHEAD
⟩ Make the onions for the Adana Kebab with Sumac Onions.

UP TO 1 DAY AHEAD
⟩ Assemble, fill, and roll the Sigara Böreği.
⟩ Make the Cacık.
⟩ Make the meat mixture for the kebabs and shape onto skewers.

UP TO SEVERAL HOURS AHEAD
⟩ Make the Ezme Salad.
⟩ Prepare the pouches for the Katmer and keep them covered with a damp towel or plastic wrap. Pop them into the oven to bake when it's time for dessert.

UP TO 1 HOUR AHEAD
⟩ Fry the böreği. Keep them warm in a 200-degree oven.

SIGARA BÖREĞİ

Serves 4

Total Time: 1 hour

WHY I LOVE THIS RECIPE Böreği are an essential part of Turkish cooking; the savory pastries can be made in many different ways and can be served at practically any time of day. Sigara böreği, which translates as "cigarette böreği," is named for its shape. These crispy, slender cylinders are filled with a Turkish white cheese similar to feta, parsley, and sometimes an assortment of spices and scallions. I use feta for its availability and add scallions for a nice allium punch that cuts the richness of the feta. But I skip the spices to give the pastry a more traditional taste. This is minimal ingredients with optimal rewards. They are best warm, but even as they cool, they're still so crispy and delicious. Dip them in the cacık or enjoy them on their own.

8	ounces feta cheese, crumbled (2 cups)
½	cup minced fresh parsley
4	scallions, finely chopped
15	(14 by 9-inch) phyllo sheets, thawed and cut in half diagonally into triangles
1½	quarts vegetable oil for frying

1 Combine feta, parsley, and scallions in bowl. Stack two phyllo triangles on top of each other on clean, dry counter with shortest edge of triangle closest to you (keep remaining triangles covered with damp dish towel). Spoon 1 tablespoon filling in thin layer over bottom of triangle, leaving ½-inch border at bottom and sides.

2 Using pastry brush, brush water onto top 1 inch of phyllo triangle. Fold in bottom corners of phyllo over filling and gently roll to form tight cylinder. Transfer to parchment paper–lined plate. (Do not stack.) Repeat with remaining phyllo triangles and filling, filling two at a time if you feel comfortable with it. (Sigara böreği can be refrigerated in single layer in airtight container for up to 24 hours.)

3 Heat oil in large Dutch oven over medium heat to 350 degrees. Set wire rack in rimmed baking sheet. Line rack with paper towels. Using tongs, transfer 5 böreği to oil and fry, adjusting burner if necessary to maintain oil temperature of 340 to 360 degrees, until golden brown, 2 to 4 minutes. Transfer to prepared rack. Return oil to 350 degrees and repeat with remaining böreği. Let cool for at least 5 minutes before serving.

ERICA'S TIPS

› These are traditionally made with yufka dough, which is not quite as thin as phyllo. If you have access to yufka, you can use 30 triangle leaves here instead of the phyllo sheets.

› Phyllo dough is also available in larger, 18 by 14-inch sheets; if using, cut them in half to make 14 by 9-inch sheets. Don't thaw the phyllo in the microwave; let it sit in the refrigerator overnight or on the counter for 4 to 5 hours.

› As you're making the pastries, cover the phyllo dough that you're not using with a damp dish towel. Shape the pastries on a dry work surface to keep the dough from sticking.

› Phyllo dough can easily tear, but this recipe is very forgiving and uses two pieces of dough per pastry. If one piece rips, not to worry: Just arrange it back together and carefully proceed.

CACIK

Makes 1½ cups

Total Time: 10 minutes, plus 1 hour chilling

WHY I LOVE THIS RECIPE   One of Turkey's most popular side dishes, this yogurt and cucumber mixture can be defined as a dip, a sauce, or even a soup depending on who you ask. This means that there are a plethora of variations based on preference. I like a cacık with a thicker consistency, so I opt for a thick, unstrained yogurt with a high milk fat percentage. This cacık is rich, creamy, and full of flavor, with a balanced infusion of garlic, lemon, and mint. It's perfect for dipping the böreği, topping the kebabs, or even just eating on its own.

2	tablespoons extra-virgin olive oil, plus extra for serving
2	teaspoons lemon juice
1	teaspoon dried mint
1	garlic clove, minced
½	teaspoon table salt
1	cup plain whole-milk Greek yogurt
½	cup finely chopped Persian or English cucumber

Whisk oil, lemon juice, mint, garlic, and salt in medium bowl until salt has dissolved. Stir in yogurt until well combined, then stir in cucumber. Cover and refrigerate for at least 1 hour or up to 24 hours. Drizzle with extra oil just before serving.

ERICA'S TIPS

> In order to get the desired thick and creamy consistency, use a strained yogurt. I love Fage 5% because it has just the right amount of tanginess, and it stays creamy and thick even after adding the cucumbers.

> The refrigeration time ensures that the garlic has time to infuse into the yogurt and balances the flavor, so don't skip it.

EZME SALAD

Serves 4

Total Time: 15 minutes

WHY I LOVE THIS RECIPE   This flavorful tomato-based salad is popular throughout southern Anatolia and is offered as one of many meze at kebab restaurants around Gaziantep. Since there is a lot of liquid from the tomatoes and cucumbers—it's almost the consistency of a salsa— it's best to enjoy this salad the day you make it. The spices, herbs, and pomegranate molasses create acidic and sweet flavors that complement the richness of the kebabs.

3	tablespoons extra-virgin olive oil
2	tablespoons lemon juice
2	tablespoons pomegranate molasses
1	tablespoon sumac
1	teaspoon Aleppo pepper
¾	teaspoon table salt
3	tomatoes, cored and finely chopped (3 cups)
5	ounces Persian or English cucumbers, chopped fine (1 cup)
¼	cup finely chopped red bell pepper
4	scallions, chopped fine
½	cup minced fresh parsley
¼	cup minced fresh mint

Whisk oil, lemon juice, molasses, sumac, Aleppo pepper, and salt in large bowl. Stir in tomatoes, cucumbers, bell pepper, scallions, parsley, and mint. Serve.

ERICA'S TIPS

> This salad is supposed to be very wet. You can make it ahead, but to keep the vegetables from turning soggy, don't make it more than 6 to 8 hours before serving.

> Pomegranate molasses, which is readily available in large supermarkets and online, is essential to achieve the balance of flavors in this salad.

TURKISH DRINKS

> **AYRAN** This simple, refreshing beverage is made with plain yogurt diluted with water and lightly seasoned with salt. It's nourishing and satisfying, and the flavors will cool the spicy heat of the kebabs.

>  **MINT LEMONADE** To enjoy it as they do in Gazientep during the summer months, add lots of finely chopped fresh mint to lemonade—it should be an almost 50-50 combination. The mint forms a layer of "mint foam" that rises to the top of the pitcher, so be sure to stir it before you pour to ensure that you get a balance of lemonade and mint.

> **ÇAY** Ending a meal with a beautiful tulip-shaped glass of black tea is customary and essential in Turkey, whether you're dining in or dining out. A cup of tea is a sign of hospitality, and a good host will never let a guest's glass get below halfway full.

ADANA KEBAB WITH SUMAC ONIONS

Serves 4

Total Time: 1 hour, plus 30 minutes chilling

WHY I LOVE THIS RECIPE Most traditionally made with lamb, Adana kebab is exceptionally tender, juicy, and flavorful due to the reasonably fatty cuts used. Typically, the meat is finely hand chopped and mixed with chopped sweet peppers and spices before being formed around skewers and grilled. As a workaround, I've chosen 80 percent lean ground lamb, which provides enough fat to keep the kebabs juicy. I've also brought the cooking indoors to a grill pan. The sumac onions kick these kebabs up a notch, adding flavor punch and counterbalancing the richness of the meat.

SUMAC ONIONS

- 2 red onions, halved and sliced thin
- ½ teaspoon table salt
- ½ cup minced fresh parsley
- 1 tablespoon extra-virgin olive oil
- 1 tablespoon sumac

KEBABS

- ¼ cup finely chopped red bell pepper
- ¼ cup finely chopped green bell pepper
- 1 pound 80 percent lean ground lamb
- 2 garlic cloves, minced
- 1½ teaspoons table salt
- 1 teaspoon ground cumin
- 1 teaspoon pul biber
- ½ teaspoon sumac
- 2 tablespoons vegetable oil
- 4 (8 by 10-inch) pieces lavash or 8-inch pitas

1 FOR THE ONIONS Gently massage onions with salt in large bowl to soften, 1 to 2 minutes. Add parsley, oil, and sumac and toss to combine; set aside until ready to serve. (Onions can be refrigerated for up to 2 days.)

2 FOR THE KEBABS Place bell peppers in center of clean dish towel. Gather ends of towel together, twist tightly, and squeeze over sink to drain as much liquid as possible. Using your hands, knead peppers, lamb, garlic, salt, cumin, pul biber, and sumac in bowl until thoroughly combined and mixture starts to get sticky, about 5 minutes. Cover and refrigerate for 30 minutes.

3 Divide mixture into 8 equal portions. Using lightly moistened hands, shape each portion into 5-inch-long cylinder about 1½ inches in diameter. Thread each portion onto 12-inch round metal skewer, reshaping as needed and using fingers to flatten meat slightly on two sides and create horizontal indentations. (Skewers can be refrigerated for up to 24 hours.)

4 Heat large shallow grill pan or griddle over medium-high heat for 5 minutes. Add oil and heat until just smoking. Lay the skewers in pan flat side down and cook until well browned and meat registers 160 degrees, 2 to 3 minutes per side. If using pitas, 2 minutes before removing kebabs from pan, arrange pitas on top to warm through. Serve each lavash or pita with 2 kebabs per person. Serve with onions.

ERICA'S TIPS

› You will need 8 (12-inch) round metal skewers. Alternatively, you can use 4 flat metal skewers (which are traditional). If using flat skewers, you can shape 2 portions of meat onto each skewer, if you like.

› You will need a large (at least 12-inch) grill pan or griddle.

› Squeezing the peppers in step 2 is important. Otherwise, the mixture will be too wet and will not adhere to the skewers.

› You can substitute Aleppo pepper for the pul biber.

KATMER

Serves 4

Total Time: 30 minutes

WHY I LOVE THIS RECIPE As with böreği, there are different versions of katmer throughout Turkey. In western Turkey, katmer can refer to a savory, layered, buttery flatbread. But in the southern city of Gaziantep, katmerci are pastry shops dedicated to sweet, flaky versions of katmer. Traditionally, the crispy pastries are made with yufka, a pastry similar to phyllo dough, that's filled with kaymak (a sweet, thick cream), brushed with clarified butter, and sprinkled with sugar and plenty of chopped premium Antep fıstık—the local pistachios. This katmer is sweet and crunchy like really good baklava but so much simpler to make at home.

8	(14 by 9-inch) phyllo sheets, thawed
5	tablespoons unsalted butter, melted, divided
¼	cup sugar, divided
6	tablespoons unsalted, roasted pistachios, finely chopped, divided
¼	cup mascarpone cheese, divided
1	pint premium vanilla ice cream

1   Adjust oven rack to middle position and heat oven to 400 degrees. Line baking sheet with parchment paper.

2   Stack two phyllo sheets on top of each other on clean, dry counter and brush top with 1 tablespoon melted butter. Sprinkle 1 tablespoon sugar and 1 tablespoon pistachios in 4-inch square in center of phyllo. Dollop six ½-teaspoon mounds of mascarpone over pistachios. Fold both long sides of phyllo over filling, then fold short sides of phyllo over filling to create 4-inch square package. Transfer package seam side down to prepared sheet. Repeat with remaining phyllo, 3 tablespoons melted butter, 3 tablespoons sugar, 3 tablespoons pistachios, and 3 tablespoons mascarpone.

3   Brush tops of katmer with remaining 1 tablespoon melted butter and bake until golden brown and bubbling, about 6 minutes. Serve warm with ice cream, sprinkled with remaining pistachios.

ERICA'S TIPS

> Since it can be difficult to find kaymak outside of specialty stores, I developed this recipe using mascarpone, which is similar to kaymak in terms of texture, consistency, and flavor.

> Phyllo dough is also available in larger 18 by 14-inch sheets; if using, cut them in half to make 14 by 9-inch sheets. Don't thaw the phyllo in the microwave; let it sit in the refrigerator overnight or on the counter for 4 to 5 hours.

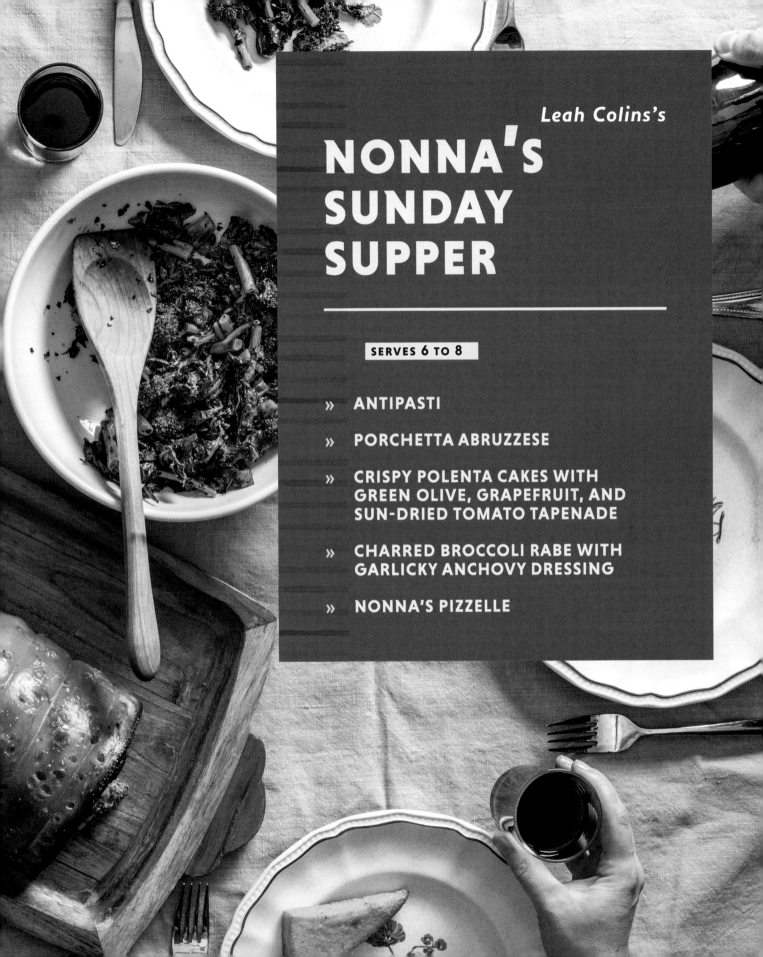

Leah Colins's

NONNA'S SUNDAY SUPPER

SERVES 6 TO 8

» **ANTIPASTI**

» **PORCHETTA ABRUZZESE**

» **CRISPY POLENTA CAKES WITH GREEN OLIVE, GRAPEFRUIT, AND SUN-DRIED TOMATO TAPENADE**

» **CHARRED BROCCOLI RABE WITH GARLICKY ANCHOVY DRESSING**

» **NONNA'S PIZZELLE**

Leah Colins

To come into my home for dinner means that you are joining our family for the evening. With this menu, I pay tribute to my South Philly nonna and my five aunties who introduced me to the kitchen. Big shared platters to be enjoyed in overabundance, with lots of laughter served alongside, highlight this family-style eating at its finest. The main star here is the porchetta, with roots in the cuisine of Italy's Abruzzo region, whose people emigrated en masse to Philadelphia. I grew up eating all versions of roast pork and broccoli rabe sandwiches, and for special occasions, a whole roasted pig known as porchetta abruzzese. My version doesn't require a whole pig, and there is no day-of prep: All the prep work can be done in advance, so all that is needed on the day of your dinner is to roast the porchetta low and slow, welcoming guests into your home with its incredible aroma. This satisfying meal definitely has winter-weather vibes, and it's perfect for a festive celebration.

MY GAME PLAN

UP TO 1 WEEK AHEAD
› Make Nonna's Pizzelle.

UP TO 3 DAYS AHEAD
› Stuff, roll, and tie the Porchetta Abruzzese and refrigerate it on its prepared roasting rack, uncovered. (Note that you must refrigerate the assembled porchetta for at least 1 day before roasting it.)

UP TO 2 DAYS AHEAD
› Make the pickled vegetables for the Antipasti (refrigerate the drained vegetables and the vinegar mixture separately).
› Make the tapenade for the Crispy Polenta Cakes with Green Olive, Grapefruit, and Sun-Dried Tomato Tapenade.

UP TO 1 DAY AHEAD
› Cook and cool the polenta for the polenta cakes, then refrigerate it in its loaf pan.

UP TO A COUPLE OF HOURS AHEAD
› Prep the broccoli rabe and transfer to the baking sheet (but wait to broil it until right before you're ready to serve).
› Roast the porchetta. It's large, so it will stay warm, and it frees up your oven for the quick broil of the broccoli rabe.

STREAMLINE
› If you're in a time pinch, store-bought pizzelle make for a great and easy alternative. I promise that my nonna would still approve.

ANTIPASTI

Serves 6 to 8

Total Time: 1 hour

WHY I LOVE THIS RECIPE An Italian meal often starts with antipasti, a selection of meats, cheeses, and preserved vegetables. A combination of quick pickled and store-bought antipasti platter staples makes this appetizer easy to prep ahead and assemble quickly, yet it's so impressive with its vibrant array of colors, flavors, and textures. I marinate onions, zucchini, and artichokes in a seasoned red wine vinegar mixture for one element. For another, cherry tomatoes, pepperoncini, and salami tossed in a simple dressing make an exciting mix of pickled, fresh, and cured flavors. To finish, add cheeses, olives, and a generous sprinkle of fresh basil.

1	cup red wine vinegar
⅓	cup water
2	garlic cloves, minced
2	teaspoons dried oregano
2	teaspoons sugar
1	teaspoon table salt
¼	teaspoon red pepper flakes
1	red onion, halved and sliced ¼ inch thick
1	zucchini, trimmed and cut ¼ inch thick
9	ounces frozen artichoke hearts, thawed and patted dry
2	tablespoons extra-virgin olive oil, divided
12	ounces cherry tomatoes, halved
3	(¼-inch-thick) slices salami (6 ounces), cut into 1-inch-long matchsticks
½	cup jarred sliced pepperoncini
3	(¼-inch-thick) slices provolone cheese (6 ounces), cut into 1-inch-long matchsticks
6	ounces fresh mozzarella cheese, sliced thin
½	cup pitted kalamata olives
¼	cup chopped fresh basil

1 Bring vinegar, water, garlic, oregano, sugar, salt, and pepper flakes to boil in medium saucepan over medium-high heat. Add onion and zucchini; reduce heat to medium-low; and simmer, stirring occasionally, until vegetables are nearly tender, about 5 minutes. Stir in artichokes and cook until onion and zucchini are tender, about 3 minutes. Transfer pickled vegetables to bowl and let cool to room temperature, about 30 minutes.

2 Drain vegetables in fine-mesh strainer set over bowl; reserve ¼ cup vinegar mixture. (Pickled vegetables and reserved vinegar mixture can be refrigerated separately for up to 2 days.) Toss vegetables with 1 tablespoon oil in bowl. Whisk reserved vinegar mixture and remaining 1 tablespoon oil together in separate large bowl. Add tomatoes, salami, and pepperoncini and toss to coat. Season with salt and pepper to taste. Arrange pickled vegetables and tomato-salami mixture attractively on large serving board or platter. Nestle provolone, mozzarella, and olives around board. Sprinkle with basil and serve.

LEAH'S TIPS

› There's no wrong way to assemble an antipasti platter, so get creative. You can create individual rows or piles of items or layer items on top of one another to let their flavors meld.

› Serve with store-bought thin breadsticks; grissini are ideal.

PORCHETTA ABRUZZESE

Serves 6 to 8

Total Time: 3¾ hours, plus 1 day chilling and 30 minutes resting

WHY I LOVE THIS RECIPE "Special" and "impressive" are the first words that come to mind when describing this company-worthy roast. It highlights all my favorite elements of a pig roast (the crackly skin, juicy pork belly, and succulent loin) without needing to roast an entire pig. To create it, I liberally season a tenderloin of pork and a slab of pork belly with lots of garlic, fennel, and fresh herbs for that signature porchetta flavor profile. A touch of orange zest and orange slices shingled in the roast add a bright citrus balance. Rolling the tenderloin within the slab of pork belly and tying it all together in a neat cylinder ensures that the tenderloin cooks to its proper temperature while wrapped in the pork belly "blanket," which cooks to a higher temperature. Your guests will be wowed.

- 1 tablespoon fennel seeds, toasted
- 1 teaspoon black peppercorns
- 1 tablespoon minced fresh sage
- 1 tablespoon minced fresh rosemary
- 1 teaspoon crushed red pepper flakes
- 5 garlic cloves, minced
- 1 tablespoon kosher salt, divided
- 1 teaspoon grated orange zest, plus 1 orange
- 1 (6- to 7-pound) skin-on center-cut fresh pork belly, about 1½ inches thick
- 1 (1-pound) pork tenderloin, trimmed

1 Pulse fennel seeds and peppercorns in spice grinder until coarsely ground, about 10 pulses. Add sage, rosemary, and pepper flakes and pulse until finely chopped, about 10 pulses. Transfer mixture to small bowl and stir in garlic, 2 teaspoons salt, and orange zest; set aside. Cut away peel and pith from orange. Halve orange, then slice crosswise into ¼-inch-thick pieces.

2 Set wire rack in aluminum foil–lined rimmed baking sheet. Place pork belly, skin side up, on cutting board and trim edges to create uniform rectangular shape. Using paring knife or metal skewer, poke holes spaced 1 inch apart through skin. Using meat mallet, pound pork all over to tenderize, about 2 minutes. Flip belly skin side down with short side parallel to counter edge. Using sharp knife, cut 1-inch crosshatch pattern about ¼ inch deep.

3 Rub tenderloin and flesh side of belly all over with herb rub. Layer orange slices in single row across center of belly. Center tenderloin on top of orange slices. (If necessary, tuck under thin end of tenderloin to be even with edge of belly.)

4 Tightly roll belly away from you around tenderloin, then tie at 1-inch intervals with kitchen twine. Sprinkle with remaining 1 teaspoon salt. Transfer roast to prepared rack and refrigerate, uncovered, for at least 1 day or up to 3 days.

5 Remove porchetta from refrigerator. Adjust oven rack to middle position and heat oven to 500 degrees. Roast porchetta for 40 minutes. Reduce temperature to 325 degrees and continue to roast until pork belly registers 195 degrees and pork tenderloin registers at least 145 degrees, 2½ to 3 hours, rotating sheet halfway through roasting. Let porchetta rest for at least 30 minutes (and up to 2 hours). Discard twine and slice porchetta 1 inch thick. Serve.

LEAH'S TIPS

> If you don't have a spice grinder, you can use a mortar and pestle.

> The shape of the pork belly is important for creating a uniform porchetta. Talk to your butcher and request a belly that is about 14 by 11 inches and uniform thickness.

> For extra-crisp skin, you can increase the oven temperature to 500 degrees at the end of roasting and continue to cook for 5 to 10 minutes, until the skin is deep brown begins to puff in spots.

PREPPING PORCHETTA

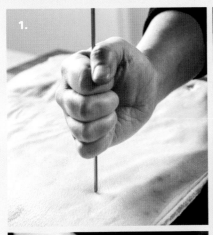

1. Trim edges of skin-side-up pork belly to create rectangle. Using paring knife or metal skewer, poke holes 1 inch apart through skin. Using meat mallet, pound pork all over to tenderize.

2. Flip belly skin side down with short side parallel to counter edge. Cut 1-inch crosshatch pattern about ¼ inch deep.

3. Layer orange slices across center of seasoned belly and center tenderloin on top of orange slices. Tuck under thin end of tenderloin to be even with edge of belly, if necessary.

4. Tightly roll belly away from you around tenderloin, then tie at 1-inch intervals with kitchen twine.

CRISPY POLENTA CAKES WITH GREEN OLIVE, GRAPEFRUIT, AND SUN-DRIED TOMATO TAPENADE

Serves 6 to 8

Total Time: 1¼ hours, plus 2 hours cooling and 3 hours chilling

WHY I LOVE THIS RECIPE Crispy on the outside and creamy on the inside, seared polenta cakes are an excellent addition to any hearty meal. After cooking the polenta on the stovetop, you'll pour it into a loaf pan and let it firm up in the refrigerator before slicing it into triangles. Searing the cakes in a nonstick skillet achieves a golden exterior, and serving with the bold tapenade adds loads of robust flavor.

TAPENADE

- 1   red grapefruit
- ⅓   cup pitted green olives, chopped fine
- ⅓   cup oil-packed sun-dried tomatoes, patted dry and chopped fine
- 1   shallot, halved and sliced thin
- 2   tablespoons extra-virgin olive oil
- 1   teaspoon red wine vinegar
- 1   tablespoon chopped fresh basil or mint

POLENTA

- 4   tablespoons unsalted butter
- ¼   cup extra-virgin olive oil, divided
- 2   garlic cloves, peeled and smashed
- ½   teaspoon minced fresh rosemary
- 7   cups water
- ½   teaspoon table salt
- ½   teaspoon pepper
- 1½ cups cornmeal
- 2   ounces Pecorino Romano cheese, grated (1 cup)
- ¼   cup half-and-half

1 FOR THE TAPENADE Cut away peel and pith from grapefruit. Cut grapefruit into 8 wedges, then slice crosswise into ½-inch-thick pieces. Place grapefruit in strainer set over bowl and let drain for 15 minutes; measure out 1 tablespoon juice. Combine juice, olives, tomatoes, shallot, oil, and vinegar in bowl. Stir in grapefruit and let sit for 15 minutes. Season with salt and pepper to taste. (Tapenade can be refrigerated for up to 2 days; bring to room temperature before serving.) Just before serving, stir in basil.

2 **FOR THE POLENTA** Line 8½ by 4½-inch loaf pan with parchment paper and lightly spray with vegetable oil spray. Heat butter and 2 tablespoons oil in Dutch oven over medium heat until butter is melted. Add garlic and cook until fragrant and beginning to brown, 2 to 4 minutes. Stir in rosemary and cook until fragrant, 30 seconds. Discard garlic.

3 Add water, salt, and pepper to butter mixture. Increase heat to medium-high and bring to boil. Whisking constantly, add cornmeal in slow, steady stream. Reduce heat to medium-low and cook, whisking frequently and scraping sides and bottom of pot, until mixture is thick and cornmeal is tender, about 20 minutes.

4 Off heat, whisk in Pecorino and half-and-half. Transfer polenta to prepared pan, smooth top, and let cool completely, about 2 hours. Once cool, cover pan with plastic wrap and refrigerate until completely chilled, at least 3 hours or up to 24 hours.

5 Run small knife around edge of polenta, then flip onto cutting board; discard parchment. Trim edges to create uniform loaf, then cut loaf crosswise into eight 1-inch-thick slices. Cut each slice diagonally into two triangles. You should have 16 polenta triangles.

6 Adjust oven rack to middle position and heat oven to 225 degrees. Set wire rack in rimmed baking sheet and lightly spray with vegetable oil spray. Heat remaining 2 tablespoons oil in 12-inch nonstick skillet over medium-high heat until shimmering. Place 8 polenta triangles in skillet and cook until golden brown, 4 to 6 minutes per side. Transfer to prepared rack and keep warm in oven. Repeat with remaining 8 polenta triangles; transfer to sheet and keep warm until ready to serve. Serve with tapenade.

LEAH'S TIPS

› I recommend traditional cornmeal for its desirable texture and relatively short cooking time. Stone-ground or coarse cornmeal will take longer.

› I prefer to use an 8½ by 4½-inch loaf pan, which creates a more uniform loaf, but a 9 by 5-inch loaf pan will work.

› The polenta cakes are just as delicious served at room temperature as they are served warm.

CHARRED BROCCOLI RABE WITH GARLICKY ANCHOVY DRESSING

Serves 6 to 8

Total Time: 20 minutes

WHY I LOVE THIS RECIPE Broiling broccoli rabe takes mere minutes and creates deep caramelization, which I like to enhance with garlic, anchovy, and lemon zest. Golden raisins add a welcome sweet touch. Thanks to this broiling method, you can skip the typical step of blanching the broccoli rabe to temper its natural bitterness.

¼	cup extra-virgin olive oil, divided
1½	pounds broccoli rabe
1	anchovy fillet, minced
1	garlic clove, minced
½	teaspoon grated lemon zest, plus lemon wedges for serving
½	teaspoon table salt
¼	teaspoon red pepper flakes
2	tablespoons golden raisins

1 Adjust oven rack 4 inches from broiler element and heat broiler. Brush rimmed baking sheet with 1 tablespoon oil. Trim and discard bottom 1 inch of broccoli rabe stems. Cut tops (leaves and florets) from stems, then cut stems into 1-inch pieces (keep tops whole).

2 Whisk remaining 3 tablespoons oil, anchovy, garlic, lemon zest, salt, and pepper flakes together in bowl. Toss broccoli rabe with oil mixture on prepared sheet. Broil until exposed broccoli rabe leaves are well browned, 2 to 4 minutes. Using tongs, toss to expose unbrowned leaves. Return sheet to oven and continue to broil until most leaves are lightly charred and stalks are crisp-tender, 2 to 4 minutes. Transfer to serving platter and stir in raisins. Serve with lemon wedges.

NONNA'S PIZZELLE

Makes about 24 cookies
Total Time: 45 minutes

WHY I LOVE THIS RECIPE This recipe is near and dear to my heart, as it is adapted directly from my grandmother's pizzelle recipe. My mother, sister, and now my baby daughter all continue to make this recipe together every holiday season. Nonna's handwritten version of the recipe was inspired by Fante's Kitchen Shop in South Philly, which has been around since the early 1900s. When my grandmother was alive, we used her original pizzelle iron that she had purchased from Fante's. The star of this recipe is the flavor combination of anise and orange that comes through in every crispy, buttery bite. Pizzelle are perfect for dipping into good coffee or espresso and also pair well with gelato or berries.

LEAH'S TIP
› Keep a close eye on the pizzelle as they cook, as they can go from perfectly golden to burnt very quickly.

2	cups (10 ounces) all-purpose flour
¼	teaspoon table salt
3	large eggs
1	cup (7 ounces) granulated sugar
10	tablespoons unsalted butter, melted and cooled
2	teaspoons grated orange zest plus ¼ cup juice
1½	teaspoons anise seeds
1½	teaspoons vanilla extract
	Confectioners' sugar (optional)

1 Whisk flour and salt together in bowl. Using stand mixer fitted with paddle, beat eggs and granulated sugar on medium-high speed until pale yellow and fluffy, about 3 minutes, scraping down sides of bowl as needed. Slowly add melted butter and beat until incorporated, about 1 minute. Add orange zest and juice, anise seeds, and vanilla and beat until incorporated, about 1 minute.

2 Reduce speed to low, add flour mixture, and mix until just combined, about 1 minute. Increase speed to medium and beat until dough is satiny and smooth, 3 to 5 minutes. (It will look broken at first but will come together to form cohesive dough that is slightly sticky.)

3 Preheat the pizzelle maker according to the manufacturer's instructions. Spray iron with vegetable oil spray. Drop 1½-tablespoon portions of batter into center of each pizzelle mold. Close cover and cook until golden, 30 to 60 seconds. Using heatproof spatula, gently slide cookies off of iron and transfer to wire rack. Let sit until cool and crisp, about 10 minutes. Repeat with remaining batter, spraying iron with additional vegetable oil spray if pizzelle begin to stick. (Pizzelle can be stored for up to 1 week in an airtight container.) Dust pizzelle with confectioners' sugar before serving, if desired.

Nicole Konstantinakos
and Alex Montiel's

A NIGHT AT LA CUCHARA DE SAN TELMO

SERVES 8

» **ALMEJAS EN SALSA VERDE**
(Clams in Green Sauce)

» **TXIPIRONES ENCEBOLLADOS A LA PLANCHA**
(Griddled Squid with Sweet Onions)

» **ENSALADA DE TOMATE ASADO CON JAMÓN IBÉRICO Y IDIAZÁBAL**
(Roasted Tomato Salad with Ibérico Ham and Idiazábal Cheese)

» **COSTILLAS AL VINO TINTO**
(Braised Beef Short Ribs in Red Wine Sauce)

» **TARTA DE QUESO DE LA VIÑA CON CARAMELO DE SAGARDOA**
(La Viña–Style Cheesecake with Salted Caramel Cider Sauce)

Nicole
Konstantinakos

Tucked away in a corner of the Parte Vieja in Donostia–San Sebastián, a shimmering coastal city in Spain's Basque Country, is a small pintxos bar that stole my heart, La Cuchara de San Telmo. I had read about La Cuchara before heading to Donostia in 2006 between sous-chef jobs in NYC. I'd been exploring the Parte Vieja for days and was having trouble locating La Cuchara. One scorching afternoon, when most of the city had retreated into la hora de la siesta, I found myself in the Plaza Zuloaga, drawn in by the luminous facade of the San Telmo Museum and the breeze off the ocean. I spied an inviting wisp of an alley and thought, "Wouldn't it be funny if La Cuchara were down there?" Funny indeed, since that ramble led me not only to La Cuchara and its founder, Alex Montiel (who was hanging a massive painting on an exterior wall, part of the daily ritual of transforming a stretch of the alley into an enchanting dining terrace), but to a job working in La Cuchara's tiny kitchen. These recipes represent some of our favorite pinxtos that you might encounter on a night at La Cuchara de San Telmo. On egin!

OUR GAME PLAN

UP TO 2 WEEKS AHEAD
❯ Make the Caramelo de Sagardoa for the Tarta de Queso de La Viña.

UP TO 1 WEEK AHEAD
❯ Make the Vinagreta.

UP TO 4 DAYS AHEAD
❯ Make the Crema de Garbanzos con Refrito.

UP TO 3 DAYS AHEAD
❯ Make the Mayonesa de Ajo and the Picada.
❯ Make the cheesecake.

UP TO 1 DAY AHEAD
❯ Make the filling for the Txipirones Encebollados a la Plancha and stuff the squid.
❯ Braise the short ribs and strain and reduce the braising liquid to make the sauce for the Costillas al Vino Tinto.
❯ Roast the tomatoes for the Ensalada de Tomate Asado con Jamón Ibérico y Idiazábal.

UP TO SEVERAL HOURS AHEAD
❯ Scrub the clams for the Almejas en Salsa Verde.
❯ Reheat the chilled short ribs in the sauce. We sometimes use our slow cooker to hold the completed braise at serving temperature starting about an hour before serving.

STREAMLINE
❯ This is meant to be a pintxos feast! However, there will still be plenty of food if you make only one of the seafood dishes rather than both.

ALMEJAS EN SALSA VERDE
(Clams in Green Sauce)

Serves 8

Total Time: 45 minutes

WHY WE LOVE THIS RECIPE Salsa verde appears in popular cuisines around the world, including Italian, French, Mexican, Chilean, German, and Spanish. The Basque salsa verde is made from garlic, (sometimes) onion, white wine, fish broth, and parsley, and is slightly thickened with flour. The sauce is used to poach fish and clams, sometimes with vegetables such as peas, chard, spinach, asparagus, or potatoes. This is by far one of our favorite ways to cook and enjoy clams, especially as a small plate. Some recipes call for cooking the salsa and the clams separately (presumably to avoid getting grit from the clams in the sauce), but we strongly prefer cooking well-scrubbed clams directly in the sauce to take full advantage of their sweet, briny juices.

3	tablespoons extra-virgin olive oil, plus extra for drizzling
1	small onion, chopped fine
6	garlic cloves, minced
⅛	teaspoon red pepper flakes
3	tablespoons all-purpose flour
¾	cup txakoli or other dry white wine
1	cup bottled clam juice
½	cup water
6	pounds littleneck clams, scrubbed
¼	cup minced fresh parsley, plus extra parsley leaves for serving

1   Heat oil in Dutch oven over medium heat until shimmering. Stir in onion, garlic, and pepper flakes and reduce heat to medium-low. Cover and cook, stirring occasionally, until onion and garlic are very soft but not browned, 20 to 25 minutes.

2   Add flour and cook, stirring constantly, until pale golden and fragrant, about 1 minute. Slowly whisk in wine until smooth. Whisk in clam juice and water and bring to boil over high heat. Cook, whisking constantly, until liquid has thickened to consistency of heavy cream, about 2 minutes.

3   Add clams, cover, and cook until about half have opened, 5 to 7 minutes. Using tongs, transfer opened clams to large bowl; replace lid and continue to cook until remaining clams have opened, 1 to 3 minutes. Transfer remaining clams to large bowl. Discard any clams that refuse to open.

4   Reduce heat to medium-low and simmer until sauce has thickened slightly, about 3 minutes. Off heat, whisk in parsley. Divide clams evenly among serving bowls and ladle ½ cup cooking liquid over each bowl. Drizzle with extra oil and sprinkle with extra parsley leaves. Serve.

> **NICOLE AND ALEX'S TIP**
> › Eastern littleneck clams average 8 to 10 clams per pound. You can substitute other small, hard-shelled clams, such as Manila clams, cockles, or Pacific littlenecks, but their sizes (therefore their numbers per serving) and cook times will vary. Don't use larger clams, such as cherrystones or quahogs, or soft-shelled clams (sometimes sold as steamers).

TXIPIRONES ENCEBOLLADOS A LA PLANCHA
(Griddled Squid with Sweet Onions)

Serves 8

Total Time: 1½ hours

WHY WE LOVE THIS RECIPE Like many dishes for which La Cuchara is known, this hot, made-to-order pintxo is a reinterpreted and miniaturized version of a traditional dish; in this case, the Basque squid preparation known as txipirones encebollados a lo Pelayo. Believed to have originated over a century ago in the seaside town of Getaria (the heart of the txakoli-producing region), the dish features small squid sautéed and served with caramelized onions. At La Cuchara, squid bodies are stuffed with a mixture of slow-poached sweet onions and tentacles (sometimes with squid ink, a nod to another traditional preparation of squid in ink sauce), seared on the plancha, and served with a trio of vibrant sauces.

5	tablespoons extra-virgin olive oil, divided
1½	pounds sweet onions, halved and sliced thin
3	garlic cloves, minced
½	cup txakoli or other dry white wine
1	tablespoon squid or cuttlefish ink (optional)
8	medium squid bodies, plus 2 ounces tentacles, chopped (¼ cup), divided
½	cup Mayonesa de Ajo (page 268)
½	cup Vinagreta (page 268)
½	cup Picada (page 269)

1 Heat 2 tablespoons oil in Dutch oven over medium heat until shimmering. Stir in onions and garlic and reduce heat to medium-low. Cover and cook, stirring occasionally, until onions are very soft but not browned, 20 to 25 minutes. Stir in txakoli and squid ink, if using, and cook until wine is reduced by about half, 2 to 4 minutes. Add squid tentacles and cook, stirring occasionally, until tender and liquid is thick and sticky, 15 to 20 minutes. Season with salt and pepper to taste; let cool completely.

2 Using small spoon, portion about 2 tablespoons filling into each squid body, pressing on filling gently to create ½-inch space at top (you may have some filling left over). Thread toothpick through opening of each squid to secure closed. (Stuffed squid can be refrigerated for up to 24 hours.)

3 Heat 1 tablespoon oil in 12-inch skillet over low heat for at least 5 minutes. Using paper towel, wipe out skillet, leaving thin film of oil on bottom and sides. Increase heat to high and let skillet heat for 2 minutes. Pat squid dry with paper towels, then gently rub with remaining 2 tablespoons oil. Add squid to skillet and cook without moving until very well browned on first side, 3 to 5 minutes, adjusting heat as needed if skillet begins to scorch. Flip squid and continue to cook until very well browned on second side and squid is opaque throughout, 3 to 5 minutes.

4 Dollop 1 tablespoon mayonesa onto each plate and top with squid. (Alternatively, transfer squid to cutting board, halve on the bias, then transfer to plates.) Drizzle each portion with 1 tablespoon vinagreta and 1 tablespoon picada. Serve.

> ### NICOLE AND ALEX'S TIPS
> › Vidalia, Maui, or Walla Walla sweet onions will all work here.
>
> › Be sure not to overstuff the squid; the bodies shrink and the filling swells while cooking, so they will burst open if packed too full.

ENSALADA DE TOMATE ASADO CON JAMÓN IBÉRICO Y IDIAZÁBAL

(Roasted Tomato Salad with Ibérico Ham and Idiazábal Cheese)

Serves 8

Total Time: 1¼ hours

WHY WE LOVE THIS RECIPE This dish takes an unlikely cue from a backyard cookout in Massachusetts, when Alex grilled up a pile of glorious, peak-of-season heirloom tomatoes (the seedlings for which were gifted by Nicole's college professor and tomato whisperer, Harold Ward), spread them over a platter, and topped them with a few things we had on hand. Alex was inspired to add a similar dish to the menu at La Cuchara featuring magnificent Basque tomatoes. Rather than grill or griddle the tomatoes, he moved their preparation to a hot oven, roasting them with garlic and conserving all their juices, then topping them with garlicky croutons, cured Ibérico ham, tangy sheep's milk cheese, and a generous glug of extra-virgin olive oil.

- 8 tomatoes, cored
- 2 garlic cloves, minced
- ½ cup extra-virgin olive oil, divided, plus extra for drizzling
- 1 teaspoon table salt
- ¼ teaspoon pepper
- 8 (½-inch thick) slices baguette
- ¼ cup Vinagreta (page 268)
- 4 (1-ounce) slices jamón Ibérico, torn into 1-inch pieces
- 2 ounces Idiazábal cheese, shaved
- 1 tablespoon fresh thyme leaves

1 Adjust oven rack to lower-middle position and heat oven to 500 degrees. Arrange tomatoes cored sides up on rimmed baking sheet. Spoon minced garlic into cored divot of each tomato. Drizzle tomatoes with ¼ cup oil (taking care that the oil remains mostly on the tomatoes rather than on the baking sheet) and sprinkle with salt and pepper.

2 Roast until tomatoes are easily pierced with paring knife but still hold their shape, 20 to 30 minutes. Let cool to room temperature on sheet, about 15 minutes. If desired, use paring knife to gently peel and discard tomato skins. (Roasted tomatoes can be refrigerated for up to 1 day; bring to room temperature before serving.)

3 Swirl 2 tablespoons oil in 10- or 12-inch skillet until evenly coated. Arrange bread in even layer in skillet and cook over medium-low heat until deep golden brown on first side, 6 to 8 minutes. Drizzle tops of bread with remaining 2 tablespoons oil, flip, and continue to cook until deep golden brown on second side, 5 to 7 minutes. Transfer bread to plate, let cool slightly, then tear into rough 2-inch pieces.

4 Using spatula, transfer tomatoes to shallow serving bowls, then use back of spatula to gently press down onto tomatoes and break into large pieces. Drizzle tomatoes with vinagreta. Arrange bread, jamón, and cheese over tomatoes, sprinkle with thyme, and drizzle generously with extra oil. Serve.

NICOLE AND ALEX'S TIPS

› Choose the very best tomatoes you can find. A mix of varieties will bring bold colors to the salad.

› You can substitute jamón serrano or prosciutto for the jamón ibérico.

› You can substitute Manchego, Roncal, Zamorano, Pecorino Romano, or other hard sheep's milk cheeses for the Idiazábal.

› We prefer a crusty, chewy, artisan-style baguette or other rustic white bread here. You may need to toast the bread in batches in the skillet.

COSTILLAS AL VINO TINTO
(Braised Beef Short Ribs in Red Wine Sauce)

Serves 8

Total Time: 5½ hours, plus 2 hours cooling

WHY WE LOVE THIS RECIPE While braised meat may not be the first thing that comes to mind when imagining pintxos, one of La Cuchara's most appreciated traditional dishes presented in miniature is just that: a tender medallion of braised beef cheek in a velvety Rioja wine sauce, served over a garlicky garbanzo puree. Since beef cheeks (an economical cut in Basque butcher shops) are not readily available stateside, we find collagen-rich, finely marbled beef short ribs to be an excellent alternative. For a dinner party, we love that we can prepare this dish ahead of time (the recipe offers a couple of options); we reheat the braise conveniently in our slow cooker or Instant Pot (on the Sauté or Keep Warm setting).

6	pounds bone-in English-style short ribs
1	teaspoon table salt
1	teaspoon pepper
3	cups dry red wine, divided
2	tablespoons extra-virgin olive oil
1	head garlic, outer papery skins removed, halved horizontally
2	large onions, chopped
1	large carrot, peeled and chopped
8	cups beef broth
2	bay leaves
1	tablespoon cornstarch
1	recipe Crema de Garbanzos con Refrito (page 269), warmed
¼	cup Vinagreta (page 268)
½	cup Picada (page 269)
	Flake sea salt

1   Adjust oven rack to lower-middle position and heat oven to 450 degrees. Sprinkle short ribs with salt and pepper. Arrange ribs bone side down in single layer in large roasting pan. Roast until meat begins to brown, 30 to 45 minutes; drain off all liquid and fat. Return short ribs to oven and continue to roast until meat is well browned, 15 to 20 minutes. Transfer ribs to large plate; discard rendered fat.

2   Reduce oven temperature to 300 degrees. Using oven mitts (pan handles will be hot), place now-empty pan over medium heat (over 2 burners, if possible). Add 2½ cups wine; bring to simmer; and cook, scraping up any browned bits, until wine is reduced by about half, about 3 minutes.

3   Heat oil in Dutch oven over medium heat until shimmering. Add garlic, cut sides down, and cook without moving until lightly browned, 3 to 5 minutes. Add onions and carrot and cook, stirring occasionally, until softened and lightly browned, 8 to 12 minutes. Stir in reduced wine, scraping up any browned bits, then stir in broth and bay leaves and bring to boil. Nestle short ribs into liquid and return to boil. Cover pot and transfer to oven. Cook until short ribs are very tender and beginning to separate from bones, 2½ to 3 hours. Remove pot from oven and let cool, uncovered, to room temperature, 2 to 3 hours.

4   Using slotted spoon, transfer short ribs to platter. Discard bones and any large pieces of fat or vegetables that cling to meat; set meat aside. Working in batches, strain braising liquid through fine-mesh strainer into fat separator, pressing on solids to extract as much liquid as possible; discard solids.

5   Return defatted liquid to now-empty pot, bring to boil over high heat, and cook until liquid is reduced to about 3 cups, 30 to 45 minutes. Whisk remaining ½ cup wine and cornstarch together in small bowl until cornstarch has dissolved, then whisk mixture into sauce. Return sauce to boil, reduce heat to medium-low, and cook until sauce is thickened and thinly coats back of spoon, 4 to 6 minutes. Season with salt and pepper to taste. (Sauce and meat can be refrigerated separately for up to 2 days. Bring sauce to boil before proceeding with step 6.)

6   Nestle short ribs into sauce and return to boil. Reduce heat to medium-low and simmer until short ribs are heated through, 6 to 10 minutes, turning meat occasionally. Dollop crema de garbanzos onto each serving plate. Divide ribs evenly among plates and spoon 2 tablespoons sauce over each portion. Drizzle with vinagreta and picada and sprinkle with flake sea salt to taste. Serve.

NICOLE AND ALEX'S TIP

> English-style short ribs contain a single rib bone. Look for ribs with 1 to 1½ inches of meat on top of the bone.

LA HORA DEL VERMUT

Greet your guests with a Marianito (a cocktail of sweet vermouth, with or without a splash of gin and/or old-fashioned aromatic bitters, and garnished with olives and orange peel). Alongside, offer some salty snacks, such as anchovy-stuffed manzanilla olives and olive oil–fried potato chips. (In Donostia, our favorite chips are Sarriegui, San Jeronimo, and San Nicasio brands. In the U.S., look for Bonilla and Torres brands.) With dinner itself, we opt for txakolina, a slightly effervescent Basque white wine, or sagardoa, a dry fermented apple cider.

MAYONESA DE AJO

Makes about 1 cup
Total Time: 10 minutes

- ½ cup sunflower oil or vegetable oil
- ½ cup extra-virgin olive oil, plus extra as needed
- 1 large egg
- 2 garlic cloves, chopped
- ¼ teaspoon table salt
- 2 tablespoons water, plus extra as needed

1 Combine sunflower oil and olive oil in small liquid measuring cup or pitcher. Combine 2 tablespoons oil mixture, egg, garlic, and salt in immersion blender cup or 2-cup liquid measuring cup. Place immersion blender flush against bottom of cup and pulse mixture until garlic is minced and mixture is evenly combined, about 5 pulses.

2 With immersion blender running, slowly stream in half of remaining oil mixture, tilting and lifting blender wand slightly, until very thick, creamy emulsion forms, about 1 minute. Add 2 tablespoons water, then process until mixture is slightly thinned and evenly combined. While slowly streaming in remaining oil mixture, process until mixture forms thick yet pourable consistency, about 1 minute. If mayonesa is too thick, add up to 2 tablespoons water, 1 tablespoon at a time, processing until thoroughly combined between each addition. If mayonesa is too thin, add up to 2 tablespoon olive oil, 1 tablespoon at a time, processing until thoroughly combined between each addition. (Mayonesa can be refrigerated for up to 3 days.)

NICOLE AND ALEX'S TIPS

> We prefer using an immersion blender and its accompanying cup for the Mayonesa de Ajo, Vinagreta, and Picada. If you don't have one, you can use a standard blender instead, scraping down the sides of the blender jar as needed.

> The egg in the mayonesa is not cooked; if you prefer, you can use ¼ cup pasteurized liquid egg.

> Leftover mayonesa is great for serving with potatoes or on a sandwich.

VINAGRETA

Makes about 1 cup
Total Time: 5 minutes

- ¾ cup extra-virgin olive oil, divided
- ¼ cup balsamic vinegar

Add ¼ cup oil and vinegar to immersion blender cup or 2-cup liquid measuring cup. Place immersion blender flush against bottom of cup and pulse mixture until combined, about 5 pulses. With immersion blender running, slowly stream in remaining oil, tilting and lifting blender wand slightly, until creamy emulsion forms, about 1 minute. (Vinagreta can be refrigerated for up to 1 week; blend to re-emulsify before serving.)

PICADA

Makes about 1 cup
Total Time: 15 minutes

½ cup plus 2 tablespoons extra-virgin olive oil, divided, plus extra as needed
1 (½-inch-thick) slice baguette, torn into pieces
¼ cup whole or slivered blanched almonds
6 garlic cloves, peeled
2 cups chopped fresh parsley
2 tablespoons water, plus extra as needed
¼ teaspoon table salt

1 Swirl 2 tablespoons oil in 10- or 12-inch skillet until evenly coated. Add bread, almonds, and garlic and cook over low heat, stirring often, until mixture is lightly toasted, 3 to 5 minutes. Transfer mixture to cutting board, let cool to room temperature, then coarsely chop.

2 Combine parsley, water, salt, toasted bread mixture, and remaining ½ cup oil in immersion blender cup or 2-cup liquid measuring cup. Using immersion blender, process mixture until smooth and pourable, about 1 minute, tilting and lifting blender wand slightly and scraping down sides of bowl as needed. Adjust consistency with extra water as needed. (Picada can be refrigerated for up to 3 days; bring to room temperature and stir to recombine before serving.)

NICOLE AND ALEX'S TIPS

› We prefer a crusty, artisan-style baguette or other rustic white bread here rather than commercial or supermarket baguettes, which tend to have spongy crumbs and soft crusts.

› You can substitute other nuts, such as hazelnuts or walnuts, for the almonds.

CREMA DE GARBANZOS CON REFRITO
(Garlicky Chickpea Puree)

Makes about 3 cups
Total Time: 35 minutes

¼ cup extra-virgin olive oil
6 garlic cloves, sliced thin
2 (15-ounce) cans chickpeas
1 tablespoon lemon juice, plus extra for seasoning

1 Cook oil and garlic in small saucepan over medium-low heat, stirring often, until garlic is crisp and golden, about 5 minutes. Using slotted spoon, transfer garlic to paper towel–lined plate. Transfer oil to 1-cup liquid measuring cup or small pitcher.

2 Bring chickpeas and their liquid to boil in now-empty saucepan over medium-high heat. Reduce heat to medium-low and cook until chickpeas are very soft, 15 to 20 minutes. Set strainer over bowl and drain chickpeas, reserving liquid.

3 Process chickpeas, ½ cup reserved cooking liquid, toasted garlic, and lemon juice in food processor until smooth, about 1 minute, scraping down sides of bowl as needed. With processor running, slowly add garlic oil in steady stream until completely incorporated and mixture is smooth, about 2 minutes. Adjust consistency with additional reserved cooking liquid as needed to achieve thick yet spreadable consistency. Season with salt and extra lemon juice to taste. Transfer puree to now-empty saucepan and cover to keep warm. (Puree can be refrigerated for up to 4 days; reheat over low heat before serving, adjusting consistency with water as needed.)

TARTA DE QUESO DE LA VIÑA CON CARAMELO DE SAGARDOA

(La Viña–Style Cheesecake with Salted Caramel Cider Sauce)

Serves 8 to 12

Total Time: 1 hour, plus 2 hours cooling

WHY WE LOVE THIS RECIPE Dessert is not always on the menu at La Cuchara, and when it is, it's usually simple—a quenelle of chocolate ganache, a spoonful of Torta del Casar cheese with apricot compote, a scoop of melon-verbena ice cream. So when diners ask for recommendations for dessert spots nearby, Alex sends them to La Viña, birthplace of the 5-ingredient, caramelized crustless cheesecake developed by chef Santiago Rivera more than 30 years ago and now celebrated and imitated all over the world. We follow Santi's original recipe but with a twist: To complement the cheesecake's slightly toasted exterior, we add a tangy cider-caramel sauce inspired by a sauce made by Ana Rodriquez, chef de cuisine at La Cuchara.

7	large eggs, room temperature
2	cups (14 ounces) sugar
2¼	pounds (36 ounces) cream cheese, room temperature
1	cup heavy cream, room temperature
¼	cup (1¼ ounces) all-purpose flour
1	recipe Caramelo de Sagardoa

1 Adjust oven rack to middle position and heat oven to 425 degrees. Spray or lightly sprinkle two approximately 16 by 12-inch pieces of parchment paper evenly with cold water. Crumple each piece of parchment into ball, then gently uncrumple. Overlap parchment pieces slightly to form approximately 16-inch square. Press parchment into bottom and sides of 9-inch springform pan. Fold overhanging parchment outward, over edge of pan. Using scissors or kitchen shears, trim overhanging parchment to about 1 inch past edge of pan.

2 Process eggs and sugar in large (14-cup) food processor until mixture is frothy and pale yellow, about 1 minute. Add cream cheese, heavy cream, and flour and pulse until cream cheese is broken into large, even pieces, 8 to 10 pulses. Process until mixture is completely smooth, about 2 minutes, scraping down sides of bowl and breaking up any large clumps of cream cheese (processor bowl will be very full).

3 Transfer batter to prepared pan and place pan on rimmed baking sheet. Bake until top of cheesecake is deeply browned, edges are set, and center of cheesecake registers 155 degrees, 45 to 55 minutes (center will be very jiggly). Remove cheesecake from oven and transfer to cooling rack. Let cheesecake cool in pan for at least 2 hours.

4 Remove side of pan. Gently peel parchment away from sides of cheesecake until parchment is flush with counter. To slice, dip sharp knife in very hot water and wipe dry after each cut. Serve slightly warm (after 2 hours cooling) or at room temperature with Caramelo de Sagardoa. (Cheesecake can be refrigerated for up to 3 days; let sit at room temperature for 1 to 2 hours before serving.)

NICOLE AND ALEX'S TIPS

> Use full-fat block cream cheese.

> To ensure that the cheesecake cooks properly within the given time, be sure all ingredients are at room temperature.

> We strongly recommend using an instant-read thermometer in step 3.

> We prefer to make this the day of the dinner to enjoy its tender, just-cooled texture, but it's still great if you make it ahead.

> Don't be surprised if your cheesecake rises far above the rim of the pan while baking and/or small cracks appear on the surface; the cake will settle and the cracks will disappear as it cools.

CARAMELO DE SAGARDOA
(Salted Caramel Cider Sauce)

Makes about 1 cup
Total Time: 1 hour

1	(750-ml) bottle Basque hard cider
1⅔	cups (11⅔ ounces) sugar
¾	cup heavy cream
¼	teaspoon table salt

1 Bring cider and sugar to boil in large heavy-bottomed saucepan over medium-high heat. Cook without stirring until mixture is syrupy and full of large bubbles and registers about 250 degrees, 25 to 35 minutes.

2 Reduce heat to medium-low and continue to cook, swirling saucepan occasionally, until mixture is deep amber–colored and registers 320 to 330 degrees, 10 to 15 minutes longer. (Watch caramel closely during final minutes of cooking, since temperature can increase quickly.)

3 Off heat, carefully whisk in cream and salt (mixture will bubble and steam). Continue to whisk until sauce is smooth. Let sauce cool slightly before serving, about 15 minutes. (Sauce will thicken as it cools. Cooled sauce can be refrigerated for up to 2 weeks; reheat before serving.)

NICOLE AND ALEX'S TIPS

› If you can't find Basque cider, substitute another dry hard cider.

› You can reheat the sauce either in a microwave or in a small saucepan over low heat, whisking often, until it's warm and smooth.

› Leftover caramel sauce is great for drizzling over French toast or pancakes; it's also a wonderful topping for ice cream, fresh fruit, or pound cake.

Bridget Lancaster's

WINTER COMFORT DINNER

SERVES 6

» **VIN CHAUD**

» **SHORT RIBS BOURGUIGNON**

» **VERY RUSTIC! MASHED POTATOES**

» **CIDER-DRESSED GREENS**

» **APPLE CHARLOTTE**

Bridget Lancaster

The dark, somber months of winter set the perfect stage to enjoy a comforting dinner with friends and family. Time seems to move more slowly when it's cold outside, so I love to tackle recipes that might be a little bit of a project. To ensure that I have plenty of opportunities to socialize at my own affair, I like to choose a couple components of the meal that can be at least partially made ahead of time. When guests arrive, I'll take their mittens and place a glass of vin chaud in their hands. The hot, spiced wine, which I'll often pair with a very simple cheese board, perfumes the house and buys me time to suss out any last-minute cooking. The wine itself foreshadows the food that's yet to come: short ribs bourguignon. Braises like this are a natural fit for dinner parties, since they are so impressive for guests and your hard work was done a day or more ago. The sides are simple, supporting but not outshining those short ribs. The cider in the greens also gives a clue to the evening's showstopping closer, apple charlotte. Time to stoke the fire and light the candles. Company is here.

UP TO 1 WEEK AHEAD
> Make the Vin Chaud.

UP TO 3 DAYS AHEAD
> Make the short ribs and sauce for the Short Ribs Bourguignon; refrigerate them separately.

UP TO 2 DAYS AHEAD
> Make the Very Rustic! Mashed Potatoes.
> Make the crème anglaise and filling for the Apple Charlotte.

UP TO 1 DAY AHEAD
> Assemble the apple charlotte in its pan and refrigerate.

UP TO A FEW HOURS AHEAD
> Prep the greens and make the cider-shallot dressing for the Cider-Dressed Greens.

STREAMLINE
> There's no getting around the fact that the Apple Charlotte is a project recipe. Although it's really a superstar, no one will judge you if you buy an apple pie for dessert instead!

VIN CHAUD

Makes 6 to 8 cocktails

Total Time: 1½ hours

WHY I LOVE THIS RECIPE Versions of this mulled wine are often served at European outdoor Christmas markets, and it's one of the easiest ways to serve your guests a soul-warming cocktail. The spices—toasted just for a moment to deepen their presence—flavor a fruity red wine in all the right ways. I love that the drink also can be tailored to suit the imbiber. I've chosen to use cinnamon (my favorite) as the spice base, with star anise, cardamom, and vanilla playing backup. But you can use cloves, nutmeg, mace, or other whole spices as you wish, or garnish mugs with thin slices of orange, apple, pear, or fresh cranberries.

- 2   cinnamon sticks, broken into pieces, plus extra for serving
- 6   green cardamom pods, cracked
- 2   whole star anise pods, plus extra for serving
- 1   teaspoon allspice berries, cracked
- ½   teaspoon black peppercorns, cracked
- 2   (750-ml) bottles fruity red wine such as Merlot, Grenache, or Gamay
- ½   cup sugar, plus extra for seasoning
- 1   (2-inch) piece ginger, sliced ½ inch thick
- 1   vanilla bean
- 2   ounces Cognac, brandy, or eau de vie

1 Toast cinnamon, cardamom, star anise, allspice, and peppercorns in large saucepan over medium heat, shaking saucepan occasionally until fragrant, 1 to 3 minutes. Slowly add wine, sugar, ginger, and vanilla and bring to simmer. Reduce heat to low and partially cover. Simmer gently, stirring occasionally, until flavors meld, about 1 hour.

2 Line fine-mesh strainer with coffee filters and set over large bowl. Strain wine mixture through prepared strainer; discard solids. Return wine mixture to now-empty saucepan, stir in cognac, and season with extra sugar to taste. (Vin chaud can be refrigerated for up to 1 week; bring to brief simmer before serving.) Serve in warmed mugs, garnishing individual portions with extra cinnamon sticks and/or star anise, if desired.

BRIDGET'S TIPS

> Don't split the vanilla bean; it will overwhelm the vin chaud's flavor. After steeping it, pat the vanilla bean dry. You can use it in the Apple Charlotte; or cut it in half lengthwise, scrape out the seeds, then combine the bean and seeds with 1 cup sugar and store in an airtight container for up to 3 months. Use the vanilla sugar in baking or for sweetening beverages.

> An eau de vie such as Calvados or Poire Williams is excellent here.

> If you have a small slow cooker, you can use that to keep the vin chaud warm and steaming.

SHORT RIBS BOURGUIGNON

Serves 6

Total Time: 5½ hours, plus 24 hours chilling

WHY I LOVE THIS RECIPE This is what I would make for Julia Child if she were coming for dinner. Rendering short ribs in the oven is easy, and using a roasting pan allows the meat to cook evenly in the liquid during the long, hands-off braising that follows. When ready to serve, I finish the short ribs and vegetables together in a Dutch oven on the stovetop. Like most braises, this dish is better when made in advance; in fact, it's absolutely engineered that way.

6	pounds bone-in English-style short ribs, 4 to 5 inches long, 1 to 1½ inches of meat on top of bone
1¾	teaspoons table salt, divided
1	teaspoon pepper, plus ½ teaspoon black peppercorns
6	ounces salt pork, cut into ½-inch pieces
⅓	cup all-purpose flour
4	cups beef broth
1	(750-ml) bottle dry red wine, such as Pinot Noir, divided
1	tablespoon tomato paste
2	onions, chopped coarse
2	carrots, peeled and cut into 2-inch lengths
2	large celery ribs, chopped coarse
1	garlic head, cloves separated and crushed
2	bay leaves
¾	ounce dried porcini mushrooms, rinsed
12	sprigs fresh parsley, plus 3 tablespoons minced parsley
5	sprigs fresh thyme
8	ounces frozen pearl onions, thawed
2	teaspoons sugar
1	pound cremini or white mushrooms, trimmed, halved if medium or quartered if large
2–4	tablespoons brandy (optional)

1 Adjust oven rack to lower-middle position and heat oven to 450 degrees. Trim short ribs; reserve trimmings. Pat ribs dry with paper towels and sprinkle with 1½ teaspoons salt and pepper. Arrange ribs bone side down in single layer in large roasting pan and roast until meat begins to brown, about 45 minutes.

2 Pour off accumulated fat and juice from pan. Return 2 tablespoons fat to pan (reserve remaining fat). Scatter salt pork and reserved trimmings around ribs and continue to roast until meat is well browned, about 20 minutes.

3 Remove pan from oven and reduce temperature to 300 degrees. Transfer ribs to large plate; set aside. Sprinkle flour over rendered fat in pan and whisk until no dry flour remains. Whisk in broth, 2½ cups wine, and tomato paste until combined. Add chopped onions, carrots, celery, garlic, bay leaves, peppercorns, porcini mushrooms, parsley sprigs, and thyme sprigs to pan. Nestle ribs bone-side up into braising liquid. Braising liquid should reach about three-quarters up side of ribs; add water as needed. Return roasting pan to oven and cook, uncovered, for 2 hours.

4 While ribs are cooking, bring pearl onions, ½ cup water, 2 tablespoons reserved fat, and sugar to boil in 12-inch skillet over medium-high heat. Cover, reduce heat to low, and cook until onions are tender, 5 to 7 minutes. Uncover, increase heat to medium-high and cook until liquid evaporates, about 3 minutes. Add cremini mushrooms and remaining ¼ teaspoon salt and cook until vegetables are browned and glazed, about 10 minutes. Transfer onion-mushroom mixture to large plate and let cool to room temperature. Cover vegetables and refrigerate until ready to use. Add ¼ cup water to skillet and scrape with wooden spoon to loosen browned bits; set aside.

5 Remove pan from oven. Flip ribs so that meat is above braising liquid and add liquid from skillet. Return pan to oven and cook, uncovered, until fork slips easily in and out of meat, 1 to 1½ hours.

6 Transfer ribs to large plate, removing excess vegetables that may cling to meat and discarding loose bones that have fallen away from meat. Strain braising liquid through fine-mesh strainer set over large bowl, pressing on solids to extract as much liquid as possible; discard solids. Let ribs and liquid cool separately to room temperature, then cover and refrigerate for at least 24 hours or up to 3 days.

7 Using wide, shallow spoon, skim excess fat from surface of braising liquid. Transfer defatted liquid to Dutch oven, add remaining wine, and bring to boil over medium-high heat. Reduce to simmer and cook, stirring frequently, until sauce is slightly thickened, about 15 minutes. Reduce heat to medium-low, stir in onion-mushroom mixture, and nestle ribs into sauce. Cover and simmer gently until heated through, about 8 minutes. Stir in brandy, if using, and season with salt and pepper to taste. Serve, sprinkling parsley over individual portions.

BRIDGET'S TIP

› A wide slotted spoon is best for serving; it will prevent the bones from falling off the meat when removing the ribs from the Dutch oven.

VERY RUSTIC! MASHED POTATOES

Serves 6

Total Time: 45 minutes

WHY I LOVE THIS RECIPE   There are a million recipes for mashed potatoes, but this one is more guidelines than recipe, and I love that. I call them "Very Rustic!" as kind of a joke (in our house, "rustic" often refers to winging it). You can use any kind of potato you want and choose to peel or not. Mash the spuds until they are completely smooth or leave 'em lumpy. Thin out the mash a lot or a little. Toss in some fresh chives or parsley if you want. Totally up to you. Change the method, change the potatoes, change your expectations.

- 3   pounds potatoes, peeled if desired, cut into 1-inch pieces
- 6   tablespoons unsalted butter, melted
- 8   ounces (1 cup) crème fraîche
      Heavy cream or milk

1   Place potatoes in Dutch oven or large pot and add enough water to cover by 1 inch. Bring to boil over high heat; reduce heat to medium and simmer until potatoes break apart when paring knife is inserted, about 20 minutes.

2   Drain potatoes, then return to pot. Cook over low heat until potatoes are thoroughly dried, 1 to 2 minutes. Using potato masher, mash potatoes to desired consistency. Using rubber spatula, stir in melted butter until combined, then fold in crème fraîche. Adjust consistency with heavy cream or milk as desired. Season with salt and pepper to taste. Serve.

BRIDGET'S TIPS

› If you're in doubt whether the potatoes are tender enough to mash, let them cook a little more. They should almost fall apart when tested with a knife.

› I like to spoon some of the mash into a wide, shallow, rimmed bowl and then spoon the short ribs and sauce over most of the mash.

› If you make the potatoes ahead, stir in ½ cup heavy cream when adjusting the consistency in step 2 (the mixture will look soupy). Transfer the potatoes to a microwave-safe serving bowl, cover, and refrigerate. To serve, microwave the potatoes on high, stirring occasionally, until heated through, about 4 minutes.

CIDER-DRESSED GREENS

Serves 6

Total Time: 35 minutes

WHY I LOVE THIS RECIPE   A fresh, slaw-like salad is one of my favorite ways to serve vegetables. These assertive greens with their tart dressing cut through the decadence of the short ribs. You can use any color of chard here; the minerally flavor goes perfectly with the sweet, tangy cider. I've also switched out the pecans for hazelnuts or almonds on occasion, and sometimes I'll steam a handful of dried currants along with the shallot.

- 3   tablespoons apple cider
- 2   teaspoons cider vinegar
- ¼   teaspoon plus ⅛ teaspoon table salt, divided
- 1   shallot, halved lengthwise and sliced thin crosswise
- 3   tablespoons extra-virgin olive oil
- 1½   pounds Swiss chard, stems sliced ¼ inch thick, leaves cut into ⅛-inch thick ribbons
- ½   cup pecans, chopped
- 1½   cups baby arugula or spinach, chopped

1   Whisk cider, vinegar, and ¼ teaspoon salt together in small bowl. Add shallot, cover tightly, and microwave until steaming, 30 to 60 seconds. Uncover, stir, and let cool to room temperature, about 15 minutes.

2   Heat oil in 12-inch skillet over medium-high heat until shimmering. Add chard stems and remaining ⅛ teaspoon salt and cook until just starting to brown, about 3 minutes. Reduce heat to medium-low; add pecans; and cook, stirring constantly, until nuts are toasted, 2 to 3 minutes. Add chard leaves and arugula, one handful at a time, and cook until slightly wilted, about 5 minutes. Add shallot mixture and toss greens until evenly coated. Continue to cook until chard leaves start to soften, 1 to 2 minutes. Season with salt and pepper to taste. Serve.

BRIDGET'S TIP

› Look for younger chard, which tends to be less bitter.

APPLE CHARLOTTE

Serves 6

Total Time: 2¼ hours, plus 1 hour chilling

WHY I LOVE THIS RECIPE This impressive dessert involves apples encased in a buttery, sugared, golden bread crust. Apple charlotte was never something that I felt a desire to make at home—until I tasted one with a deep caramelly apple interior, which lifted the dessert to a whole new level. It's a bit messy to serve (I kind of dig that), but once you've scooped the charlotte into bowls and topped it with sauce, your guests will go gaga.

CRÈME ANGLAISE
- ½ vanilla bean
- 1 cup whole milk
- ½ cup heavy cream
- 5 large egg yolks
- ¼ cup sugar
- Pinch table salt

CHARLOTTE
- 4 tablespoons unsalted butter, divided; plus 6 tablespoons melted butter for brushing
- 2 pounds Golden Delicious apples, peeled, cored, and cut into ¾-inch pieces
- ¼ teaspoon table salt
- ¼ teaspoon ground cinnamon (optional)
- ⅔ cup sugar, plus 3 tablespoons for dusting
- ⅓ cup water
- 2 tablespoons heavy cream
- 10 slices hearty white sandwich bread, crusts removed

1 FOR THE CRÈME ANGLAISE Cut vanilla bean in half lengthwise. Using tip of paring knife, scrape out seeds. Heat seeds, pod, milk, and cream in medium saucepan over medium heat until steaming, about 3 minutes. Off heat, cover and let steep for 20 minutes. Uncover, return mixture to medium heat, and heat until steaming, about 1 minute.

2 Set fine-mesh strainer over medium bowl. Whisk egg yolks, sugar, and salt in medium bowl until pale yellow, about 1 minute. Slowly whisk ½ cup hot milk mixture into yolk mixture to temper. Return mixture to saucepan and cook over low heat, stirring constantly with wooden spoon, until mixture thickens slightly, coats back of spoon with thin film, and registers 175 to 180 degrees, 5 to 8 minutes. Immediately pour mixture through strainer into bowl. Transfer to clean, airtight

container and press piece of plastic wrap flush against surface to prevent skin from forming. Cover and refrigerate until chilled, at least 1 hour or up to 2 days.

3 FOR THE CHARLOTTE Melt 1 tablespoon butter in 12-inch nonstick skillet over medium-high heat. Add apples and salt, cover, and cook until apples start to soften and release juices, 5 to 8 minutes. Uncover and continue to cook until apples are very soft and most of liquid has evaporated, 6 to 12 minutes. Stir in cinnamon, if using, and set aside.

4 Bring sugar and water to boil in large saucepan over medium-high heat. Cook, without stirring, until mixture begins to turn straw-colored around edge of pan, 6 to 8 minutes. Reduce heat to medium-low and continue to cook, swirling pan occasionally, until mixture is medium amber colored, 2 to 4 minutes.

5 Off heat, carefully whisk in cream (mixture will bubble and steam) and 2 tablespoons butter. Fold in apples, transfer to bowl, and let cool completely, about 30 minutes. (Filling can be refrigerated for up to 2 days.)

6 Adjust oven rack to middle position and heat oven to 375 degrees. Grease large charlotte mold with remaining 1 tablespoon butter. Dust with 3 tablespoons sugar, then shake and rotate mold to coat it evenly; shake out excess sugar. Using rolling pin, flatten bread and brush one side of each slice with melted butter. Line bottom and sides of prepared mold with bread, buttered side facing in, overlapping slices by ½ inch, and trimming bread as needed to create even layer without gaps. Reserve unused bread.

7 Spoon apple mixture into bread-lined mold and use rubber spatula to firmly pack down mixture; mixture will not fill mold completely. (You can cover and refrigerate for up to 1 day, if you like.) Cover exposed bread along edges of mold with aluminum foil and place mold on rimmed baking sheet. Bake for 15 minutes. Remove sheet from oven and discard foil. Fold down exposed bread over apple filling, then arrange reserved bread, buttered side down, in even layer on top to cover filling completely. Return sheet to oven and bake until top is deep golden brown, 20 to 25 minutes.

8 Transfer sheet to wire rack and let charlotte cool in mold for 10 minutes. Carefully invert charlotte onto serving plate and continue to cool for at least 10 minutes. Serve slightly warm or at room temperature with crème anglaise.

BRIDGET'S TIPS

> You will need a large charlotte mold, approximately 7½ inches in diameter and 4 inches deep. Alternatively, you can use a 9 by 5-inch loaf pan; the charlotte won't look as impressive but I promise it will taste just as delicious.

> Stir a tablespoon of Calvados into the filling along with the apples!

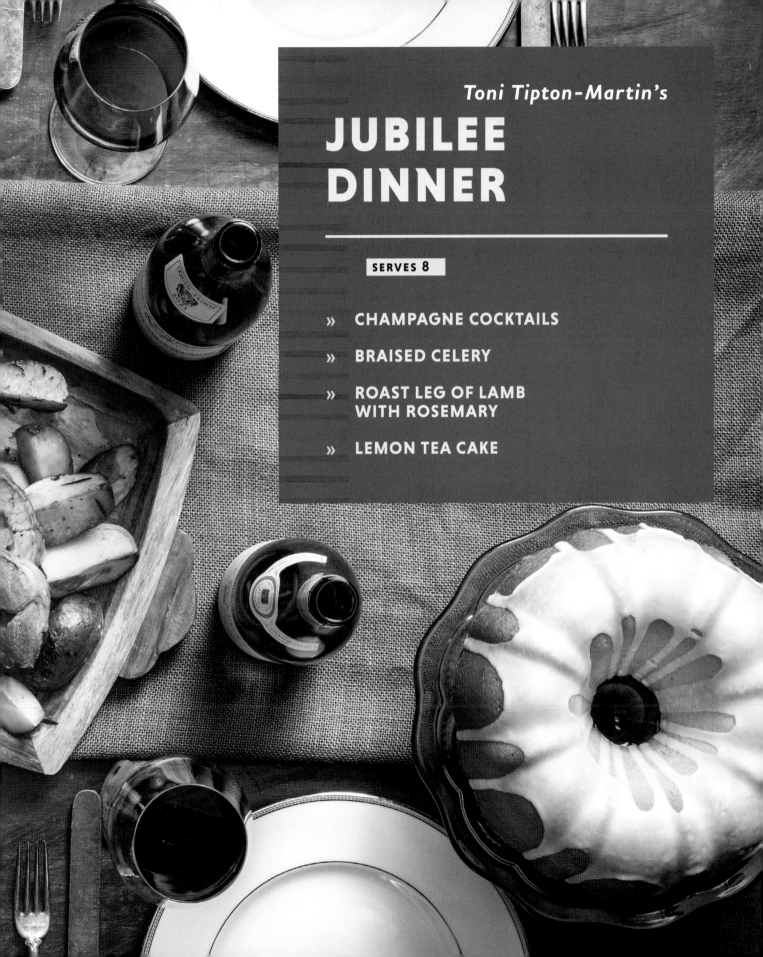

Toni Tipton-Martin's

JUBILEE DINNER

SERVES 8

» **CHAMPAGNE COCKTAILS**

» **BRAISED CELERY**

» **ROAST LEG OF LAMB WITH ROSEMARY**

» **LEMON TEA CAKE**

Toni Tipton-Martin

At my dinner table, stories don't take the place of small talk, they spur it. Even before I wrote *Jubilee: Recipes from Two Centuries of African American Cooking*, I was always creating themed menus. Perhaps it is because I spent so many years as a newspaper food editor, thinking about the ways that food, culture, and celebrations entwine. I know everyone serves special dishes and traditional family recipes on major holidays. But my party-planning strategy leans on these themes all year round. In February, jambalaya and gumbo celebrate Mardi Gras. An Easter or Mother's Day brunch features lamb, eggs, and spring vegetables—foods that honor new birth. I created this menu as an homage to Black cookbook authors who gave us something to talk about when they shared bits of themselves in their recipe books. These recipes invite us to escape into another world as we dine and share the delicious journey with friends.

MY GAME PLAN

UP TO 2 DAYS AHEAD

› Butterfly the lamb for the Roast Leg of Lamb with Rosemary if your butcher hasn't done it for you.

› Bake the Lemon Tea Cake and pour the lemon syrup onto it.

UP TO 1 DAY AHEAD

› Prep the celery for the Braised Celery; store in the refrigerator in a zipper-lock bag.

UP TO SEVERAL HOURS AHEAD

› Chill the flute glasses for the Champagne Cocktails.

› Squeeze the grapefruits and chill the juice for the cocktails.

› Season and tie the leg of lamb.

› Glaze the cake.

CHAMPAGNE COCKTAILS

Makes 8 cocktails

Total Time: 10 minutes

WHY I LOVE THIS RECIPE This beautiful cocktail is my special tribute to Tom Bullock, famed bartender at the St. Louis Country Club and author of the 1917 cocktail classic, *The Ideal Bartender*. I also took my cue from home cooks who adapted the recipe by replacing the original Champagne with American sparkling wine. Think of it as a dressed-up mimosa, prepared in small batches and served regally in chilled flutes.

8	maraschino cherries with stems
8	teaspoons grenadine
	West Indian orange bitters
2	cups ruby red grapefruit juice (2 to 3 grapefruits)
1	(750-ml) bottle American brut sparkling wine, chilled

Add 1 cherry, 1 teaspoon grenadine, 2 dashes bitters, ¼ cup grapefruit juice, and 2 to 3 ounces sparkling wine to each chilled flute glass. Top off with remaining wine to fill glasses. Serve.

TONI'S TIPS

> Chill the glasses for at least 30 minutes before making the cocktail.

> Prosecco or cava also works well, if you prefer.

> I often make these with old-fashioned, bright red maraschino cherries; you can certainly use the dark burgundy, Italian-style maraschino cherries in their place.

BRAISED CELERY

Serves 8

Total Time: 55 minutes

WHY I LOVE THIS RECIPE I created this dish one Easter Sunday, with the taste of a dish served at Mary Mac's Tea Room in Atlanta still on my lips and recipes published in 1912 by S. Thomas Bivins on my mind. Bivins wrote *The Southern Cook Book*, a massive work of more than 600 recipes, including his take on the dish known in fine-dining restaurants as Celery Victor. I give the dish body, just as Bivins did, with beurre manié—a French technique that uses a flour-butter paste at the last minute to thicken most any dish.

1	tablespoon olive oil
2	bunches celery (about 2 pounds), trimmed and cut into 3-inch pieces
½	onion, chopped coarse
2	cups chicken broth
1	teaspoon table salt
	Pinch red pepper flakes
	Pinch ground nutmeg (optional)
1	tablespoon unsalted butter, cut into small pieces
1	tablespoon all-purpose flour
¼	cup heavy cream

1 Heat oil in Dutch oven over medium heat until shimmering. Add celery and onion and cook until softened, 10 to 12 minutes. Add broth; salt; pepper flakes; and nutmeg, if using. Simmer until celery is tender, about 30 minutes.

2 Meanwhile, rub together butter and flour with fingertips until well mixed and resembling a smooth, thick paste.

3 Whisk butter-flour mixture into cooking liquid until completely dissolved. Stir in cream. Simmer, uncovered, until thickened, 2 to 3 minutes more. Season with salt and pepper to taste, and serve.

TONI'S TIP

> Edna Lewis, the grande dame of Southern cooking, prepared her version of this dish using meat drippings. So, if you like, substitute 1 tablespoon lamb drippings for the olive oil.

ROAST LEG OF LAMB WITH ROSEMARY

Serves 8

Total Time: 1¾ hours

WHY I LOVE THIS RECIPE Edna Lewis's third cookbook, *In Pursuit of Flavor*, is not as popular as her other titles, but I love it. She describes her secret for coaxing the natural goodness from the flavorful lamb leg: "I rub the outside of the tied-up leg with butter to help it brown, to add flavor, and to keep it from drying out. Deglaze the pan with less than 1 tablespoon of water and scrape up all the browned bits and juices. Turn into a warm bowl and pass with the slices of lamb after it is carved," with small roasted potatoes. Heavenly.

1	(4- to 5-pound) boneless leg of lamb, trimmed
¼	cup extra-virgin olive oil, divided, plus extra for pan
¼	cup minced fresh parsley, plus 4 sprigs, divided
2	tablespoons minced fresh rosemary, plus 4 sprigs, divided
6	garlic cloves, minced
1	tablespoon table salt, divided
1	teaspoon pepper, divided
20	small red potatoes, quartered

1   Adjust oven rack to middle position and heat oven to 375 degrees. Open lamb leg and place fat side down on cutting board; pat dry with paper towels. Drizzle lamb with 2 tablespoons oil. Combine minced parsley, minced rosemary, and garlic in small bowl. Rub over entire surface of lamb. Season with 1½ teaspoons salt and ½ teaspoon pepper. Roll up lamb into as tight a cylinder as you can and tie with kitchen twine at 1-inch intervals. Rub lamb with remaining 2 tablespoons oil and season with remaining 1½ teaspoons salt and ½ teaspoon pepper.

2   Place parsley and rosemary sprigs in bottom of lightly greased roasting pan. Arrange potatoes on top of herbs. Add lamb to pan, resting it on potatoes, and roast uncovered until lamb registers 135 degrees for medium-rare or 140 degrees for medium, 1 to 1½ hours.

3   Transfer roast to carving board, tent with aluminum foil, and let rest for 10 minutes. Meanwhile, transfer potatoes to serving platter and strain pan juices into measuring cup. Let juices sit or refrigerate until fat rises to top, then skim off fat. (If using drippings to make the Braised Celery, reserve 1 tablespoon.) Remove and discard twine from roast, slice roast thin, and transfer to serving platter with potatoes. Pass juices separately for drizzling.

TONI'S TIPS

›   Ask your butcher to butterfly the lamb leg for you. If you like, ask for the bone too. You can stash it in the freezer and, when you're ready, simmer it for stock or use it to flavor soup.

›   If I season and tie the roast ahead, I usually do it earlier in the same day that I'm planning to cook it. You can do it up to 1 day ahead, but be aware that the salt will draw out some of the moisture from the meat.

›   Look for potatoes that measure 1 to 2 inches in diameter.

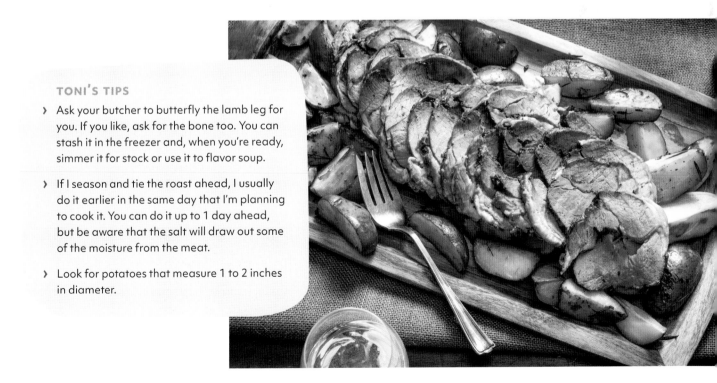

LEMON TEA CAKE

Serves 10 to 12

Total Time: 1½ hours, plus 1 hour cooling and 1 hour setting

WHY I LOVE THIS RECIPE Malinda Russell's classic lemon cake from her 1866 book, *A Domestic Cook Book*, reminds me of much more modern versions, which get extra moisture from a sweet lemon syrup that is poured over the cake after it bakes. The sweet lemon glaze is a contemporary addition, an update of the lightly browned butter glaze that pioneers poured over classic pound or butter cakes. It is lovely as it drips along the peaks and valleys created by the Bundt pan. The end result is a cake loaded with lemon flavor.

CAKE

- 16 tablespoons (8 ounces) unsalted butter, room temperature, plus extra for pan
- 3 cups (15 ounces) all-purpose flour
- ½ teaspoon baking powder
- ½ teaspoon baking soda
- 1 teaspoon table salt
- ¼ cup grated lemon zest, plus ¾ cup lemon juice, divided (4 to 5 lemons)
- 1 cup buttermilk
- 1 teaspoon vanilla extract
- 2½ cups (17½ ounces) granulated sugar, divided
- 5 large eggs

LEMON GLAZE

- 3½ tablespoons lemon juice (1 to 2 lemons)
- 2 cups (8 ounces) confectioners' sugar, sifted

1 FOR THE CAKE Preheat oven to 325 degrees. Coat 10-inch Bundt pan with butter. Dust lightly with flour, shaking to remove any excess.

2 Whisk flour, baking powder, baking soda, and salt in small bowl; set aside. Combine ¼ cup lemon juice, buttermilk, and vanilla in small bowl; set aside.

3 Using stand mixer fitted with paddle attachment, beat butter on medium speed until light, about 2 minutes. With mixer running, add 2 cups granulated sugar (1 cup at a time) until incorporated. Continue beating until light and fluffy, 3 to 5 minutes, scraping down sides of bowl as needed. With mixer still on medium speed, add eggs, 1 at a time, beating after each addition until completely incorporated. Beat in lemon zest.

4 Reduce mixer speed to low and beat in flour mixture in 3 additions, alternating with lemon juice–buttermilk mixture. Mix just until batter is smooth. Pour batter into prepared pan and bake until toothpick inserted in center comes out clean, 50 to 60 minutes. Transfer pan to wire rack.

5 Meanwhile, combine remaining ½ cup sugar and remaining ½ cup lemon juice in small saucepan. Bring to boil, then reduce heat and simmer for 1 minute. Remove from heat and stir; set syrup aside to cool slightly.

6 Poke holes over cake surface with wooden skewer. Spoon lemon syrup over entire surface, allowing syrup to soak in between spoonfuls and using all of syrup. Let cake cool in pan for 10 minutes, then invert cake onto wire rack set in rimmed baking sheet. Let cake cool completely, about 1 hour. (You can make the cake to this point up to 2 days ahead; store at room temperature, covered loosely with plastic wrap.)

7 FOR THE GLAZE Whisk lemon juice and confectioners' sugar in small bowl until smooth.

8 Drizzle glaze over top, letting it drip down sides. Let glaze set before slicing and serving, about 1 hour.

> **TONI'S TIPS**
> - If you like, you can divide the batter evenly between two 8-inch loaf pans. The baking time will be the same. (Unlike with the Bundt pan, poke holes for the syrup in what will be the top of the cake.)
> - To ensure that the glaze sets properly, let the syrup-soaked cake cool out of the pan for several hours before drizzling it with the glaze.
> - You will have leftover cake, which is a very good thing. It keeps for up to 1 week, and it also freezes beautifully.

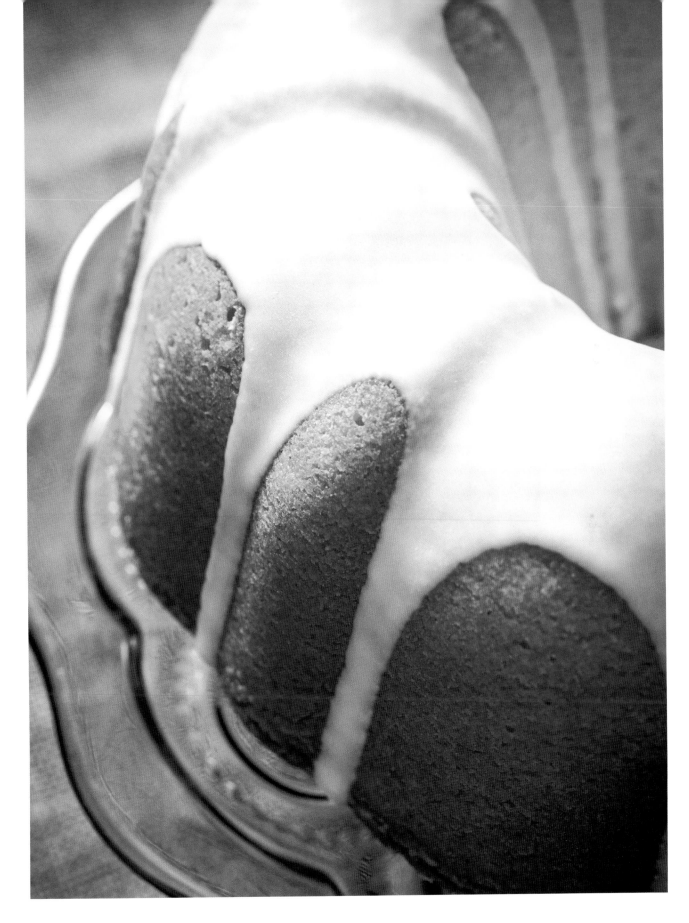

NUTRITIONAL INFORMATION FOR OUR RECIPES

To calculate the nutritional values of our recipes per serving, we used The Food Processor SQL by ESHA research. When using this program, we entered all the ingredients, using weights wherever possible. We also used our preferred brands in these analyses. Any ingredient listed as "optional" was excluded from the analyses. If there is a range in the serving size, we used the highest number of servings to calculate nutritional values. We did not include additional salt or pepper for food that's seasoned to taste.

	CALORIES	TOTAL FAT (G)	SAT FAT (G)	CHOL (MG)	SODIUM (MG)	TOTAL CARB (G)	DIETARY FIBER (G)	TOTAL SUGARS (G)	ADDED SUGARS (G)	PROTEIN (G)
LET'S GET TOGETHER										
Everyday Long-Grain White Rice	130	0.5	0	0	5	5	29	1	0	2
Pearl Couscous Pilaf	110	1	0	0	25	22	1	0	0	4
Boiled Red Potatoes with Butter and Herbs	140	4	2.5	10	30	24	3	2	0	3
Chickpeas with Garlic and Parsley	180	11	1.5	0	480	16	5	1	0	5
Easiest-Ever Biscuits	340	20	13	60	470	35	1	3	2	6
Compound Butter										
Herb Butter	110	12	7	30	35	1	0	0	0	0
Herb-Mustard Butter	120	12	7	30	190	0	0	0	0	0
Herb-Lemon Butter	100	12	7	30	0	0	0	0	0	0
Simplest Salad	70	7	1	0	0	1	0	0	0	0
Make-Ahead Vinaigrette	200	22	3	0	210	2	0	2	2	0
Make-Ahead Sherry-Shallot Vinaigrette	210	22	3	0	210	2	0	2	2	0
Make-Ahead Balsamic-Fennel Vinaigrette	210	22	3	0	210	4	1	3	2	0
Make-Ahead Cider-Caraway Vinaigrette	200	22	3	0	210	2	0	2	2	0
Cucumber Water	5	0	0	0	10	1	0	0	0	0
Cucumber Water with Lemon and Mint	5	0	0	0	10	1	0	0	0	0
Cucumber Water with Lime and Ginger	5	0	0	0	10	2	0	1	0	0
Cucumber Water with Orange and Tarragon	10	0	0	0	10	2	0	1	0	1
Iced Black Tea	0	0	0	0	10	1	0	0	0	0
Iced Raspberry-Basil Black Tea	35	0	0	0	10	8	2	5	3	1
Iced Ginger-Pomegranate Black Tea	25	0	0	0	10	7	1	5	3	0
Iced Apple-Cinnamon Black Tea	15	0	0	0	5	4	1	3	1	0

	CALORIES	TOTAL FAT (G)	SAT FAT (G)	CHOL (MG)	SODIUM (MG)	TOTAL CARB (G)	DIETARY FIBER (G)	TOTAL SUGARS (G)	ADDED SUGARS (G)	PROTEIN (G)
LATE-SUMMER DINNER FOR CLOSE FRIENDS										
"Caprese" Salad with Fried Green Tomatoes and Basil Vinaigrette	930	66	22	175	850	57	2	6	0	32
Penne with Caramelized Zucchini, Parsley, and Sumac	560	21	4.5	10	610	79	4	10	0	19
Salty Apple-Raspberry Crisp with Walnuts	740	40	17	75	340	91	6	49	27	11
MODERN TENDERLOIN DINNER										
Easy Beef Tenderloin with Harissa Spice Rub	410	15	6	145	600	15	1	13	13	51
Cilantro-Mint Relish	130	14	2	0	70	2	1	0	0	0
Baby Red Potatoes with Lemon and Chives	200	9	5	25	490	27	3	2	0	3
Arugula and Baby Kale Salad with Dates, Oranges, and Almonds	170	12	1.5	0	230	18	4	13	0	2
Chocolate Pots de Creme with Dulce de Leche and Bourbon Whipped Cream	580	40	24	200	160	54	0	47	9	7
VIET-CAJUN SHRIMP BOIL										
Fresh Spring Rolls with Mango and Marinated Tofu and Hoisin-Peanut Sauce	320	16	2.5	0	600	3.5	4	10	1	14
Viet-Cajun Shrimp Boil	880	45	23	585	6330	50	7	11	2	72
Piña Coladas with Mint and Lime	410	9	9	0	80	60	2	54	10	1
MY MAINE EVENT										
Gin Camps	150	0	0	0	15	12	0	11	11	0
Roasted Oysters on the Half Shell with Dijon Crème Fraîche	90	7	4.5	35	150	1	0	1	0	2
Maine-Style Lobster Rolls	520	19	8	185	1890	59	0	9	0	30
House Salad	120	11	1.5	0	125	5	2	3	0	2
Lime Possets with Raspberries	560	44	28	135	35	42	3	38	33	4
NACHO AVERAGE BARBECUE										
Nachos!	1000	61	26	215	3010	53	3	23	13	58
Grill-Smoked Pork Butt	440	31	12	140	1150	1	0	0	0	37
Ancho Chile Barbecue Sauce	70	1.5	0	0	490	14	1	10	8	1
Pickled Hominy, Red Onions, and Jalapeños	60	0	0	0	320	11	1	7	5	0
Big-Batch Green Chile Queso	300	23	14	75	960	8	1	6	0	17
Candied Bacon S'mores	570	25	8	15	450	77	1	47	34	12
BAO BAR										
Star Anise– and Ginger-Braised Pork	350	23	9	105	630	5	0	3	2	29
Crispy Sesame Chicken	210	12	2	60	410	13	1	0	0	14
Crispy Sesame Tofu	170	11	1.5	0	350	13	1	1	0	5
Sweet-and-Spicy Quick Pickled Carrots	25	0	0	0	190	6	2	3	0	1
Hoisin-Lime Sauce	90	4.5	0.5	0	500	13	0	7	0	1
Sriracha Mayo	150	16	2.5	10	290	2	0	1	0	0
Guava Sorbet with Fresh Fruit	240	0	0	0	30	60	1	50	10	2

	CALORIES	TOTAL FAT (G)	SAT FAT (G)	CHOL (MG)	SODIUM (MG)	TOTAL CARB (G)	DIETARY FIBER (G)	TOTAL SUGARS (G)	ADDED SUGARS (G)	PROTEIN (G)
VEGETARIAN DUMPLING PARTY										
Vegetable Dumplings	390	14	2	0	480	56	5	5	0	8
Soy-Mirin Dipping Sauce	25	0	0	0	930	4	0	4	0	1
Chili Crisp	130	13	2	0	170	4	2	1	0	1
Gai Lan with Oyster Sauce	110	6	1	0	310	12	4	2	1	3
No-Churn Lime-Pineapple Swirl Ice Cream	480	33	21	105	180	45	0	42	11	6
SUMMERTIME AND THE GRILLING IS EASY										
Creamy Herb Dip	70	1.5	1	10	70	5	0	3	0	9
Grilled Lemon-Garlic Chicken with New Potatoes	740	47	12	195	1440	25	1	3	3	52
Summer Tomato Salad	90	7	1	0	85	6	2	3	0	1
Grilled Peaches with Butter Cookies and Ice Cream	390	19	10	50	170	52	2	38	11	5
THE GREAT BRITISH PICNIC										
English 75	110	0	0	0	0	12	0	11	3	0
Sage and Scallion Scotch Eggs	390	21	6	270	460	27	1	1	0	22
Brown Butter–Poached Potted Shrimp	360	25	14	130	630	23	0	3	0	11
Coronation Chicken	330	19	3	70	200	12	3	7	0	26
Cucumber and Asparagus Salad	40	2	0	0	190	4	1	2	0	2
Nectarines and Berries in Elderflower and Sparkling Wine	110	0.5	0	0	10	24	4	18	3	2
TAKE ME BACK TO TUSCANY										
Antipasti with Schiacciata	1020	55	20	135	3620	73	3	14	2	55
Brothy White Beans with Sun-Dried Tomatoes and Garlic	240	11	1.5	0	520	28	14	1	0	9
Farro and Kale Salad with Fennel, Olives, and Pecorino	370	23	2	5	1620	34	5	2	0	9
Bistecca alla Fiorentina with Portobellos and Grilled Bread	730	48	9	110	1290	40	1	5	0	38
Gelato with Olive Oil, Sea Salt, and Amaretti Crumble	440	28	10	40	280	44	0	42	0	5
POLENTA AND PALOMAS										
Palomas for a Crowd	230	0	0	0	440	26	0	9	9	1
Creamy Baked Polenta	340	13	7	35	1150	44	6	0	0	12
Grilled Shrimp with Calabrian Chiles, Lemon, and Parmesan	200	10	2.5	195	1350	3	0	0	0	22
Grilled Ratatouille	210	15	2	0	260	19	6	10	0	4
Grilled Corn "Caprese" Salad	310	23	7	25	500	17	3	5	0	12
Grilled Pound Cake with Pineapple and Honey Mascarpone	570	33	14	95	310	67	2	46	30	7
A COZY ICELANDIC EVENING										
Icelandic-Style Creamy Fish Soup	380	10	5	205	1340	23	2	6	0	46
Simple Crusty Bread	350	6	3	10	700	61	2	0	0	11

	CALORIES	TOTAL FAT (G)	SAT FAT (G)	CHOL (MG)	SODIUM (MG)	TOTAL CARB (G)	DIETARY FIBER (G)	TOTAL SUGARS (G)	ADDED SUGARS (G)	PROTEIN (G)
MIDWESTERN BRUNCH										
Simple Green Juice	120	0.5	0	0	30	28	6	19	0	2
Carrot-Pineapple-Ginger Juice	100	0	0	0	105	24	4	14	0	2
Goetta	380	16	6	80	680	31	5	1	0	29
Brunch Salad with Creamy Parmesan Dressing	190	12	4	125	440	12	1	2	0	9
Blueberry Swirl Buns with Lemony Cream Cheese Icing	420	13	7	70	430	66	3	29	25	8
NOT DOG PARTY										
Spiked Sparkling Lemonade	240	0	0	0	95	28	0	25	24	0
Smoky Carrot Dogs	170	8	1	0	1080	22	6	11	0	4
Lentil Chili Dog Sauce	170	8	1	0	710	22	5	4	0	6
Spiced Cheez Sauce	140	7	1	0	320	18	2	1	0	3
Chicago-Style Neon Relish	60	0	0	0	470	15	1	13	12	1
Jalapeño Relish	5	0	0	0	160	1	1	1	0	0
Peanut Butter–Chocolate Chunk Cookies	670	36	14	0	480	83	4	55	53	13
APPETIZERS FOR DINNER										
Cider Bourbon Cocktails	210	0	0	0	5	20	0	18	6	0
Gazpacho in Cucumber Cups	50	3	0	0	160	6	1	3	0	1
Biscuit Crackers with Red Lentil Dip	170	9	4	15	670	18	2	3	1	4
Mushroom, Fontina, and Chive Flatbread	340	8	3.5	15	780	56	0	8	0	13
Corn, Pepperoni, and Burrata Flatbread	390	12	5	25	910	58	1	8	0	15
Roasted Jerk Chicken Wings	210	15	3.5	80	800	4	1	2	2	14
Salted Chocolate Chip Cookie Ice Cream Sandwiches	290	14	8	45	230	40	0	26	17	4
ROAD TRIP DINNER PARTY										
Sticky Spiced Nuts with Orange, Honey, and Rosemary	330	23	2.5	5	320	27	5	20	17	10
Mediterranean Layered Dip	300	23	7	30	740	17	0	6	0	12
"The Italian" Stromboli	630	28	12	100	1750	65	2	11	0	31
Browned Butter RKTs	450	12	7	30	410	85	0	44	44	4
OKTOBERFEST AT HOME										
Beer-Caraway Pretzels	320	4	2	10	4210	57	2	2	2	9
Bavarian-Inspired Mustard Sauce	80	2	0	0	760	15	0	14	13	1
Schweinebraten	570	38	15	155	2250	14	2	6	3	40
Browned Butter Sauerkraut	120	12	7	30	420	4	2	2	1	1
Käsespätzle	410	19	10	145	950	43	2	2	0	18
Black Forest Brownies	690	23	13	100	40	106	4	83	52	7
PORKADISE FOUND										
The Spiked Swine	180	2	0.5	5	95	5	0	4	3	2
Salami Get This Straight Salad	250	19	5	25	860	13	2	2	0	8
Piggy Peppers	250	18	3	10	870	17	4	6	0	8
Crispy, Spicy Swineapple Ribs	900	64	18	170	1530	43	1	23	10	37
Sticky Sweet Sow Bars	550	22	10	85	520	80	1	56	42	9

	CALORIES	TOTAL FAT (G)	SAT FAT (G)	CHOL (MG)	SODIUM (MG)	TOTAL CARB (G)	DIETARY FIBER (G)	TOTAL SUGARS (G)	ADDED SUGARS (G)	PROTEIN (G)
AUTUMN VEGETARIAN SALADS + DESSERT										
Romaine and Radicchio Salad with Roasted Squash and Pickled Pears	220	15	2.5	0	720	20	4	9	3	3
White Bean and Arugula Salad with Frico Crumble	240	13	4	15	600	19	5	2	0	11
Sweet Potato and Lentil Salad with Fried Shallots	300	14	4	10	520	34	8	4	0	13
Spiced Panna Cotta with Candied Maple Pecans	370	30	15	70	180	22	1	21	16	5
VEGETARIAN LUNCHEON										
Pear-Mint Sparkling Iced Green Tea	60	0	0	0	15	12	2	9	4	2
Red Leaf and Watercress Salad with Fennel, Apple, Parmesan, and Hazelnuts	140	11	2.5	5	220	8	2	4	0	4
Celery Root Galette with Blue Cheese and Walnuts	630	41	18	100	870	55	6	12	7	13
Gingered Pear and Cranberry Cobbler	410	9	5	20	350	79	9	44	20	4
DOUBLE-DATE NIGHT										
Bijou Cocktails	220	0	0	0	5	17	0	15	12	0
Smoked Salmon Crisps	80	5	2	0	25	230	3	0	0	6
Sautéed Chilean Sea Bass with Creamy Coconut Rice and Baby Bok Choy	600	22	11	95	1040	50	2	2	0	51
Raspberry Napoleons with Bittersweet Chocolate Sauce	620	44	26	200	280	56	0	36	25	6
MEXICAN BRUNCH										
Hibiscus Margaritas	270	0	0	0	100	66	1	64	59	0
Chilaquiles Verdes with Sheet-Pan Fried Eggs	570	36	8	200	690	49	6	7	0	18
Fruit Stand Salad with Chile and Lime	170	0.5	0	0	25	43	7	31	0	3
Mexican Chocolate Conchas	470	23	10	60	470	59	3	13	13	9
GUMBO WEATHER GET-TOGETHER										
Big-Batch Sazeracs	150	0	0	0	0	4	0	4	4	0
Fried Oyster Po'Boy Sliders	360	17	2.5	5	1200	49	4	7	0	9
Smoky Chicken and Andouille Gumbo	880	56	13	180	1450	31	4	7	1	66
Bananas Foster Bread Pudding	940	45	22	295	890	107	5	63	42	16
MIDWESTERN FAMILY CLASSICS										
Pork Chop Potato Bake Casserole	610	40	19	100	1300	31	0	2	0	31
Southern Punch Bowl Seven-Layer Salad	560	43	10	285	850	20	5	11	4	24
Vintage Triple-Layer "Christmas" Jell-O	360	7	4	25	300	64	0	60	52	10
TRADITIONAL ANATOLIAN DINNER										
Sigara Böreği	490	30	12	50	870	42	1	3	0	14
Cacık	140	13	6	10	320	2	0	2	0	4
Ezme Salad	150	11	1.5	0	450	13	2	8	0	2
Adana Kebab with Sumac Onions	520	27	8	75	1490	42	2	5	0	29
Katmer	600	41	22	100	250	50	1	27	23	9

	CALORIES	TOTAL FAT (G)	SAT FAT (G)	CHOL (MG)	SODIUM (MG)	TOTAL CARB (G)	DIETARY FIBER (G)	TOTAL SUGARS (G)	ADDED SUGARS (G)	PROTEIN (G)
NONNA'S SUNDAY SUPPER										
Antipasti	620	46	21	125	2820	13	4	5	1	37
Porchetta Abruzzese	820	56	19	245	720	3	1	1	0	75
Crispy Polenta Cakes with Green Olive, Grapefruit, and Sun-Dried Tomato Tapenade	300	22	7	25	360	24	3	2	0	5
Charred Broccoli Rabe with Garlicky Anchovy Dressing	90	8	1	0	200	4	2	2	0	3
Nonna's Pizzelle	380	17	10	110	100	53	1	25	25	6
A NIGHT AT LA CUCHARA DE SAN TELMO										
Almejas en Salsa Verde	160	6	1	35	680	7	0	1	0	14
Txipirones Encebollados a la Plancha	630	46	6	295	240	30	2	4	0	24
Ensalada de Tomate, Asado con Jamón Ibérico, y Idiazábal	430	25	5	20	940	41	2	4	0	13
Costillas al Vino Tinto	680	42	10	80	1320	37	5	4	0	38
Tarta de Queso de la Viña con Caramelo de Sagardoa	1110	67	39	350	550	109	0	103	91	15
WINTER COMFORT DINNER										
Vin Chaud	290	0	0	0	10	22	0	17	16	0
Short Ribs Bourguignon	800	45	17	135	1980	30	4	10	2	46
Very Rustic! Mashed Potatoes	410	26	17	85	55	37	4	4	0	6
Cider-Dressed Greens	150	14	1.5	0	350	7	3	3	0	3
Apple Charlotte	630	26	13	205	520	88	5	57	36	11
JUBILEE DINNER										
Champagne Cocktails	140	0	0	0	10	7	0	4	2	0
Braised Celery	80	6	3	10	400	5	2	2	0	2
Roast Leg of Lamb with Rosemary	450	17	4	120	1940	33	4	3	0	42
Lemon Tea Cake	540	18	10	120	340	90	1	62	60	7

CONVERSIONS AND EQUIVALENTS

Some say cooking is a science and an art. We would say that geography has a hand in it too. Flours and sugars manufactured in the United Kingdom and elsewhere will feel and taste different from those manufactured in the United States. So we cannot promise that the loaf of bread you bake in Canada or England will taste the same as a loaf baked in the States, but we can offer guidelines for converting weights and measures. We also recommend that you rely on your instincts when making our recipes. Refer to the visual cues provided. If the dough hasn't "come together in a ball" as described, you may need to add more flour—even if the recipe doesn't tell you to. You be the judge.

The recipes in this book were developed using standard U.S. measures following U.S. government guidelines. The charts below offer equivalents for U.S. and metric measures. All conversions are approximate and have been rounded up or down to the nearest whole number.

EXAMPLE:

1 teaspoon = 4.9292 milliliters, rounded up to 5 milliliters
1 ounce = 28.3495 grams, rounded down to 28 grams

VOLUME CONVERSIONS

U.S.	METRIC
1 teaspoon	5 milliliters
2 teaspoons	10 milliliters
1 tablespoon	15 milliliters
2 tablespoons	30 milliliters
¼ cup	59 milliliters
⅓ cup	79 milliliters
½ cup	118 milliliters
¾ cup	177 milliliters
1 cup	237 milliliters
1¼ cups	296 milliliters
1½ cups	355 milliliters
2 cups (1 pint)	473 milliliters
2½ cups	591 milliliters
3 cups	710 milliliters
4 cups (1 quart)	0.946 liter
1.06 quarts	1 liter
4 quarts (1 gallon)	3.8 liters

WEIGHT CONVERSIONS

OUNCES	GRAMS
½	14
¾	21
1	28
1½	43
2	57
2½	71
3	85
3½	99
4	113
4½	128
5	142
6	170
7	198
8	227
9	255
10	283
12	340
16 (1 pound)	454

CONVERSIONS FOR COMMON BAKING INGREDIENTS

Baking is an exacting science. Because measuring by weight is far more accurate than measuring by volume, and thus more likely to produce reliable results, in our recipes we provide ounce measures in addition to cup measures for many ingredients. Refer to the chart below to convert these measures into grams.

INGREDIENT	OUNCES	GRAMS
FLOUR		
1 cup all-purpose flour*	5	142
1 cup cake flour	4	113
1 cup whole-wheat flour	5½	156
SUGAR		
1 cup granulated (white) sugar	7	198
1 cup packed brown sugar (light or dark)	7	198
1 cup confectioners' sugar	4	113
COCOA POWDER		
1 cup cocoa powder	3	85
BUTTER†		
4 tablespoons (½ stick or ¼ cup)	2	57
8 tablespoons (1 stick or ½ cup)	4	113
16 tablespoons (2 sticks or 1 cup)	8	227

* U.S. all-purpose flour, the most frequently used flour in this book, does not contain leaveners, as some European flours do. These leavened flours are called self-rising or self-raising. If you are using self-rising flour, take this into consideration before adding leaveners to a recipe.

† In the United States, butter is sold both salted and unsalted. We generally recommend unsalted butter. If you are using salted butter, take this into consideration before adding salt to a recipe.

OVEN TEMPERATURES

FAHRENHEIT	CELSIUS	GAS MARK
225	105	¼
250	120	½
275	135	1
300	150	2
325	165	3
350	180	4
375	190	5
400	200	6
425	220	7
450	230	8
475	245	9

CONVERTING TEMPERATURES FROM AN INSTANT-READ THERMOMETER

We include doneness temperatures in many of the recipes in this book. We recommend an instant-read thermometer for the job. Refer to the table above to convert Fahrenheit degrees to Celsius. Or, for temperatures not represented in the chart, use this simple formula:

Subtract 32 degrees from the Fahrenheit reading, then divide the result by 1.8 to find the Celsius reading.

EXAMPLE:

"Roast chicken until thighs register 175 degrees."

To convert:
175°F – 32 = 143°
143° ÷ 1.8 = 79.44°C, rounded down to 79°C

INDEX

Note: Page references in *italics* indicate photographs.

S